# solutions@syngress.com

With more than 1,500,000 copies of our MCSE, MCSD, CompTIA, and Cisco study guides in print, we continue to look for ways we can better serve the information needs of our readers. One way we do that is by listening.

Readers like yourself have been telling us they want an Internet-based service that would extend and enhance the value of our books. Based on reader feedback and our own strategic plan, we have created a Web site that we hope will exceed your expectations.

**Solutions@syngress.com** is an interactive treasure trove of useful information focusing on our book topics and related technologies. The site offers the following features:

- One-year warranty against content obsolescence due to vendor product upgrades. You can access online updates for any affected chapters.

- "Ask the Author"™ customer query forms that enable you to post questions to our authors and editors.

- Exclusive monthly mailings in which our experts provide answers to reader queries and clear explanations of complex material.

- Regularly updated links to sites specially selected by our editors for readers desiring additional reliable information on key topics.

Best of all, the book you're now holding is your key to this amazing site. Just go to **www.syngress.com/solutions**, and keep this book handy when you register to verify your purchase.

Thank you for giving us the opportunity to serve your needs. And be sure to let us know if there's anything else we can do to help you get the maximum value from your investment. We're listening.

## www.syngress.com/solutions

D1222979

SYNGRESS®

SYNGRESS®

# DESIGNING A
# Wireless Network

Jeffrey Wheat

Randy Hiser

Jackie Tucker

Alicia Neely

**Andy McCullough** Technical Editor

| KEY | SERIAL NUMBER |
| --- | --- |
| 001 | PL94T945T5 |
| 002 | AKLRT4JKN6 |
| 003 | VM55R3N54N |
| 004 | S6TF4B39UN |
| 005 | 8ZSC7U6N7H |
| 006 | NFG4BYQ2M4 |
| 007 | 44DVHT746T |
| 008 | N5FL9565MR |
| 009 | 83N5MYFW4S |
| 010 | GT6YHM7F3C |

PUBLISHED BY
Syngress Publishing, Inc.
800 Hingham Street
Rockland, MA 02370

**Designing a Wireless Network**

Printed in the United States of America

1 2 3 4 5 6 7 8 9 0

ISBN: 1-928994-45-8

Technical Editor: Andy McCullough
Technical Reviewer: Rick Murphy
Co-Publisher: Richard Kristof
Acquisitions Editor: Catherine B. Nolan
Developmental Editor: Kate Glennon

Freelance Editorial Manager: Maribeth Corona-Evans
Cover Designer: Michael Kavish
Page Layout and Art by: Shannon Tozier
Copy Editor: Adrienne Rebello
Indexer: John Hulse

Distributed by Publishers Group West in the United States and Jaguar Book Group in Canada.

# Acknowledgments

We would like to acknowledge the following people for their kindness and support in making this book possible.

Richard Kristof and Duncan Anderson of Global Knowledge, for their generous access to the IT industry's best courses, instructors, and training facilities.

Ralph Troupe, Rhonda St. John, and the team at Callisma for their invaluable insight into the challenges of designing, deploying, and supporting world-class enterprise networks.

Karen Cross, Lance Tilford, Meaghan Cunningham, Kim Wylie, Harry Kirchner, Kevin Votel, Kent Anderson, and Frida Yara of Publishers Group West for sharing their incredible marketing experience and expertise.

Mary Ging, Caroline Hird, Simon Beale, Caroline Wheeler, Victoria Fuller, Jonathan Bunkell, and Klaus Beran of Harcourt International for making certain that our vision remains worldwide in scope.

Anneke Baeten, Annabel Dent, and Laurie Giles of Harcourt Australia for all their help.

David Buckland, Wendi Wong, Daniel Loh, Marie Chieng, Lucy Chong, Leslie Lim, Audrey Gan, and Joseph Chan of Transquest Publishers for the enthusiasm with which they receive our books.

Kwon Sung June at Acorn Publishing for his support.

Ethan Atkin at Cranbury International for his help in expanding the Syngress program.

Joe Pisco, Helen Moyer, Paul Zanoli, Alan Steele, and the great folks at InterCity Press for all their help.

Philip Allen at Brewer & Lord LLC for all his work and generosity.

# Acknowledgements from the Contributors

This book is written for all those who have considered the possibilities of leveraging wireless technologies and have labored to challenge the existing way we interact in our day-to-day activities in order to promote a greater quality of life. For we know that there is a balance between what can be accomplished technically and that which should be.

We would like to thank Syngress Publishing for the opportunity to bring our ideas and visions to print. Catherine Nolan and others at Syngress Publishing were key to our success. We would also like to thank our families for putting up with the many long hours and late nights spent writing this book. Lastly, we would like to thank Lucent Technologies for putting us in the position to write this book.

# Contributors

**Anthony Bruno** (CCIE #2738, CCDP, CCNA-WAN, MCSE, NNCSS, CNX-Ethernet) is a Principal Consultant with Lucent Worldwide Services. As a consultant, he has worked with many customers in the design, implementation, and optimization of large-scale, multi-protocol networks. Anthony has worked on the design of wireless networks, Voice over technologies, and Internet access. Formerly, he worked as an Air Force Captain in network operations and management where he implemented wireless LANs on the base network. Anthony completed his master's degree in Electrical Engineering from the University of Missouri-Rolla in 1994 and his B.S. in Electrical Engineering from the University of Puerto Rico-Mayaguez in 1990. He is the co-author of *CCDA Exam Certification Guide* and has performed technical reviews for several Cisco professional books.

**Jeffrey A. Wheat** (Lucent WaveLAN Wireless Certification, FORE ATM Certification) is a Principal Member of the Consulting Staff at Lucent Worldwide Services. He currently provides strategic direction and architectural design to Lucent Service Provider and Large Enterprise customers. His specialties include convergence and wireless architectures, and he is an ATM and Testing Methodology Subject Matter Expert within Lucent. Jeff's background with Lucent includes design engagements with Metricom, Sprint ION, Sprint PCS, Raytheon, and Marathon Oil. Prior to Lucent, he spent 11 years working for the U.S. Intelligence Agencies as a Network Architect and Systems Engineer. Jeff graduated from the University of Kansas in 1986 with a B.S. in Computer Science and currently resides in Kansas City with his wife Gabrielle and their two children, Madison and Brandon.

**Dustin Coffel** is a Network Systems Consultant with Lucent Technologies Enhanced Services and Sales. He provides network consulting and technical support for Lucent products to any Lucent customers in the central region of the United States. Dustin holds a bachelor's degree from Kansas State University in Electrical Engineering with an emphasis in Wireless Communication Systems. He resides in the Kansas City area with his family.

**Randy Hiser** is a Senior Network Engineer for Sprint's Research, Architecture & Design Group, with design responsibilities for home distribution and DSL self-installation services for Sprint's Integrated On Demand Network. He is knowledgeable in the areas of multimedia services and emerging technologies, has installed and operated fixed wireless MMDS facilities in the Middle East, and has patented network communication device identification in a communications network for Sprint. Randy lives with his wife Deborah and their children, Erin, Ryan, Megan, Jesse, and Emily in Overland Park, KS.

**Christian Barnes** (CCNA, CCDA, MCSE, CNA, A+) is a Network Consultant for Lucent Technologies in Overland Park, KS. His career in the IT industry began with supporting NT and Netware servers and NT workstations for a large banking company in Western New York. It quickly evolved into support of high-level engineers and LAN and WAN administrators as they attempted to troubleshoot and design their networks, and then on to consulting. Chris has a wife and four sons.

**Alicia Neely** (CCNA, CCDA) is currently a Consultant with Lucent Enhanced Services and Sales. Her experience includes optical networking and internetworking. Alicia graduated from the University of Kansas with a B.S. and is pursuing an MBA.

**Donald Lloyd** (CCSA, CCSE, CCNA) is a Distinguished Member of Lucent Worldwide Services' Consulting Staff. His specialties include Juniper and Cisco routers, network design assessments, network security architecture, wireless network design, and network optimization. Donald's background includes several start-up ventures, a successful career with International Network Services, and now Lucent Technologies. Donald has developed and taught classes on wireless technologies, TCP/IP, BGP Routing, Multicast Networking, Implementing Juniper Routers in a Cisco-based Network, and Implementing DNS in a Enterprise or Global network. His areas of expertise include large-scale DNS architecture and design, IP Network design, IP routing using BGP, IS-IS, or OSPF, and network security assessments. He lives in Tulsa, OK.

**Chuck Fite** is a Consultant currently working for Iconixx Systems Engineering on Sprint ION. He has been a technical writer, a test technician, and a business analyst in the computer and telecommunications industries for the past eight years. Chuck received a B.S. in Physics and an M.A. in Rhetoric and Professional Communication from Iowa State University.

**Jackie Tucker** is a Kansas-based Technical Consultant with over 14 years experience in technical writing, interface design, and Web development. She has participated in all phases of software design at several software companies, including a long tenure at Informix Software, Inc., worked extensively on Sprint ION, and is currently consulting in the network division of Sprint Corporation. She graduated with honors from St. Mary College with a B.S. in Computer Science and from Baker University with a M.S. in Management. After work, Jackie spends as much time as possible with her husband Bob, and her two little girls, Sarah and Jessie, in a sports-filled household.

**Michael Snodgrass** serves as Distinguished Member of Consulting Staff with Lucent Technologies Worldwide Services and provides strategic and technical consulting associated with a wide variety of networking disciplines. As a Senior Network Systems Consultant, he provides services across the entire realm of network engineering, including network planning, design, router and switch configuration, enterprise and service provider network management, and 5ESS and 7R/E Core Service Provider Circuit and packet switching and access. His other experiences include network troubleshooting and optimization, application design, and UNIX system administration. Michael also has two decades of industry experience, which includes four years at International Network Services, ten years of Service Provider experience with Southwestern Bell Corporation in a senior role supporting Regional Bell Operating Companies through Bellcore (Bell Communications Research, now Telecordia Technologies), and reservation system application and network design for United Airlines. Michael holds multiple degrees from Southwest Missouri State University in Springfield, MO.

**Darren Bonawitz** is a Network Systems Engineer with Lucent Worldwide Service. Darren started his career pursuing entrepreneurial endeavors in electronic commerce. In January of 2001, he joined Lucent Worldwide Service as a Network Systems Engineer bringing his knowledge of the desktop platform and a general understanding of a broad range of technologies in areas such as remote access, ATM, frame relay, and wireless. In addition, his background includes consulting with universities and corporate clients on a pre- and post-sales basis, business/technology planning, and a proven dedication to customer service. He studied Electrical Engineering with an emphasis in Communication Systems at Kansas State University. In 2000, Darren was nominated for Kansas Young Entrepreneur of the Year and he was also recently recognized by *The Los Angeles Times* for commitment to online customer service.

# Technical Editor and Contributor

**Andy McCullough** (BSEE, CCNA, CCDA) has been in network consulting for over seven years. He is currently working at Lucent Enhanced Services and Sales as a Distinguished Member of the Consulting Staff. Andy has done architecture and design work for several global customers of Lucent Technologies including Level 3 Communications, Sprint, MCI/WorldCom, the London Stock Exchange, and British Telecom. His areas of expertise include network architecture and design, IP routing and switching, and IP Multicast. Prior to working for Lucent, Andy ran a consulting company and a regional ISP.

Andy is co-author of *Building Cisco Remote Access Networks* (Syngress Publishing, ISBN: 1-928994-13-X). He is also an assistant professor teaching networking classes at a community college in Overland Park, KS.

# Technical Reviewer

**Rick Murphy** (MCP, MCNE) is the CTO of vTown Inc. and the President of vLogic Inc. He is also a Senior Instructor with Global Knowledge Networks. Rick began programming and providing service and support for computer networks, full-time in 1983. He has designed and implemented over 200 local and wide area networks for regional municipalities and businesses. As Chief Technology Officer for vTown, Inc., he designs wireless network and content delivery systems for resort communities to be used as a public service by quests and residents. As an author and course director for Global Knowledge, Rick has taught IP Over Wireless Broadband, Wireless IP Infrastructure Electronic Delivery versions (Web and CD), Frame Relay Internetworking, and Building Broadband Networks. He resides in Brighton, CO.

# Contents

Foreword                                                                    xxv

## Chapter 1 Introduction to Wireless: From Past to Present                 1

Introduction                                                                2
Exploring Past Discoveries That Led to Wireless                             4
    Discovering Electromagnetism                        4
    Exploring Conduction                                6
    Inventing the Radio                                 6
    Mounting Radio-Telephones in Cars                   8
    Inventing Computers and Networks                    9
    Inventing Cell Phones                               11
Exploring Present Applications for Wireless                                 12
    Applying Wireless Technology to
    Vertical Markets                                     13
        Using Wireless in Delivery Services       14
        Using Wireless for Public Safety          14
        Using Wireless in the Financial World     15
        Using Wireless in the Retail World        15
        Using Wireless in Monitoring
          Applications                           16
    Applying Wireless Technology to Horizontal
    Applications                                        16
        Using Wireless in Messaging               17
        Using Wireless for Mapping                17
        Using Wireless for Web Surfing            17
Exploring This Book on Wireless                                             18

**Apply Wireless Technologies to Horizontal Applications**

Along with the many vertical markets and applications, you can apply wireless technologies to horizontal applications, meaning that delivery services, public safety, finance, retail, and monitoring can all use and benefit from them.

Summary                                          19
Solutions Fast Track                             20
Frequently Asked Questions                       21

**Chapter 2 Radio Elements
and Frequency Spectrums                          23**
Introduction                                     24
Transmitting Radio Signals Over EM Waves         24
    Anatomy of a Waveform                        25
        Modulating a Radio Signal                27
Propagating a Strong Radio Signal                34
    Understanding Signal Power and
        Signal-to-Noise Ratio                    35
    Attenuation                                  36
        Rain Attenuation                         39
    Bouncing                                     39
    Refracting                                   41
    Line of Sight                                42
    Penetration                                  43
Understanding the Wireless Elements              45
    Generic Radio Components                     45
    Antennas                                     49
        Omnidirectional Antennas                 50
        Directional Antennas                     51
    Base Stations and Mobile Stations            56
    Access Points                                57
Channelizing the Frequency Spectrum             57
    Channelizing                                 59
        Channel Bandwidth                        59
        Channel Spacing and Buffer Zones         60
        Multichannel Systems and Channel
            Offsets                              61
    Extending the Number of Channels
    (Frequency Reuse)                            61
        Seven Cell Frequency Reuse               62
        Multiple Accessing                       63

**Learn the Properties of
Waveforms**

$a$ = Amplitude

$v$ = Velocity of Propagation

$\tau$ = Period

$\lambda$ = Wavelength

$f$ = Frequency

Regulating Wireless Communications          64
  Regulatory Agencies          64
    The Need to Know          65
  Regulations for Low Power, Unlicensed
    Transmitters          66
Summary          68
Solutions Fast Track          69
Frequently Asked Questions          71

## Chapter 3 TCP/IP and the OSI Model          73

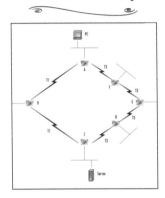

**Learn to Configure
and Maintain Routes
for Full Connectivity**

Static Routing in a
Multihop, Multipath
Network

Introduction          74
Exploring the OSI and DoD Models          74
  Layer 1: The Physical Layer          75
  Layer 2: The Data-Link Layer          75
  Layer 3: The Network Layer          77
  Layer 4: The Transport Layer          78
  Layer 5: The Session Layer          78
  Layer 6: The Presentation Layer          79
  Layer 7: The Application Layer          80
  OSI and DoD Correlation          81
Understanding the Network Access Layer          81
  Using Bridging          82
  The Ethernet Protocol          85
    Understanding the ARP Process          86
  Wireless Protocols          87
  Other Network Access Protocols          88
Understanding the Internet Layer          88
  The Internet Protocol          89
    IP Addressing          91
    Conserving Address Space with VLSM          93
    Routing          95
  The Internet Control Message Protocol          101
Understanding the Host-to-Host Layer          101
  User Datagram Protocol          102
  Transmission Control Protocol          102
Managing the Application Layer          105
  Monitoring Tools: SNMP          105

Assigning Addresses with DHCP                       105
Conserving with Network Address
    Translation                                     106
Summary                                             110
Solution Fast Track                                 111
Frequently Asked Questions                          113

**Chapter 4 Identifying Evolving Wireless Technologies and Standards                  115**

**Understand Bluetooth
Piconet and Scatternet
Configuration**

Introduction                                        116
Fixed Wireless Technologies                         117
    Multichannel Multipoint Distribution Service    117
    Local Multipoint Distribution Services          119
    Wireless Local Loop                             120
    Point-to-Point Microwave                        121
    Wireless Local Area Networks                    122
    Why the Need for a Wireless LAN Standard?       123
        What Exactly Does the 802.11 Standard
            Define?                                 125
        Does the 802.11 Standard Guarantee
            Compatibility across Different Vendors? 128
        802.11b                                     130
        802.11a                                     131
        802.11e                                     132
Developing WLANs through the 802.11
Architecture                                        133
    The Basic Service Set                           133
    The Extended Service Set                        135
        Services to the 802.11 Architecture         135
    The CSMA-CA Mechanism                           138
        The RTS/CTS Mechanism                       138
        Acknowledging the Data                      139
    Configuring Fragmentation                       140
    Using Power Management Options                  140
    Multicell Roaming                               140
    Security in the WLAN                            141

Developing WPANs through the 802.15
Architecture                                            143
  Bluetooth                                             144
  HomeRF                                                147
  High Performance Radio LAN                            147
Mobile Wireless Technologies                            148
  First Generation Technologies                         150
  Second Generation Technologies                        150
  2.5G Technology                                       150
  Third Generation Technologies                         151
  Wireless Application Protocol                         151
  Global System for Mobile Communications               153
  General Packet Radio Service                          155
  Short Message Service                                 155
Optical Wireless Technologies                           156
Summary                                                 157
Solutions Fast Track                                    159
Frequently Asked Questions                              163

## Chapter 5 Designing a Wireless Network     165

Introduction                                            166
Exploring the Design Process                            166
  Conducting the Preliminary Investigation              167
  Performing Analysis of the Existing
    Environment                                         168
  Creating a Preliminary Design                         169
  Finalizing the Detailed Design                        169
  Executing the Implementation                          170
  Capturing the Documentation                           171
Identifying the Design Methodology                      172
  Creating the Network Plan                             173
    Gathering the Requirements                          173
    Baselining the Existing Network                     175
    Analyzing the Competitive Practices                 176
    Beginning the Operations Planning                   176
    Performing a Gap Analysis                            176
    Creating a Technology Plan                           177

**Create a Detailed Physical Design**

- Equipment model
- Cabling details
- Rack details
- Environment requirements
- Physical location of devices
- Detailed RF design

Creating an Integration Plan                              178
Beginning the Collocation Planning                        178
Performing a Risk Analysis                                179
Creating an Action Plan                                   179
Preparing the Planning Deliverables                       180
Developing the Network Architecture                       180
    Reviewing and Validating the Planning
        Phase                                             181
    Creating a High-Level Topology                        181
    Creating a Collocation Architecture                   182
    Defining the High-Level Services                      182
    Creating a High-Level Physical Design                 183
    Defining the Operations Services                      183
    Creating a High-Level Operating Model                 184
    Evaluating the Products                               184
    Creating an Action Plan                               185
    Creating the Network Architecture
        Deliverable                                       186
Formalizing the Detailed Design Phase                     186
    Reviewing and Validating the Network
        Architecture                                      186
    Creating the Detailed Topology                        187
    Creating a Detailed Service Collocation
        Design                                            188
    Creating the Detailed Services                        188
    Creating a Detailed Physical Design                   189
    Creating a Detailed Operations Design                 190
    Creating a Detailed Operating Model
        Design                                            190
    Creating a Training Plan                              191
    Developing a Maintenance Plan                         192
    Developing an Implementation Plan                     192
    Creating the Detailed Design Documents                192
Understanding Wireless Network Attributes
from a Design Perspective                                 193
    Application Support                                   194
    Subscriber Relationships                              196

Physical Landscape                                    197
Network Topology                                      200
Network Security                                      201
Summary                                               203
Solutions Fast Track                                  204
Frequently Asked Questions                            206

**Use Two Wireless
Outdoor Routers to
Create Redundancy**

## Chapter 6 Designing a Wireless Enterprise Network: Hospital Case Study    209

Introduction                                          210
  Applying Wireless in an Enterprise Network          210
Introducing the Enterprise Case Study                 211
  Assessing the Opportunity                           211
  Evaluating Network Requirements                     213
  Assessing the Satellite Buildings' Physical
    Landscape                                         214
  Evaluating the Outside Physical Landscape           214
  Evaluating the Current Network                      216
  Evaluating the Hospital Conference Room
    Networking Landscape                              216
Designing a Wireless Solution                         217
  Project 1: Providing Satellite Building Access      218
  Project 2: Providing Wireless Technology
    to the Conference Rooms                           219
  Project 3: Providing Building-to-Building
    Connectivity                                      220
  Describing the Detailed Design of the
    Building Links                                    222
Implementing and Testing the Wireless Solution        224
  Project 1: Implementing the Satellite
    Building LAN Access                               224
  Project 2: Implementing the Hospital
    Conference Room                                   224
  Project 3: Implementing the
    Building-to-Building Connectivity                 225
  Reviewing the Hospital's Objectives                 227
Lessons Learned                                       228

Summary                                            229
Solutions Fast Track                               230
Frequently Asked Questions                         232

**Chapter 7 Designing a Wireless Industrial**
**Network: Retail Case Study                       233**
Introduction                                       234
  Applying Wireless Technology in an Industrial
    Network                                        235
Introducing the Industrial Case Study              235
  Assessing the Opportunity                        236
  Defining the Scope of the Case Study             238
  Reviewing the Current Situation                  238
Designing and Implementing the Wireless
  Network                                          239
  Creating the High-Level Design                   239
  Creating a Detailed Design                       240
    Obtaining a Physical Map                       242
  Determining User Density                         247
    Identifying Constraints                        248
    Conducting the Walk-Through                    249
    Identifying RF Interface Sources               249
    Plan the RF Pattern for the Network            249
Planning the Equipment Placement                   250
  Determining Where to Place the Access
    Points                                         251
    Determining the RF Channel
      Optimization                                 254
    Identifying IP Addresses                       255
  Implementing the Wireless Network                255
    Selecting the Hardware                         256
  Installing the Wireless Components               258
    Setting Up IP Information                      258
    Installing the Access Points                   258
    Install the AP Manager Software                260
    Installing the PC Card in Shipping/
      Receiving                                    260

**Create an Installation
Checklist and Verify
the Steps on the List**

- Set up the IP
  information

- Install the access points

- Install the AP Manager
  software

- Test the wireless
  network

- Review the client's
  objectives

Testing the Wireless Network               260
Reviewing the Client's Objectives          261
Lessons Learned                            262
Summary                                    263
Solutions Fast Track                       264
Frequently Asked Questions                 266

## Chapter 8 Designing a Wireless Campus Network: University Case Study          269

Introduction                                              270
Applying Wireless Technology in a Campus
Network                                                   270
Introducing the Campus Case Study                         271
Assessing the Opportunity                                 271
Defining the Scope of the Case Study                      272
Designing the Wireless Campus Network                     273
The Design Approach                                       273
Determining the Functional Design
Requirements                                              273
Tracking the Administration Needs                         274
Tracking the Athletic Needs                               275
Tracking the Academic Department
Needs                                                     276
Tracking Student Union Needs                              277
Tracking Student Needs                                    277
Constraints and Assumptions                               277
Identifying the Assumptions                               279
Identifying the Constraints                               281
Planning the Equipment Placement: Detailed
Design Requirements                                       283
Providing Detailed Administration
Requirements                                              283
Providing Detailed Athletic
Department Requirements                                   285
Providing Detailed Academic
Department Requirements                                   288

**Establish High-Level Inter-Building Connectivity**

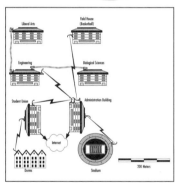

Providing Detailed Student Union
    Department Requirements 290
Providing Detailed Student Requirements 291
Implementing the Wireless Campus Network 292
    Implementing the Physical Deployment 293
    Implementing the Logical Deployment 294
Lessons Learned 295
Summary 296
Solutions Fast Track 297
Frequently Asked Questions 299

## Chapter 9 Designing a Wireless Home Network: Home Office Case Study  301

Introduction 302
    Advantages of a Home Network 302
    Advantages of a Wireless Home Network 304
Introducing the Wireless Home Network
  Case Study 305
    Assessing the Opportunity 305
    Defining the Scope of the Case Study 306
Designing the Wireless Home Network 306
    Determining the Functional Requirements 307
        Determining the Needs of Management 307
        Determining the Needs of the Family 308
        Talking to the IT Department 308
    Creating a Site Survey of the Home 309
      Assessing the Functional Requirements 310
      Analyzing the Existing Environment 310
      Identifying Current Technology Options
        and Constraints 312
      Investigating Costs 313
      Weighing Costs and Benefits 313
      Assessing the Existing Environment 314
    Developing a Preliminary Design 315
      Choosing Vendor Solutions 317
    Developing a Detailed Design 318
Implementing the Wireless Home Network 319

**Learn to Build a Wireless Home Network**

- Assembling the network components
- Determining Broadband configuration
- Installing the hardware
- Installing and configuring the software
- Testing the network

Assembling the Network Components              319
Determining Broadband Configuration            320
Installing the Hardware                        321
Installing and Configuring the Software        322
    Installing and Configuring the Software
        for the Home Firewall                  322
    Installing and Configuring the Software
        for the Wireless Access Point          324
Testing the Network                            326
Designing a Wireless Home Network for Data,
    Voice, and Beyond                          326
    Current State of the Home Wireless
        Marketplace                            327
    A Proposed Solution for the Future         329
Lessons Learned                                330
Summary                                        332
Solutions Fast Track                           332
Frequently Asked Questions                     335

**Designing a Wireless Network Fast Track    337**

**Index                                      357**

# Foreword

Over the last ten years, the impact of wireless communications on the way we live and do business has been surpassed only by the impact of the Internet. Cell phones, pagers, and wireless Personal Digital Assistants (PDAs) have become so commonplace in our lives that it is easy to forget that ten years ago, they were a rarity. But wireless communications is still in its infancy, and the next stage of its development will be in supplementing or replacing the network infrastructure that was traditionally "wired" as well as enabling network infrastructures that previously could only be imagined. From local coffee shops to commercial inventory control systems, within restaurants and throughout public airports, accessing central pools of information and communicating directly between users and among the devices themselves, wireless commerce is beginning to challenge the exchange system that our modern world currently embraces.

No longer are we restricted by the shortfalls of processing and battery power, operating system efficiencies, or heat dissipation within the small footprint of the mobile device. Rather, we are limited only by the practical application of these technologies. How will we access information? How will we integrate multiple hardware and software technologies into intelligent and useable form factors? Not all business models necessarily imply the use of a single terminal to supply the user with voice, video, and data services. Ergonomic factors may dictate that voice services are maintained privately while data exchange and video information is easily viewable from a specified distance, perhaps on complementary devices.

As network engineers, we will be charged with the seamless distribution of information between seemingly incompatible software and hardware standards. In addition, we will be challenged by narrower bandwidths to develop highly efficient means of transport in order to fully leverage wireless technologies. This book is meant as both a primer for wireless technologies and as a guide on how to design and implement a wireless data network.

We've written this book for our peers in the IT community with the hope that we can save them some of the "ramp-up" time we've invested over the last several years in designing and working with wireless networks. While no previous wireless, IP, or design experience is required to understand this book, some knowledge in all three areas is recommended. Upon completion of this book, you should have a good understanding of:

- How wireless communication works.
- The physics behind wireless communications.
- What components make up a wireless network.
- The Transmission Control Protocol/IP (TCP/IP) and how it relates to the conventions of the Open Systems Interconnection (OSI) Reference Model.
- The various wireless technologies available today.
- The methodologies used to design and implement a wireless network.

In laying a foundation for understanding these concepts, the construct of this book provides the reader with historical references as well as applicable case studies. Due to the vast differences between the types of wireless networks, we have tried to keep our design recommendations at a high-level.

Chapter 1 covers the history of wireless communications. It starts at the discovery of electro-magnetism and takes you through the technology developments leading up to the present day. Following the historical overview, we discuss the applications that operate over wireless technologies and the markets where wireless networking is becoming more prevalent.

Chapter 2 moves into the detailed physics behind wireless communications. It also covers the various components that make up wireless networks, including base stations, and antennas. This chapter will provide you with the level of understanding necessary to be able to better understand how wireless communication devices operate. Following the discussion on network components, we discuss some of the regulations involved with wireless communications. When building a wireless network, it is important to know and understand what regulations you possibly have to follow.

Chapter 3 departs from wireless and switches gears to TCP/IP. When designing and implementing networks today, it is important to have a good understanding of the network layer protocol that will run over them. The most popular network protocol today is TCP/IP. This chapter will cover both the OSI model and the TCP/IP protocol suite, identifying specific examples and correlations to wireless networking. Due to the complexity of both of these topics, this chapter is simply an overview of each and is meant as only an introduction.

Chapter 4 identifies some of the many wireless-networking technologies. From Bluetooth to LMDS to 802.11, this chapter explains the workings of the most popular technologies today. The chapter covers four functional wireless areas including:

- Fixed Wireless Technologies
- Mobile Wireless Technologies
- Wireless LANs and PANs
- Optical Wireless Technologies

The emphasis of this chapter is on Wireless LANs, since it is prevalent in both business and residential markets today.

Chapter 5 teaches the design methodologies used by Lucent Technologies Enhanced Services and Sales, the professional services and consulting division of Lucent Technologies. It begins by exploring the design process, moving into specific wireless considerations in the design process. Next it details the design process with a high-level overview, followed by implementation considerations and documentation.

Chapters 6 through 9 are detailed case studies of fictional wireless projects based on the authors experience in the real world. The four studies include:

- An Industrial/Retail Case Study

- A Hospital Case Study

- A College Campus Case Study

- A Home/Personal Case Study

Each case study is a design project from inception to completion. While each one is unique, they all contain the same components of wireless networking and design. Each case study will be presented in a different manner, from simple story-based to detailed engineering-based. The case studies are used as a hands-on guide towards building a wireless network.

*—Andy McCullough*
*BSEE, CCNA, CCDA*

# Chapter 1

# Introduction to Wireless: From Past to Present

## Solutions in this chapter:

- **Exploring Past Discoveries That Led to Wireless**

- **Exploring Present Applications for Wireless**

- **Exploring This Book on Wireless**

- ☑ **Summary**

- ☑ **Solutions Fast Track**

- ☑ **Frequently Asked Questions**

# Introduction

You've been on an extended business trip and have spent the long hours of the flight drafting follow-up notes from your trip while connected to the airline's onboard server. After deplaning, you walk through the gate and continue into the designated public access area. Instantly, your personal area network (PAN) device, which is clipped to your belt, beeps twice announcing that it automatically has retrieved your e-mail, voice-mail, and videomail. You stop to view the videomail—a finance meeting—and also excerpts from your children's school play.

Meanwhile, when you first walked into the public access area, your personal area network device contacted home via the Web pad on your refrigerator and posted a message to alert the family of your arrival. Your spouse will know you'll be home from the airport shortly.

You check the shuttlebus schedule from your PAN device and catch the next convenient ride to long-term parking. You also see an e-mail from your MP3 group showing the latest selections, so you download the latest MP3 play list to listen to on the way home.

As you pass through another public access area, an e-mail comes in from your spouse. The Web pad for the refrigerator inventory has noted that you're out of milk, so could you pick some up on the way home? You write your spouse back and say you will stop at the store. When you get to the car, you plug your PAN device into the car stereo input port. With new music playing from your car stereo's MP3 player, you drive home, with a slight detour to buy milk at the nearest store that the car's navigation system can find.

The minute you arrive home, your PAN device is at work, down-loading information to various devices. The data stored on your PAN device is sent to your personal computer (PC) and your voicemail is sent to the Bluetooth playback unit on the telephone-answering device. The PAN device sends all video to the television, stored as personal files for playback. As you place the milk in the refrigerator, the Web pad updates to show that milk is currently in inventory and is no longer needed. The kids bring you the television remote and you check out possible movies together to download later that night.

A few weeks later, you are en route back to the airport, but this time with the family for vacation. During the drive, you try to figure out what you could have forgotten. You check the status of the home security system on the PAN device, which was indeed activated—for alarm zones, interior light, and stereo activation to make it look and sound as if people are home—and check the lawn sprinkler mode as well, which was not on, so you set it to activate in the evenings while you're away. Your spouse had already ordered the grocery and dry cleaning delivery for the day you return, from the Web pad on your refrigerator.

As you head toward the check-in lines at the airport, you walk through the designated public access area. Your PAN device beeps, showing that there is an update on your flight plans—the flight is delayed. Your teenagers, unflappable as always, make the best of the situation, flopping in the nearest chair and pulling from the carry-on bag the Web pad that they had been sure to remove from the refrigerator just before they left. They initiate a game session to pass the time. You head over to the Bluetooth kiosk to print out a new temporary message about the flight. The message you print out also includes a coupon for the new coffee shop around the corner from the gate; your spouse takes the coupon to go get some much needed caffeine for the two of you. You sit down with the kids and they relinquish the game so you can watch a movie together with a video-on-demand session on the Web pad. This helps settle the family's nerves and makes the time go by quickly.

Do these scenarios sound familiar? If they are not familiar now, they will be soon. All of the personal wireless technologies are available for purchase now or in the very near future. Innovative service providers plan to create new services and value-added services for public access areas around the world. Soon, we will be able to communicate wirelessly throughout the world. This technology is the leading edge of future technology, a new revolution in communication.

Now that you've seen a glimpse of the current and future applications of this technology, this chapter will explain some of the history behind this technology; explore how some of the modern trends in wireless communications have developed and how business and the private sector utilize wireless networks; and discuss how that service is delivered.

# Exploring Past Discoveries That Led to Wireless

*Wireless technology* is the method of delivering data from one point to another without using physical wires, and includes radio, cellular, infrared, and satellite. A historic perspective will provide you with a general understanding of the substantial evolution that has taken place in this area. The common wireless networks of today originated from many evolutionary stages of wireless communications and telegraph and radio applications. Although some discoveries occurred in the early 1800s, much of the evolution of wireless communication began with the emergence of the electrical age and was affected by modern economics as much as by discoveries in physics.

Because the current demand of wireless technology is a direct outgrowth of traditional wired 10-Base-T Ethernet networks, we will also briefly cover the advent of the computer and the evolution of computer networks. Physical networks, and their limitations, significantly impacted wireless technology. This section presents some of the aspects of traditional computer networks and how they relate to wireless networks. Another significant impact to wireless is the invention of the cell phone. This section will briefly explain significant strides in the area of cellular communication.

## Discovering Electromagnetism

Early writings show that people were aware of magnetism for several centuries before the middle 1600s; however, people did not become aware of the correlation between magnetism and electricity until the 1800s. In 1820, Hans Christian Oersted, a Danish physicist and philosopher working at that time as a professor at the University of Copenhagen, attached a wire to a battery during a lecture; coincidentally, he just happened to do this near a compass and he noticed that the compass needle swung around. This is how he discovered that there was a relationship between electricity and magnetism. Oersted continued to explore this relationship, influencing the works of contemporaries Michael Faraday and Joseph Henry.

Michael Faraday, an English scientific lecturer and scholar, was engrossed in magnets and magnetic effects. In 1831, Michael Faraday theorized that a changing magnetic field is necessary to induce a current in a nearby circuit. This theory is actually the definition of *induction*. To test his theory, he made a coil by wrapping a paper cylinder with wire. He connected the coil to a device called a *galvanometer*, and then moved a magnet back and forth inside the cylinder. When the magnet was moved, the galvanometer needle moved, indicating that a current was induced in the coil. This proved that you must have a moving magnetic field for electromagnetic induction to occur. During this experiment, Faraday had not only discovered induction but also had created the world's first electric generator. Faraday's initial findings still serve as the basis of modern electromagnetic technology.

Around the same time that Faraday worked with electromagnetism, an American professor named Joseph Henry became the first person to transmit a practical electrical signal. As a watchmaker, he constructed batteries and experimented with magnets. Henry was the first to wind insulated wires around an iron core to make electromagnets. Henry worked on a theory known as *self-inductance*, the inertial characteristic of an electric current. If a current is flowing, it is kept flowing by the property of self-inductance. Henry found that the property of self-inductance is affected by how the circuit is configured, especially by the coiling of wire. Part of his experimentation involved simple signaling.

It turns out that Henry had also derived many of the same conclusions that Faraday had. Though Faraday won the race to publish those findings, Henry still is remembered for actually finding a way to communicate with electromagnetic waves. Although Henry never developed his work on electrical signaling on his own, he did help a man by the name of Samuel Morse. In 1832, Morse read about Faraday's findings regarding inductance, which inspired him to develop his ideas about an emerging technology called the telegraph. Henry actually helped Morse construct a repeater that allowed telegraphy to span long distances, eventually making his Morse Code a worldwide language in which to communicate. Morse introduced the repeater technology with his 1838 patent for a Morse Code telegraph. Like so many great inventions, the telegraph revolutionized the communications world by replacing nearly every other means of communication—including services such as the Pony Express.

## Exploring Conduction

Samuel Morse spent a fair amount of time working on wireless technology, but he also chose to use mediums such as earth and water to pass signals. In 1842, he performed a spectacular demonstration for the public in which he attempted to pass electric current through a cable that was underwater. The ultimate result of the demonstration was wireless communication by *conduction*, although it was not what he first intended. Morse submerged a mile of insulated cable between Governor's Island and Castle Garden in New York to prove that a current could pass through wire laid in water. He transmitted a few characters successfully, but, much to his dismay, the communication suddenly halted—sailors on a ship between the islands, unseen to the spectators, raised their ship's anchor and accidentally pulled up the cable, and not knowing what it was for, proceeded to cut it. Morse faced considerable heckling from the spectators and immediately began modification to the experiment. He successfully retested his idea by transmitting a wireless signal between copper plates he placed in the Susquehanna River, spanning a distance of approximately one mile. In doing so, he became the first person to demonstrate wireless by conduction. Conduction is the flow of electricity charges through a substance (in this case, the water in the river) resulting from a difference in electric potential based on the substance.

## Inventing the Radio

After the significant discoveries of induction and conduction, scientists began to test conduction with different mediums and apply electricity to machinery. The scholars and scientists of the day worked to apply these discoveries and explore the parameters of the properties. After the theory of conduction in water was proven, new theories were derived about conduction in the air. In 1887, a German named Heinrich Hertz became the first person to prove electricity travels in waves through the atmosphere. Hertz went on to show that electrical conductors reflect waves, whereas nonconductors simply let the waves pass through the medium. In addition, Hertz also proved that the velocity of light and radio waves are equal, as well as the fact that it is possible to detach electrical and magnetic waves from wires and radiate. Hertz served as inspiration to other researchers who scrambled to duplicate his results and further develop his findings. Inventors from all across the world easily validated Hertz's experiments, and the world prepared for a new era in *radio*, the wireless transmission of electromagnetic waves.

An Italian inventor called Guglielmo Marconi was particularly intrigued by Hertz's published results. Marconi was able to send wireless messages over a distance of ten miles with his patented radio equipment, and eventually across the English Channel. In late 1901, Marconi and his assistants built a wireless receiver in Newfoundland and intercepted the faint Morse code signaling of the letter "S" that had been sent across the Atlantic Ocean from a colleague in England. It was astounding proof that the wireless signal literally curved around the earth, past the horizon line—even Marconi could not explain *how* it happened, but he had successfully completed the world's first truly long-distance communication, and the communication world would never be the same.

Today we know that the sun's radiation forms a layer of ionized gas particles approximately one hundred miles above the earth's surface. This layer, the ionosphere, reflects radio waves back to the earth's surface, and the waves subsequently bounce back up to the ionosphere again. This process continues until the energy of the waves dissipates.

Another researcher by the name of Reginald Fessenden proceeded to further develop Marconi's achievements, and he became the first person to create a radio band wave of human speech. The importance of his results was felt worldwide, as radio was no longer limited to telegraph codes.

# Mounting Radio-Telephones in Cars

In 1921, mobile radios began operating in the 2 MHz range, which is just above the Amplitude Modulation (AM) frequency range of current radios. These mobile radios were generally used for law enforcement activities only. They were not integrated with the existing wireline phone systems that were much more common at that time—since the technology was still so new, the equipment was considered experimental and not practical for mass distribution. In fact, people originally did not consider mobile radio as a technology for the public sector. Instead, the technology was developed for police and emergency services personnel, who really served as the pioneers in mobile radio.

It was not until 1924 that the voice-based wireless telephone had the ability to be bi-directional, or two-way. Bell Laboratories invented this breakthrough telephone. Not only could people now receive messages wirelessly, they could also respond to the message immediately, greatly increasing convenience and efficiency. This improved system was still not connected to landline telephone systems, but the evolution of wireless communication had taken one more major step. One issue that still plagued this early mobile radio system was the sheer size of the radio; it took up an entire trunk. Add to the size restriction, the cost of the radio system that was almost as expensive as the vehicle.

In 1935, Edwin Howard Armstrong introduced Frequency Modulation (FM). This technology not only increased the overall transmission quality of wireless radio but also drastically reduced the size of the equipment. The timing could not have been any better. World War II had begun, and the military quickly embraced FM technology to provide two-way mobile radio communication. Due to the war, companies immediately sensed the urgency to develop the FM technology rapidly, and companies such as Motorola and AT&T immediately began designing considerably smaller equipment. Many of these new inventions became possible due to the invention of the circuit board, which changed the world of electronic equipment of all types.

# Inventing Computers and Networks

Though the beginning of the computer age is widely discussed, computer discoveries can be attributed to a long line of inventors throughout the 1800s, beginning with the Englishman Charles Babbage, who in 1822 created the first calculator called the "Difference Engine." Then came Herman Hollerith, who in 1887 produced a punch card reader to tabulate the American census for 1890. Later developments led to the creation of different punch card technologies, binary representation, and the use of vacuum tubes.

The war effort in the 1940s produced the first decoding machine, the Colossus, used in England to break German codes. This machine was slow, taking about 3 to 5 seconds per calculation. The next significant breakthrough was the creation of the Electronic Numerical Integrator and Computer (ENIAC) by Americans John Presper Eckert and John W. Mauchley. The ENIAC was the first general-purpose computer that computed at speeds 1000 times greater than the Colossus. However, this machine was a behemoth, consuming over 160 Kilowatts of power—when it ran, it dimmed lights in an entire section of Philadelphia. The main reason these machines were so huge was the vacuum tube technology. The invention of the transistor in 1948 changed the computer's development and began shrinking the machinery. In the next thirty years, the computers got significantly faster and smaller.

In 1981, IBM introduced the personal computer for the home, school, and business. The number of PCs more than doubled from 2 million in 1981 to 5.5 million in 1982; more than 65 million PCs were being used ten years later. With the surge of computer use in the workplace, more emphasis was being placed on how to harness their power and make them work together. As smaller computers became more powerful, it became necessary to find a way to link them together to share memory, software, and information, and to find a way for them to communicate together. Network technology to this point consisted of a mainframe that stored the information and performed the processes hooked to several "dumb terminals" that provided the input.

Ethernet was developed in the early 1970s and was used to link multiple PCs within a physical area to form what is known as a Local Area Network (LAN). A LAN connects network devices over a short distance. Common applications include offices, schools, and the home. Sometimes businesses are composed of several LANs that are connected together. Besides spanning a short distance, LANs have other distinctive attributes. LANs typically are controlled, owned, and operated by a single person or department. LANs also use specific technologies, including Ethernet and Token Ring for connectivity. There are typically two basic components to the LAN configuration: a client and a server. The client is the node that makes a request, and the server is the node that fulfills that request. The client computer contains the client software that allows for access to shared resources on the server. Without the client software, the computer will not actively participate in either of the two network models.

Wide Area Networks (WANs) span a much wider physical distance. Usually a WAN is a widely dispersed collection of LANs. The WAN uses a router to connect the LANs physically. For example, a company may have LANs in New York, Los Angeles, Tokyo, and Sydney; this company would then implement a WAN to span the LANs and to enable communication throughout the company. WANs use different connectivity technology than LANs—typically, T1 or T3 lines, Asynchronous Transfer Mode (ATM) or Frame Relay circuits, microwave links, or higher speed Synchronous Optical Network (SONET) connections.

The largest WAN is the Internet. The Internet is basically a WAN that spans the entire globe. Home networks often implement LANs and WANs through cable modems and digital subscriber line (DSL) service. In these systems, a cable or DSL router links the home network to the provider's WAN and the provider's central gateway to reach the Internet.

A wireless local area network transmits over the air by means of base stations, or access points, that transmit a radio frequency; the base stations are connected to an Ethernet hub or server. Mobile end-users can be handed off between access points, as in the cellular phone system, though their range generally is limited to a couple hundred feet.

# Inventing Cell Phones

Wireless technology is based on the car-mounted police radios of the 1920s. Mobile telephone service became available to private customers in the 1940s. In 1947, Southwestern Bell and AT&T launched the first commercial mobile phone service in St. Louis, Missouri, but the Federal Communications Commission (FCC) limited the amount of frequencies available, which made possible only 23 simultaneous phone conversations available within a service area (the mobile phones offered only six channels with a 60 kHz spacing between them). Unfortunately, that spacing schema led to very poor sound quality due to cross-channel interference, much like the cross talk on wireline phones. The original public wireless systems generally used single high-powered transmitters to cover the entire coverage area. In order to utilize the precious frequencies allotted to them, AT&T developed an idea to replace the single high-powered transmitter approach with several smaller and lower-powered transmitters strategically placed throughout the metropolitan area; calls would switch between transmitters as they needed a stronger signal. Although this method of handling calls certainly eased some of the problems, it did not eliminate the problem altogether. In fact, the problem of too few voice channels plagued the wireless phone industry for several years.

The problem was that demand always seemed to exceed supply. Since the FCC refused to allocate more frequencies for mobile wireless use, waiting lists became AT&T's temporary solution as the company strove for the technological advances necessary to accommodate everyone. For example, in 1976, there were less than 600 mobile phone customers in New York City, but there were over 3500 people on waiting lists. Across the United States at that time, there were nearly 45,000 subscribers, but there were still another 20,000 people on waiting lists as much as ten years long. Compare this situation to today's, in which providers give away free phones and thousands of minutes just to gain a subscriber.

Cellular technology has come a long way. The term *cellular* describes how each geographic region of coverage is broken up into *cells*. Within each of these cells is a radio transmitter and control equipment. Early cellular transmission operated at 800 MHz on analog signals, which are sent on a continuous wave. When a customer makes a call, the first signal sent identifies the caller as a customer, verifies that he or she is a customer of the service, and finds a free channel for the call. The mobile phone user has a wireless phone that in connection with the cellular tower and base station, handles the calls, their connection and handoff, and the control functions of the wireless phone.

Personal communications services (PCS), which operates at 1850 MHz, followed years later. PCS refers to the services that a given carrier has available to be bundled together for the user. Services like messaging, paging, and voicemail are all part of the PCS environment. Sprint is the major carrier that typically is associated with PCS. Some cellular providers began looking into digital technology (digital signals are basically encoded voice delivered by bit streams). Some providers are using digital signals to send not only voice, but also data. Other advantages include more power of the frequency or bandwidth, and less chance of corruption per call. Coverage is based on three technologies: Code Division Multiple Access (CDMA), Time Division Multiple Access (TDMA), and Global System for Mobile Communication (GSM). A more detailed technical description of this technology can be found in Chapter 4.

# Exploring Present Applications for Wireless

Many corporations and industries are jumping into the wireless arena. Two of the industries most committed to deploying wireless technologies are airports and hotels, for business travelers' communications needs. If they are traveling in a car, they use their wireless phones. When they are at work or home, they are able to use their computers and resources to again be productive. But when staying in a hotel for the night or even a week, there are few choices—a business traveler can look for the RJ-11 jack and connect to the Internet via 56-kilobit modem, not connect at all, or connect wirelessly. When a hotel provides the correct configuration information based on the provider, and a software configuration, a business traveler with wireless capabilities can connect to their network without worrying about connection speed or out-of-date modems.

Airports offer such services to increase travelers' productivity at a time when they would otherwise be isolated from business resources. The same configuration applies: set the configuration in the wireless client software and voilà, you are connected. This wireless technology allows users to get access to the Internet, e-mail, and even the corporate intranet sites utilizing a virtual private network (VPN) solution. Now, the work (or in some cases, gaming) can be done during what used to be known as idle time. This increase in productivity is very attractive to corporations who need their increasingly mobile workforce to stay connected. This scenario is accomplished using the following scheme:

- A wireless Internet service provider contracts with the airport or hotel to set up wireless access servers and access points.

- Access points are located in specific locations to provide wireless coverage throughout the hotel or airport.

Using this scenario, anyone with an account to that service provider can get access to the Internet by walking into the location where the service is offered with their laptop, Personal Digital Assistant (PDA), or other wireless device. This access includes such applications as e-mail, Intranet connection via VPN solution, push content such as stock updates, and Web browsing. Not that this is all work and no play—you can also set up online gaming and video-on-demand sessions. In fact, nonwork scenarios open up the possible user base to children and families, multiplying the use and demand of this technology.

# Applying Wireless Technology to Vertical Markets

There are several vertical markets in addition to airports and hotels that are realizing the benefits of utilizing wireless networks. Many of these markets, including delivery services, public safety, finance, retail, and monitoring applications, are still at the beginning of incorporating wireless networks, but as time passes and the demand and popularity grows, they will integrate wireless networking more deeply.

## Using Wireless in Delivery Services

Delivery and courier services, which depend on mobility and speed, employ a wireless technology called Enhanced Specialized Mobile Radio (ESMR) for voice communication between the delivery vehicle and the office. This technology consists of a dispatcher in an office plotting out the day's events for a driver. When the driver arrives at his location, he radios the dispatcher and lets them know his location. The benefit of ESMR is its ability to act like a CB radio, allowing all users on one channel to listen, while still allowing two users to personally communicate. This arrangement allows the dispatcher to coordinate schedules for both pick-ups and deliveries and track the drivers' progress. Drivers with empty loads can be routed to assist backlogged drivers. Drivers that are on the road can be radioed if a customer cancels a delivery. This type of communication benefits delivery services in two major areas, saving time and increasing efficiency.

United Parcel Service (UPS) utilizes a similar wireless system for their business needs. Each driver carries a device that looks like a clipboard with a digital readout and an attached penlike instrument. The driver uses this instrument to record each delivery digitally. The driver also uses it to record digitally the signature of the person who accepts the package. This information is transmitted wirelessly back to a central location so that someone awaiting a delivery can log into the Web site and get accurate information regarding the status of a package.

## Using Wireless for Public Safety

Public safety applications got their start with radio communications for maritime endeavors and other potentially hazardous activities in remote areas. Through the use of satellite communications and the coordination of the International Maritime Satellite Organization (INMARSAT), these communications provided the ships with information in harsh weather or provide them a mechanism to call for help. This type of application led to Global Positioning Systems (GPS), which are now standard on naval vessels. In many cases, a captain can use the 24 satellites circling the globe in conjunction with his ship's navigational system to determine his exact location and plot his course. GPS is also used for military applications, aviation, or for personal use when tracking or pinpointing the user's location could save his or her life.

Today, there are medical applications that use wireless technology such as ambulance and hospital monitoring links. Remote ambulatory units remain in contact with the hospital to improve medical care in the critical early moments. An emergency medical technician can provide care under a doctor's instruction during transport prior to arriving in the hospital's emergency room. Standard monitoring of critical statistics are transmitted wirelessly to the hospital.

## Using Wireless in the Financial World

Wireless applications can keep an investor informed real-time of the ticker in the stock market, allowing trades and updates to be made on the go. No longer is the investor tied to his desk, forced to call into his broker to buy and sell. Now, an online investor has the opportunity to get real-time stock quotes from the Internet pushed to his wireless device. He can then make the needed transactions online and make decisions instantaneously in response to the market.

There are also services that allow you to sign up and get critical information about earmarked stocks. In this scenario, you can set an alarm threshold on a particular stock you are following. When the threshold is met, the service sends a page to you instantly. Again, this improves the efficiency of the investor.

## Using Wireless in the Retail World

Wireless point-of-sale (POS) applications are extremely useful for both merchant and customer, and will revolutionize the way retail business transactions occur. Registers and printers are no longer fixed in place and can be used at remote locations. Wireless scanners can further assist checkout systems. Wireless technology is used for connecting multiple cash registers through an access point to a host computer that is connected to the WAN. This WAN link is used to send real-time data back to a corporate headquarters for accounting information.

Another type of wireless point-of-sale application is inventory control. A handheld scanner is used for multiple purposes. The operator can check inventory on a given product throughout the day and wirelessly transfer the data back to the main computer system. This increases efficiency in that the device is mobile and small, and the data is recorded without manually having to enter the information.

## Using Wireless in Monitoring Applications

We have been using wireless technologies for monitoring for years. There are typically two types of monitoring: passive and active. Active monitoring is conducted by use of radio signals being transmitted, and any of a number of expected signals received. An example of this implementation is the use of radar guns in traffic control. In this case, the patrolman points the gun and pulls the trigger, and a specific reading of a specific target is displayed on the radar unit. Passive monitoring is a long-term implementation whereby a device listens to a transmitter and records the data. An example of this is when an animal is tagged with a transmitter and the signal is collected and data is gathered over a period of time to be interpreted at a later date.

Monitoring applications in use today include NASA listening to space for radio signals, and receiving pictures and data relayed from probes; weather satellites monitoring the weather patterns; geologists using radio waves to gather information on earthquakes.

## Applying Wireless Technology to Horizontal Applications

Along with the many vertical markets and applications, you can apply wireless technologies to horizontal applications, meaning that delivery services, public safety, finance, retail, and monitoring can all use and benefit from them. The next section gives an overview of some of the more popular horizontal trends in wireless technology.

## Using Wireless in Messaging

The new wave of messaging is the culmination of wireless phones and the Wireless Application Protocol (WAP) and Short Message Service (SMS). This service is similar to the America Online Instant Messaging service. The ability for two-way messaging, multiservice calling, and Web browsing in one device creates a powerful tool for consumers, while providing the vendors the ability to generate higher revenues. Look for wireless messaging services to be introduced in local applications, particularly within restaurants, to replace conventional wait lists.

## Using Wireless for Mapping

Mapping in a wireless environment, of course, relates back to the GPS system; GPS not only assists the maritime industry with navigation, but also commercial vehicles and private cars for safety. In a few cars out today, a GPS receiver is placed on board to prevent drivers from becoming lost. It will also display a map of the surrounding area. The signal from the GPS satellites is fed into an onboard computer, which contains an application with software that contains a topographical map. The more current the software is, the more accurate the map will be. The coordinates of the receiver are placed on the topographical map in the program, usually in the form of a dot, and a display screen provides a visible picture of where in relation to the map someone is at that moment. This is updated live as the receiver moves.

## Using Wireless for Web Surfing

In addition to the standard laptop computer connected to a wireless LAN with Internet connectivity, there has been an explosion of other wireless units that offer multiple voice and data applications integrated in one piece of equipment. Typically, personal organizer functionality and other standard calculation-type services are offered, but now, these devices are used with appropriate software to get access to the Internet. This brings the power of the Internet and the vast repository of information to the palm of the hand.

PDAs, Palm, Inc.'s handheld devices, and wireless phones with the appropriate hardware and software are now being used for Internet access at speeds of up to 56 Kbps. This is moving wireless into the realm of not only browsing the Internet, which is a big accomplishment in and of itself, but Internet gaming. As the interface of the wireless devices gets better and better, the gaming community will be able to offer high quality online games played on your PDA.

# Exploring This Book on Wireless

The chapters in this book seek to promote a greater understanding of wireless LAN technologies in a "building block" fashion. This chapter presented the history behind wireless technology. Chapter 2 examines basic radio frequency theory, to give you a foundation of understanding and appreciation for wireless technology as a LAN transport. Beyond the physical aspect of wireless LAN technologies, it is important to understand how each of the network nodes and supporting equipment interact with the LAN and WAN infrastructures.

Traditional Transmission Control Protocol/Internet Protocol (TCP/IP) networks are typically hard-wired and use IP addressing as a means of addressing other users within that infrastructure. Chapter 3 serves to build an understanding of the various protocols commonly used on the IP network and explains the overriding addressing infrastructure.

Chapter 4 provides a glimpse into the emerging technologies in the area of wireless communications. Chapter 5 seeks to bridge both the TCP/IP and wireless worlds by exploring the design process. In that chapter, we will explore the major phases of designing a wireless network and take into account the attributes that are specific to wireless technologies.

Finally, we will examine four case studies that will provide you with added insight into applying these concepts in designing and building a wireless computer network.

# Summary

In this chapter we have explored some of the history of how wireless technology evolved into what it is today. Wireless technology has been around a long time, considering the decades of development in radio and cellular telephone technology. These technologies have been quietly developing in the background while PDAs, Palm Pilots, and other hand-held wireless devices have been gaining notoriety. Other uses such as GPS and satellite communications to the home have also been developing for mainstream applications. These applications offer consumers many advantages over wireline counterparts, including flexibility, mobility, and increased efficiency and timeliness.

In surveying all that wireless has achieved, one problem still exists: needing many devices to access the various services offered. These devices can be cumbersome to carry, and the options and selection make the situation more complicated. Without question it is time for professionals to be free from having to carry a pager, a cell phone, and a PDA to get services they need. The future of wireless technology is to integrate voice and data services into one system that will allow end users to get all their requirements met in one device. The entire network infrastructure in wired technology is moving toward a converged network where voice and data are integrated into one network—the move is monumental for end-user quality and services offered, it makes sense for carriers and service providers from a revenue standpoint, and once completed, will allow services to be distributed by request. Wireless fits into that by extending the last mile of communications to the mobile user. As wireless experiences the cost reduction and benefits enhancement that it has over the previous few years, there is little to oppose the notion of a globally connected wireless world.

# Solutions Fast Track

## Exploring Past Discoveries That Led to Wireless

☑ *Wireless technology* is the method of delivering data from one point to another without using physical wires, and includes radio, cellular, infrared, and satellite.

☑ The discovery of electromagnetism, induction, and conduction provided the basis for developing communication techniques that manipulated the flow of electric current through the mediums of air and water.

☑ Guglielmo Marconi was the first person to prove that electricity traveled in waves through the air, when he was able to transmit a message beyond the horizon line.

☑ The limitations on frequency usage that hindered demand for mobile telephone service were relieved by the development of the geographically structured cellular system.

## Exploring Present Applications for Wireless

☑ Vertical markets are beginning to realize the use of wireless networks. Wireless technology can be used for business travelers needing airport and hotel access, gaming and video, for delivery services, public safety, finance, retail, and monitoring.

☑ Horizontal applications for wireless include new technology for messaging services, mapping (GPS) and location-based tracking systems, and Internet browsing.

## Exploring This Book on Wireless

☑   The chapters of this book are to be used as building blocks. The early chapters present information on wireless LAN technologies, network protocols, emerging wireless technology, and network design concepts. The last four chapters contain case studies that build on that information and illustrate a real-world implementation.

# Frequently Asked Questions

The following Frequently Asked Questions, answered by the authors of this book, are designed to both measure your understanding of the concepts presented in this chapter and to assist you with real-life implementation of these concepts. To have your questions about this chapter answered by the author, browse to **www.syngress.com/solutions** and click on the **"Ask the Author"** form.

**Q:** Why did it take so long to develop wireless technologies?

**A:** The scientific principles behind wireless technologies have been developing at the same time as wireline technologies, and include major advances for military and industrial needs—but in comparison, the potential mainstream consumer applications for wireless have not been embraced. One reason is that the FCC has strictly regulated service providers' access to the necessary frequencies.

**Q:** What is the difference between wireless voice and wireless networking?

**A:** Technologically, they are very similar. In short, wireless voice is a traditional conversation between two or more people with at least one person not connected to wires, whereas wireless networking often implies that data is transmitted rather than voice.

**Q:** What is Bluetooth, and how can I find out more about it?

**A:** We mentioned Bluetooth in the Introduction of this chapter as an illustration of how wireless devices will link together in the near future. Bluetooth is an open wireless standard intended to support short-range transmission between Bluetooth-enabled computer peripherals and low-speed data exchange between Bluetooth-enabled devices. More information about Bluetooth is provided in Chapter 4.

# Chapter 2

# Radio Elements and Frequency Spectrums

## Solutions in this chapter:

- **Transmitting Radio Signals Over Electromagnetic Waves**
- **Propagating a Strong Radio Signal**
- **Understanding the Network Elements**
- **Channelizing the Frequency Spectrum**
- **Regulating Wireless Communications**
- ☑ **Summary**
- ☑ **Solutions Fast Track**
- ☑ **Frequently Asked Questions**

# Introduction

This chapter covers the scientific principles that make wireless communication possible. Radio components and the associated frequency range is the primary mode of transmission in the wireless industry.

*Radio* is the wireless transmission and reception of electric impulses or signals by means of electromagnetic (EM) waves. Electromagnetic waves are present at all frequencies. However, currently we can utilize only a small part of this total spectrum to transmit communication signals. This small subset of frequencies is commonly referred to as the Radio Frequency (RF) spectrum and ranges from about 9 KHz to 300 GHz. Understanding the science behind the communication provides value when you are designing a wireless network, allowing you to understand potential complications such as the signal-to-noise ratio, attenuation and multipath scattering, and channel spacing.

In this chapter we will explore the basic science of EM waves, and how and why radio signals are modulated onto carrier waves; we'll look at antenna design, the relationship between wave propagation technologies and signal power, and what elements make up a wireless network. Finally, a discussion of channels will introduce different cellular schemes and how and why wireless communications are regulated.

# Transmitting Radio Signals Over EM Waves

As described in Chapter 1, the German scientist Heinrich Hertz demonstrated in 1887 that electrical energy could be transmitted through space via electromagnetic waves. Even though Professor Hertz was the first to demonstrate this phenomenon, he did not grasp the impact of his discovery. It was a young contemporary of his, an Italian named Guglielmo Marconi, who was inspired to use Hertz's discovery to transmit signals—thus the first radio was born.

Electric fields are induced by the separation of positive and negative charges. Moving charges (electric current flow) induce electric fields. Changing electric fields induce magnetic fields. Therefore, alternating current flow—such as current flow into and out of an antenna—will induce an oscillating electric field, which will then induce an oscillating magnetic field. An EM wave is the propagation of electrical energy caused by oscillating electric fields inducing oscillating magnetic fields, which then induce further oscillating electric fields, which then induce further oscillating magnetic fields, and so on.

## Anatomy of a Waveform

Radios transmit and receive signals over vast distances in the form of EM waves, at a particular frequency level that differentiates them from other electromagnetic waves in the frequency spectrum like infrared or x-rays, which we'll discuss later in the chapter. To illustrate simply, let's look at the *sinusoidal waveform*, the simplest and most common of all waveforms, which commonly is used to represent all types of waves. Figure 2.1 shows the key properties of a sinusoidal wave.

**Figure 2.1** Sinusoidal Wave

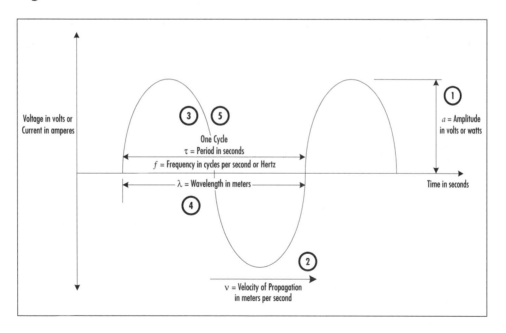

A *cycle* is the smallest portion of a waveform that, if repeated, would represent the entire waveform. Waveforms can be described as having the following properties (refer back to Figure 2.1):

1.  $a$ = Amplitude
    The measurement of a waveform above a center reference. With EM waves this is usually measured in volts or watts.

2.  $v$ = Velocity of Propagation
    The velocity of propagation of a wave is the velocity that a wave travels through a medium, and is usually measured in meters per second.

3.  $\tau$ = Period
    The period of a wave is the time it takes for one cycle to pass a fixed point and is usually measured in seconds. It is designated by the Greek letter tau ($\tau$).

4.  $\lambda$ = Wavelength
    The wavelength of a wave is the distance that the wave will propagate in one cycle and is usually measured in meters and designated by the Greek letter lambda ($\lambda$).

5.  $f$ = Frequency
    The frequency of a wave is the rate at which individual cycles pass a given point and is usually measured in cycles per second or Hertz (Hz), named after Heinrich Hertz, who discovered EM waves.

All of these properties except amplitude are related by the following formula:

$$f = 1/\tau = v/\lambda$$

The velocity of propagation for EM waves is relatively constant, and for practical purposes is equal to the speed of light ($3.00 \times 10^8$ m/s). Substituting this constant for velocity yields the following:

$$f = (3.00 \times 10^8 \text{ m/s}) / \lambda$$

Therefore, frequency (*f*) and wavelength (λ) can be used inter-changeably by using the preceding formula to convert one to the other.

Some of the most common types of signals transmitted via radio are audio signals such as voice or music. True audio signals like voice are usually near-random signals and very hard to graph and conceptualize. For our discussions, we will assume our input signal being transmitted is a 1 KHz sinusoidal wave. We will also assume the audio signal has already hit a microphone, thus converting the acoustical signal into an electric signal. If we want to transmit this 1 KHz electrical signal from point A to point B using a conductive medium such as copper wires, then we only need to connect a pair of wires to each end point: one wire is the point of reference, or *ground*, and the other wire carries the alternating signal voltage from point A to point B. However, if we want to transmit this signal without wires, it gets more complicated; the signal needs to be transmitted without interference.

## Modulating a Radio Signal

To transmit our 1 KHz wave without wires, it first must be modulated onto a *carrier wave* with a frequency many times higher than our input signal. There are several reasons why we must modulate our desired signal onto a much higher carrier signal.

The first reason is for better transmission. Most of the radio signals that we transmit are low-frequency signals. These signals do not propa-gate well as electromagnetic waves. Therefore, we use *modulation* to increase the frequency to allow more effective transmission.

The second reason is to allow multiple signals to be transmitted at the same time without interference. Your voice is in the same frequency range as my voice. Assume we both try to use a two-way radio to talk to our remote friends simultaneously. If we did not modulate our signals onto different carrier waves, then our signals would get mixed together and would be impossible to distinguish on the remote end. However, if we were to modulate our signals onto carrier waves of different frequen-cies, then our signals would not interfere with one another and we could talk simultaneously. Each specific carrier frequency is called a *channel.* We will discuss channels more when we talk about the RF spectrum.

A third reason to modulate signals onto high frequency carrier waves is due to restrictions on the antenna size. The length of an antenna is based on the length of the wave it was designed to transmit or receive. The simplest of antennas are a fraction of the wavelength, usually one half or one quarter of the wavelength. Since lower frequencies have longer wavelengths, the antennas designed for low frequencies are bigger. For example, 60 Hz is at the very lowest range of human hearing. The wavelength of a 60 Hz wave traveling at the speed of light is 3107 miles, or the distance from Boston, MA to San Francisco, CA. Therefore a one-half wavelength dipole antenna would be approximately 1500 miles long. It is easy to see this would not be a feasible length for an antenna! We will discuss antenna design in more depth later.

Now that we know a few reasons why we need to use modulation, let us talk about what it is and how a signal is modulated. When we talk about modulation, we are talking about a minimum of two waves, the *signal* and the *carrier*. Certain properties of the carrier waveform are modified (modulated) to represent the signal waveform. The signal wave is also called the modulating wave because it is the wave that modifies (or modulates) the carrier wave. The modulating wave can be anything from analog audio to a computer-generated digital square wave. The carrier wave is called the modulated wave because it is the wave that is being changed by the modulating or signal wave. Almost all carrier waves are a periodic sinusoidal wave with a frequency many, many times higher than the frequency of the modulating wave.

There are many types of modulation. Some types of modulations were developed to carry analog waveforms but since the invention of the computer, many types of modulation have been developed to carry digital waveforms. We will briefly discuss a few widely used types of modulation.

## *Analog Modulation Schemes*

There are two analog modulation schemes that are widely used and are familiar to anyone who has ever tuned a modern audio broadcast radio. These two forms of modulation are:

- Amplitude Modulation (AM)

- Frequency Modulation (FM)

Amplitude Modulation is the modulation of the amplitude of the carrier wave. Figure 2.2 illustrates the AM modulated signal.

**Figure 2.2** Amplitude Modulation (AM)

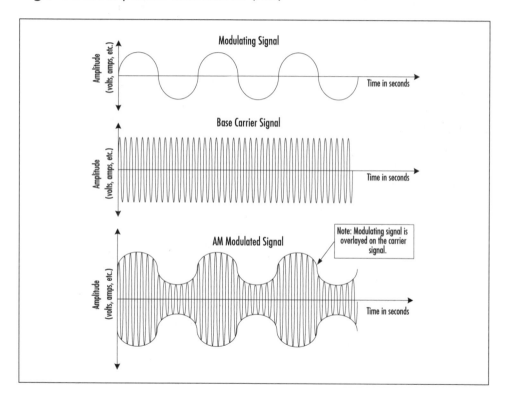

Frequency Modulation is the modulating of the frequency of the carrier wave to represent the frequency. Figure 2.3 illustrates the FM modulated signal.

**Figure 2.3** Frequency Modulation (FM)

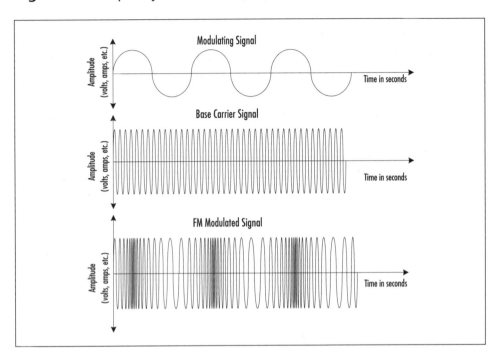

## Digital Modulation Schemes

Most sources of information that we as humans want to transmit are analog signals. Human speech, music, video, and pictures are all analog by nature. However, because computers use binary to store and process information, analog sources of information must be digitized. This means that the signal is approximately represented by a code of 1's and 0's that the computer can use to recreate the original signal as closely as possible. The error introduced when the signal is digitized is called *quantization error*. If the digitizing encoding technology is designed well, then the resulting signal so closely resembles the original signal that the differences are imperceptible to humans (such as music stored on compact discs).

As computers continue to take a more active role in capturing, storing, transmitting, and even modifying these signals, more and more information can successfully be digitized to satisfy the growing demand to transmit information over the air. This results in a growing need for modulation schemes that are designed to carry digital information.

One advantage of digital signals is the increased ease of compression. Most analog signals, once digitized, will require less space to store physically and less bandwidth to transmit due to various types of compression techniques.

Digital signals commonly are referred to as a *bit stream* and graphically are represented as a square wave (see Figure 2.4). In its simplest form, digital modulation is easier to conceptualize and easier to perform than analog modulation. That is because in the simplest form there are only two signal states to distinguish between: a bit value of one and a bit value of zero. However, digital modulation schemes get very complex as we try to maximize transmission speeds and bandwidth by combining various types of modulation. In this section we will look briefly at the following types of digital modulation in their simplest forms:

- On/Off Keying (OOK)

- Frequency Shift Keying (FSK)

- Phase Shift Keying (PSK)

- Pulse Amplitude Modulation (PAM)

On/Off Keying is the simplest form of modulation, digital or analog, and is the modulation used on the first radios built by Marconi and is the basis for Morse Code. OOK simply involves making (on) or breaking (off) the connection between the carrier signal's oscillator and the antenna in order to represent the digital signal. Figure 2.4 illustrates OOK modulation.

Frequency Shift Keying is similar to OOK, but instead of alternating between the carrier frequency (on) to no frequency (off), FSK alternates from the carrier wave frequency to the carrier wave frequency plus an *offset* frequency. The detection of this frequency change yields the transmitted digital signal. Figure 2.5 illustrates FSK modulation.

**Figure 2.4** On/Off Keying (OOK) Modulation

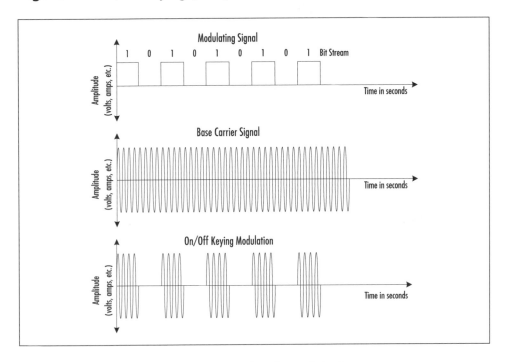

**Figure 2.5** Frequency Shift Keying (FSK) Modulation

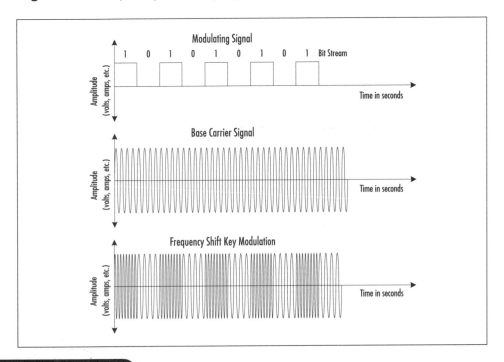

Phase Shift Keying (PSK) differs from OOK and FSK in that it does not change the frequency of the carrier wave. PSK changes the phase of the carrier wave in reference to the digital modulating wave. The detection of these phase shifts yields the transmitted digital signal. In its simplest form, PSK shifts the phase by half a wavelength, or 180 degrees. Figure 2.6 illustrates PSK modulation.

**Figure 2.6** Phase Shift Keying (PSK) Modulation

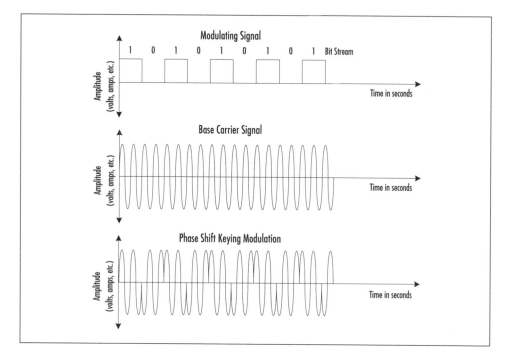

Pulse Amplitude Modulation does not vary the frequency of the carrier wave at all. As its name implies, it varies the *amplitude* of the carrier wave in reference to the digital modulating wave. Figure 2.7 illustrates PAM modulation.

Knowledge of how modulation is accomplished and of the different types is important because it applies to how computer systems communicate. FSK is the modulation technique used in frequency hopping spread spectrum (FHSS) and direct sequence spread spectrum (DSSS), used in wireless technology standards such as 802.11. In addition, modulation is also a factor in both mobile and optical wireless communications as well. This is discussed in greater detail in the Emerging Technology chapter.

**Figure 2.7** Pulse Amplitude Modulation (PAM)

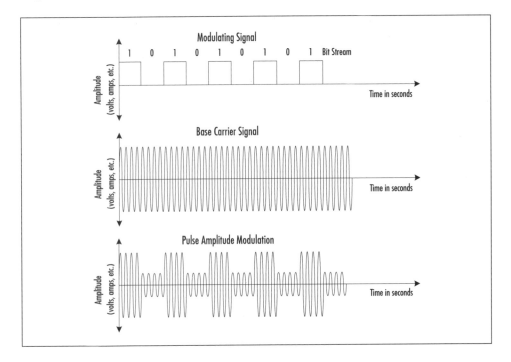

# Propagating a Strong Radio Signal

In order for wireless communications to function, the signal must have a path from the transmitter and the receiver and arrive with enough power left in the signal for the receiver to comprehend what is being sent. There are many factors that affect how a signal propagates from the transmitter to the receiver. Some of the factors that affect propagation affect low frequency signals differently than they affect high frequency signals. In this section we will look at several factors that impact the propagation of EM waves, and compare the benefits of low frequencies and higher frequencies.

# Understanding Signal Power and Signal-to-Noise Ratio

One of the principle requirements for wireless communication is that the transmitted EM wave must reach the receiver with ample power to allow the receiver to distinguish the wave from the background noise. An analogy can be made to human hearing: when someone is talking to you, they must talk loud enough for your ears to pick up the sound, and it has to be loud enough and clear enough for your brain to be able to recognize and translate the sounds into individual words.

Just as your ears and brain require a minimum volume and clarity level to be able to discern what is being said, a radio receiver also requires a minimum power level of received signal in order to discern and recreate the transmitted modulating wave. Signal strength for EM waves usually is measured in Watts, or more specifically, a logarithmic ratio of the signal strength divided by 1 milliwatt. This logarithmic ratio is called *decibels above 1 milliwatt* (dBm).

Another common property used to describe the signal strength is called the *signal-to-noise ratio* (S/N ratio). The S/N ratio does not describe the absolute power in the signal, but instead describes the power of the signal in comparison to the power of the background noise. The higher the S/N ratio, the better or more powerful the signal. If we look back at our hearing analogy, a person talking to you in a quiet room would be able to whisper to you and you would still be able to hear; however, if there was a lot of background noise present, say at a rock concert, that person would have to yell in order for you to hear. The same concepts apply to RF wireless communication. Since the S/N ratio accounts for the level of background noise, it is a very valuable and widely used indicator of signal strength.

Different modulation and encoding technologies require different minimum S/N ratios in order to function. Most digital modulation schemes require a lower S/N ratio than analog modulation schemes. The reason is the receiver of a digitally modulated carrier wave only has to distinguish between certain levels that represent a logical 1 and a logical 0. Even in the presence of a lot of noise, the receiver is able to distinguish between the predefined threshold levels and then regenerate the digital square wave. In contrast, the receiver of an analog modulated signal has an infinite number of levels that must be distinguished and maintained; it cannot assume that the received signal was supposed to be a 1 or a 0 and regenerate the signal—it must receive the signal, demodulate the signal, and then pass the resulting representation of the original signal to the next processing device, like an amplifier. Therefore, any noise added to an analog signal during propagation will alter the original signal. When the power of the modulated RF signal is several times greater than the power of the background noise, the added noise will not be noticed or can be reduced by filtering. On the other hand, when the noise is nearly as powerful as the signal, the resulting demodulated signal will be noticeably different than the original modulating signal. This is commonly called *static*.

The signal-to-noise ratio is an important aspect of network design. There are engineering rules established by vendors, specific to their equipment, to provide a set of guidelines for your design. Depending on the geographic span of your design, the S/N ratio may warrant devices to amplify or regenerate the transmitted signal.

*Attenuation*, discussed in the following section, is another important consideration in wireless networking. This will dictate the acceptable span between antennas. The engineering rules mentioned earlier also include the attenuation parameters acceptable by specific equipment.

# Attenuation

Anyone who has tried to listen to a radio while driving in rural areas knows that signals get weaker the farther you get from the source. This weakening of a signal is known as *attenuation*. There are several factors that cause attenuation besides distance, but to see how distance alone can cause attenuation we will first consider the example of propagation in free space.

Unlike audio waves (which are pressure waves and must have a medium to propagate), EM waves do not require a medium to propagate and can travel through the vacuum of space. In free space there are no other factors that cause resistance to the signal, yet there is still attenuation.

The reason is that the signal density diverges. Figure 2.8 demonstrates this phenomenon using light.

**Figure 2.8** Attenuation by Diversion of Rays from an Omnidirectional Source

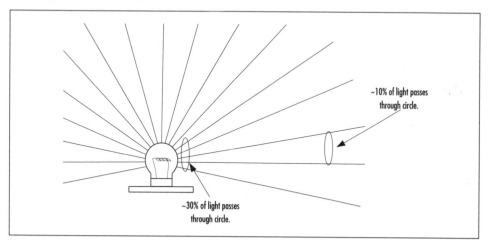

Assume that each ray of light represents an equal amount of the total light energy transmitted. It is easy to see that the rays diverge as the distance from the source increases. The result is a decrease in light intensity. Visible light waves are high frequency EM waves; therefore, this analogy also applies to EM waves in the RF spectrum as well. Since the waves are propagating in all directions, it is impossible to collect them all back at the receiver. Thus the receiver receives only a small portion of the energy transmitted, and this amount of energy received continually decreases as the distance increases and the "rays" diverge further. The affects of distance on the strength of EM waves in free space are given by the following equation:

P (proportional to) $1/r^2$

where **P** is power and **r** is the distance from the source to the receiver. The inverse square relationship means that when the distance doubles ($r \times 2$), the power received is reduced by a factor of four ($2^2 = 4$). 
Passing through objects further attenuates EM waves. The amount of attenuation depends on the frequency of the wave and the thickness and

composition of the object through which the wave is passing. Some objects, like mountains, attenuate 100 percent of the signal, thus blocking communication. This general attenuation equation gets worse when obstacles are placed in the path of the signal such as rain, buildings, mountains, and so on. The resulting affect for terrestrial EM propagation can be estimated by the equation:

P (proportional to) 1/r³

In this approximation, as the distance between transmitter and receiver doubles (r × 2), the power received is reduced by a factor of eight ($2^3 = 8$).

One way to minimize the amount the transmitted energy diverges is to use a directional antenna that focuses the waves in a specific direction. Figure 2.9 illustrates the previous example but uses an analogy of a flashlight to represent a directional antenna.

**Figure 2.9** Attenuation by Diversion of Rays from a Directional Source

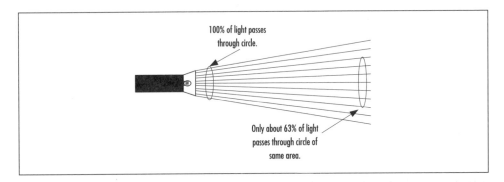

Assuming the omnidirectional light fixture in Figure 2.8 and the flashlight in Figure 2.9 both transmitted the same amount of energy, it is easy to see that the flashlight gets a stronger signal to a receiver that is the same distance away. We will talk about directional antennas in more depth later in this chapter.

EM waves do not penetrate the earth well. Therefore, for most land-based to land-based communications, the distance of the horizon is the ultimate constraint to the distance a signal can propagate. By elevating the transmitter and receiver on mountains and/or towers, however, you extend the horizon. Figure 2.10 illustrates how towers can extend the horizon.

**Figure 2.10** How Towers Can Extend Transmission Distance

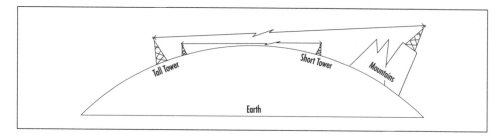

# Rain Attenuation

Rain attenuation is the attenuation to a signal due to precipitation. This affects high frequency waves more than low frequency waves because high frequency waves do not penetrate water as well.

The phenomenon of rain attenuation has been used to the advantages of some systems—for example, weather radar. Water droplets in the air that signify rain or clouds reflect and attenuate the high frequency radar signal differently than the surrounding air. This allows the radar system to paint a picture of the moisture.

# Bouncing

EM waves can pass through some objects, but they can also be reflected off of objects. In many cases, part of the signal's energy attempts to penetrate the object, while the rest of the energy of the signal is reflected. (Imagine looking into a pool of water—some of the light passes through water and is reflected off the bottom of the pool, allowing you to see the bottom. At the same time, if you readjust your focus you can see a reflection of yourself. This means that some of the light is penetrating and some of the light is reflecting.) Reflecting a signal is sometimes referred to as *bouncing* a signal and/or *scattering* a signal.

Bouncing can degrade the performance of some systems and enhance the performance of others. Both technology and the physical conditions play a factor in whether your specific application makes use of or is hindered by bouncing. For example, AM broadcast radio signals can be bounced off of the upper layers of the earth's atmosphere. Figure 2.11 illustrates how this can extend the distance a signal can be transmitted to well beyond the horizon.

**Figure 2.11** How Signal Bouncing Can Extend Transmission Distance

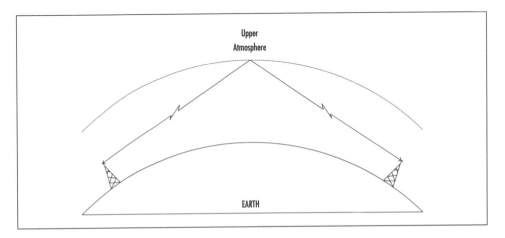

Many applications that use low frequency waves can use the layers of the atmosphere as a passive reflector, thus enhancing their distance performance; however, higher frequency waves do not bounce off the atmospheric layers well. High frequency waves penetrate through the atmospheric layers and into space without reflecting. This makes them well suited for communications with satellites. Satellites can be used as active reflectors by receiving and then retransmitting the signal to broadcast signals beyond the horizon; multiple satellites can be linked together to relay a signal completely around the world.

A specific example of using bouncing to enhance propagation is a fixed wireless telephone link this author saw in the mountains of Colorado. A house had been built up in a canyon, well beyond where the phone lines ended, but the residents wanted to have access to a phone. With a little monetary encouragement, the phone company set up a fixed wireless link to the house. However, one of the problems with choosing a wireless solution was that, obviously, the signals could not penetrate through the mountainous walls of the canyon, and the canyon was L-shaped with the house situated *around the corner* from where the last telephone access pedestal was. The fix was creative, simple, and inexpensive, albeit a little crude: a transceiver (a transmitter/receiver combination) and a directional antenna were placed at the mouth of the canyon near the last telephone access pedestal. The antenna was pointed up the canyon, aimed at a large granite rock on the far side of the L-corner of the canyon. A similar antenna was placed at the house and pointed at the same rock face. The rock actually became a reflector to bounce the signal around the corner of the canyon.

Not all results of bouncing are positive, however. One prevalent type of bouncing that adversely affects most mobile communications is called *multipath scattering*. Multipath scattering is where a signal reaches a receiver from multiple paths due to part of the signal bouncing off of various objects. If these signals arrive at the receiver out of phase, they can cancel each other. If the signals arrive in phase but are not synchronized, you can get echo signals. Echoes are probably most apparent on weak broadcast television signals where you see a main picture with a fuzzy picture just off to one side of every object in the picture. Figure 2.12 illustrates how multipath scattering occurs and demonstrates how it can cancel the signal.

One technology that makes use of multipath is Code Division Multiple Accessing (CDMA) such as Sprint's PCS phones. CDMA uses a device called a *rake receiver* to receive multiple signals and then to align them in phase so that they all amplify each other.

# Refracting

Another property that affects the path of propagation is *refraction*, that is, the bending of a wave. Just as the lens of an eyeglass bends the light waves, suspended particles and water droplets in the atmosphere can bend radio waves. A signal can refract and bend with the curve of the earth, to a certain extent

**Figure 2.12** Illustration of Multipath Scattering

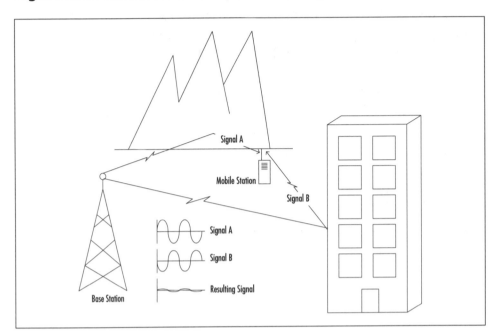

The *absolute horizon* is a straight line from the transmitter or receiver, and is tangential to the earth's surface. We have already discussed that for most cases, if both the transmitter and receiver are not above this line, communication will not work. However, if the signal bends to follow the curve of the earth, then it can reach receivers that are beyond the absolute horizon (a signal will refract with the curve of the earth only to a certain point). This distance is called the *apparent horizon*.

# Line of Sight

The straight clear path from the transmitter to the receiver is called the *line of sight*. We have already seen how this can be necessary for the propagation of some signals but we have also seen how some signals can find a path even if they don't have straight line of sight between transmitter and receiver. All signals propagate best when they have a line of sight path, but as a general rule, high frequency signals require a line of sight signal *more* than low frequency signals. Infrared transmission is particularly sensitive to obstructions in line of sight.

Usually the term *line of sight* is from the reference point of the wave being discussed. For example, assume a certain wave can pass easily through a wood wall. In this case, line of sight might mean the receiver is on one side of the wall and the transmitter is on the other. On the other hand, assume the line of sight is for a mini-dish satellite television system; you may be able to see the sky plainly through the leaves of the tree looming above, but the signal to your dish may be sufficiently attenuated by the leaves to render it useless. It is important to keep this frame of reference in mind when talking about line of sight.

# Penetration

We have been talking about signals penetrating some materials and bouncing off others. The factors that affect how well a signal will penetrate materials are type of material, thickness of material, frequency of signal, and power of signal. This is most apparent in the application of the medical x-ray. Extremely high frequency x-ray waves penetrate through the softer tissues of the body but are blocked by bone. This causes the x-ray-sensitive film to be etched with a picture that represents the bone structure.

This plays a large factor in terrestrial-based communications because of natural obstacles such as mountains, hill, and trees, and man-made obstacles like buildings. Table 2.1 gives a comparison to the penetrating power of high-, mid-, and low-frequency radio waves to various materials.

**Table 2.1** Penetration Levels of Different Frequency for Various Materials

| Material | Level of Penetration | | |
| --- | --- | --- | --- |
| | Low Frequency | Mid Frequency | High Frequency |
| Vacuum | Good | Good | Good |
| Air | Good/Bouncing | Good | Good/Rain Attenuation |
| Water | Fair | Poor | Extremely Poor |
| Earth | Poor | Poor | Poor |

Note that Table 2.1 does not include *metal* among the materials. Metal is a special case for penetration of EM waves. Let's first consider how an antenna works. At the transmitting end, a cable is hooked to an antenna. The signal travels down the cable and into the antenna. This generates an oscillating voltage potential in the antenna, which in turn generates an oscillating electric field between the antenna and the ground plane. The oscillating electric field creates an oscillating magnetic field and the magnetic fields create additional electric fields, and the wave propagates away from the antenna without wires. At the receiving end, the magnetic and electric fields induce an oscillating voltage potential in the receiving antenna. This voltage signal is carried away from the antenna by a cable.

Now let's consider a piece of metal that does *not* have a conductive path to ground and is acting as an antenna. The magnetic and electrical waves induce a voltage signal in the piece of metal. Since the antenna is not connected to ground, and there is no cable to drain the signal like in the previous example, there becomes a standing wave in the antenna. This standing wave will regenerate an electric field and the wave will propagate away from the antenna again. Therefore, as soon as a signal is received, it is retransmitted. Since part of the signal is retransmitted from each side of the piece of metal, it looks like part of the signal is being reflected and part of the signal penetrated the metal.

When this piece of metal *is* connected to ground, the EM wave hits the metal and induces a voltage in the metal. This voltage is dissipated to the ground and the signal is lost. In this case, the signal does not penetrate the metal.

The last case of penetration of metal that we will discuss is based on a principle by a scientist named Karl Friedrich Gauss and deals with metal enclosures. You may have already observed that your wireless phone does not work well in elevators. The reason is not simply that the signal cannot penetrate metal. Assume you have a metal sphere. As an EM wave hits the leading edge of the sphere, it acts like an antenna, and the wave induces a voltage in the metal. This voltage travels around the outside of the sphere to the trailing edge where the wave repropagates into the air—therefore, the signal does not penetrate to the interior of the sphere. That is one of the reasons your wireless phone does not work well in elevators or metal buildings.

These properties can be discouraging, especially since metal is so prevalent as a construction material. However, these same properties can make metal very useful as a shield from EM waves. Coaxial cable uses an outer shield of metal mesh to protect the signal that is propagating down the center conductor of the cable—the metal mesh shield acts as an antenna to receive the unwanted EM waves that would interfere with its main signal. This metal shielding is connected to ground and as the EM wave induces a voltage in the mesh, it is dissipated to ground. Now imagine that we expand that mesh shielding to surround an entire computer or an entire room. This type of shielding is important for many devices such as sensitive medical equipment, aircraft computerized flight control systems, and microwave ovens.

# Understanding the Wireless Elements

What are the wireless components in a network? Primarily, there are just two components, the antenna and the wireless device. That may seem oversimplified, but remember, a wireless network typically is not a stand-alone network. For example, a wireless local area network (LAN) is composed of access points, antennas, and wireless PC cards. The only connection that is truly "wireless" is between the antenna and the PC card. The access point is connected to the wireline network infrastructure, and the access point is then wired to the antenna.

There are numerous types of antennas, and each type is optimized for a particular environment or application. It is important to understand the distinguishing characteristics when choosing the appropriate antenna for your wireless network design. In this section, we'll also discuss mobile wireless base stations, mobile stations, and access points.

# Generic Radio Components

Generally, how is a signal manipulated during transmission? The various types of modulation and attenuation were covered earlier in this chapter;

illustrated in this section are the radio components that show the process of the signal from origin to destination. Keep in mind that these are general principles.

All radios share a basic conceptual design. In this generic design many of the specific components are commonly simplified into a "black box" schematic. Figure 2.13 highlights the generic "black box" radio components.

**Figure 2.13** Generic Radio Components

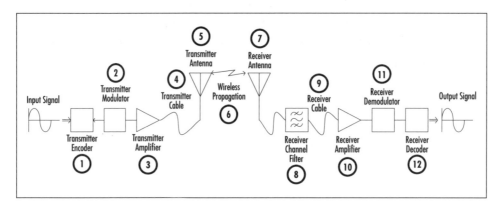

Each of the boxes in this picture represent entire subsystems of the radio; each is very complex, but simplified here as a box representing their function. The function of each of these boxes, following the system from the origin of the signal to the output of the receiver, can be described briefly as follows (refer back to Figure 2.13):

1.  **Transmitter Encoder**  The input signal enters the encoder. In this context, "encoder" is a very generic term. This could be a microphone that encodes analog sound waves into analog electrical waves or it could be a complex CDMA analog-to-digital converter. The main thing to keep in mind is that the original signal usually is modified or encoded before it is input into the modulator.

2.  **Transmitter Modulator**  As explained earlier in this chapter, the modulator box performs the modulation of the carrier wave.

3. **Transmitter Amplifier** After the signal is modulated, it is amplified so that it can be radiated with enough power to reach the receiving antenna. You may have heard radio stations boasting something like, "5000 Watts of Rock and Roll coming your way!" This is the result of a large amplifier.

4. **Transmitter Cable** Up to this point, most of the components would be located in one physical device. Sometimes even the antenna is integrated into the same box. However, the antenna is often mounted a distance away from the rest of the radio, for example outside the building for better transmission. That creates the problem of getting the signal from the amplifier to the antenna. It might seem like a simple wire connection; however, cables designed for high frequency electrical signals are significantly more complex than simple wire. They are called *transmission lines* because the signal is transmitted down the cable. The most common design for these cables is *coaxial cable*, as shown in Figure 2.14.

**Figure 2.14** Cutaway of Coaxial Cable

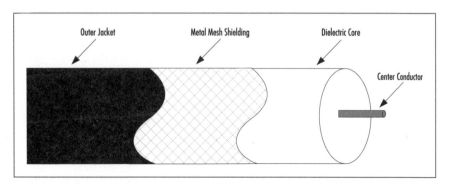

As mentioned earlier, the outer metal mesh of coaxial cable acts as a shield that shunts unwanted interference to ground. Since the shielding is tied to ground, it acts as a baseline reference. The center conductor carries the signal in reference to the outer, grounded shield. The spacing between the center conductor and the outer shield is very important and must remain constant; the dielectric material between the center conductor and the outer shield maintains this distance. Kinking coaxial cable can permanently damage the cable and can attenuate the signal, so it is important to be careful with the cable. Since the spacing is so critical to the function of a coaxial cable, splicing two cables is not as simple as connecting the inner conductor and the outer shields together. Splicing coaxial cable usually requires a splicer that looks like two connectors linked end to end and is crimped onto the cable with a special tool.

5. **Transmitter Antenna** The purpose of an antenna is to convert electrical signal to radio waves and vice versa. The antenna is one of the simplest subsystems of a radio because most antennas are passive devices, yet a tremendous amount of engineering goes into antenna design. We will discuss antennas in more depth in the next subsection.

6. **Wireless Propagation** The oscillating voltage potential in the antenna generates an oscillating electric field between the antenna and the ground plane. The oscillating electric field creates an oscillating magnetic field, the magnetic fields create additional electric fields, and the wave propagates away from the antenna.

7. **Receiver Antenna** Similar to the transmitter antenna, the receiver antenna converts the radio waves back into an electrical signal.

8. **Receiver Channel Filter** Even though antennas are designed and tuned for a specific frequency, they will still receive EM energy from the entire spectrum. Most electrical components are designed to work at a specific range of frequencies and they do not deal well with frequencies outside this range. For this reason the received signal is filtered to allow only the intended frequencies to pass to the subsequent receiver components.

9. **Receiver Cable** Same as the transmitter cable. On the transmitter end, the signal is amplified before leaving the main circuitry of the transmitter and entering the cable; therefore, cable loss is not a problem on the transmitter side. However, on the

receiver, the weak signal can be drastically affected by loss due to the length of the cable and the quality of the cable.

10. **Receiver Amplifier** The received signal is usually very weak and must be amplified before it is processed by the more complex receiver components. Some receiver designs place this amplifier or add an additional amplifier before the cable and very near the antenna to boost the received signal so that cable loss does not kill the signal as it travels from the antenna to the main receiver.

11. **Receiver Demodulator** Separates the original encoded modulating signal from the carrier signal. On a clean signal, the output of the receiver demodulator should closely represent the input of the transmitter demodulator.

12. **Receiver Decoder** Decodes the demodulated signal to get a representation of the original input signal.

As noise increases and/or the received signal strength decreases, the output of the receiver less resembles the transmitted signal until the point where it can no longer be recognized as the same signal.

# Antennas

By definition, an antenna is a conductive device used to transmit and/or receive radio waves. We mentioned earlier that antennas are passive devices and can be the simplest components in a wireless system. However, there is a tremendous amount of engineering and complex math that goes into designing antennas to meet certain needs.

Some antennas are designed to broadcast a signal in all directions, known as *omnidirectional* antennas; other antennas are designed to focus their beam in a specific direction, known as *directional* antennas. All of the antennas described in this section are used in wireless networking, however, each type is optimized in certain environments. Selecting the right antenna is crucial in designing a wireless system.

# Omnidirectional Antennas

*Omnidirectional* antennas propagate or receive signals in all directions. These types of antennas are useful in point-to-multipoint scenarios like a radio station, and for mobile devices that are constantly changing their aspect to their peer antenna.

## Half-Wavelength Dipole (Half λ Dipole)

The *half-wavelength dipole* antenna is one of the simplest antennas in design and construction. It consists of two conductors positioned end-to-end with a small gap between them. This gap usually is filled with a dielectric such as air, plastic, silicon, or rubber. The total length of the two conductors should be one half of the wavelength of the wave that they are designed to send or receive. If the antenna is designed for a range of frequencies such as the FM broadcast radio band, then the length is usually half the wavelength of the center frequency of the range. Figure 2.15 illustrates a half-wavelength dipole antenna and demonstrates its omnidirectional propagation pattern.

**Figure 2.15** Dipole Antenna and Associated Omnidirectional Beam Pattern

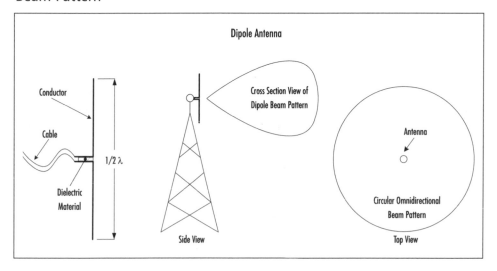

When the antenna is not near half the wavelength, the performance of the antenna is drastically affected due to a mismatch in characteristic impedances and standing wave ratios.

### Quarter-Wavelength Dipole (Quarter λ Dipole)

The *quarter-wavelength dipole* is a special version of the half-wavelength dipole. It consists of one side of a half-wavelength dipole that is mounted above a ground plane, such as the roof of a car. The ground plane acts as a reflector to simulate the second arm of a half-wavelength dipole. Quarter-wavelength dipoles do not have as high of a gain as half-wavelength dipoles, but they are close.

Quarter-wavelength dipoles are probably the most recognized form of antennas. They are found on almost all cars and "boom boxes" for AM and FM broadcast radio reception. They are also found on most hand-held transceivers such as cellular phones, wireless phones, and two-way radios.

## Directional Antennas

*Directional* antennas can take the same power coming from a transceiver and magnify the effect of the radiated signal by focusing most of the radiated power in one or two general directions. This focused radiated energy is referred to as a *beam*. Directional antennas fall into two general categories: *parabolic* and *phased array*.

Parabolic antennas function similar to a flashlight in that they use a dish-shaped reflector to concentrate the signal into a tight beam.

It is harder to visualize how phased arrays work because they involve some very complex electromagnetic theory and complex mathematics. Remember back to our discussion on concerning multipath scattering and how waves could amplify or interfere with one another based on their phase—this is the concept behind phased array antennas. Multiple antennas work together to amplify some waves and cancel other waves so that the overall sum of radiated energy is in the form of a focused beam.

## *Yagi Array Antennas*

*Yagi* antennas are named after their inventor, Dr. Hidetsugu Yagi. Yagi antennas consist of three or more dipole antennas, called *elements*, mounted on a common boom. All the elements work together as a phased array to direct the radiated energy into a focused beam. This gives Yagi antennas much higher gains than a half-wavelength dipole. Figure 2.16 illustrates the design and construction of a Yagi antenna.

**Figure 2.16** Yagi Phased Array Antenna and Associated Directional Beam Pattern

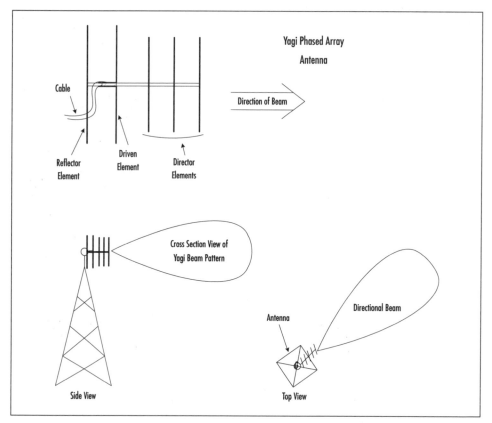

The elements are longest at the rear and gradually get shorter towards the front. The rear element is called the *reflector*. Immediately in front of the reflector is the *driven element*. In front of the driven element are one or more *director* elements.

The driven element is the only active element on a Yagi antenna and is the only element that connects to the transceiver via a cable. The remaining elements are known as parasitic elements because they feed off of the radiated power from the driven element. As we described earlier, if a piece of metal receives a signal and it is not drained from the metal, it will be re-radiated from the metal. This is how the parasitic elements of a Yagi work.

Broadcast television antennas are examples of Yagi type antennas.

## Planar Array Antennas

*Planar array* antennas are similar in concept to Yagi antennas except all elements, both active and parasitic, lie in the same plane. This results in a flat antenna that can be mounted flat on a wall, yet still have the properties and gain of a directional antenna. Figure 2.17 shows a planar array antenna.

**Figure 2.17** Planar Array Antenna and Associated Directional Beam Pattern

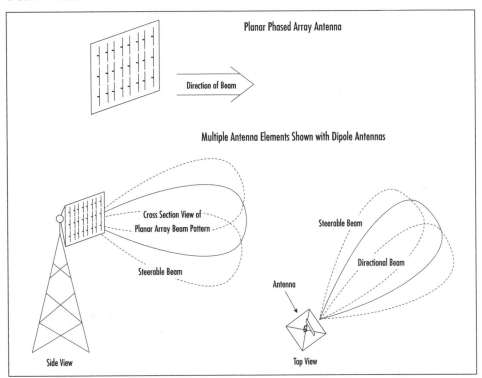

Planar arrays can have more than one active element. By changing the phase and power of the signal to hit specific active elements, the beam can be steered without the antenna physically moving. A useful application of this is on military tracking radars. A computer can adjust the input signals to the various elements of a planar array and steer the beam faster than the whole array could be moved physically, thus allowing for tracking of multiple fast-moving targets.

## Sectorized Array Antennas

*Sectorized array* antennas are a type of phased array antenna designed to split up a circular coverage area into sectors to help in channel allocation and reuse. Most sectorized antennas will have a beam width of about 120° that allow them to divide a circle into three sectors. Sectorized antennas are commonly used in wireless phone applications and can be seen on wireless phone towers all over America. Figure 2.18 illustrates how sectorized antennas work to divide a coverage area.

**Figure 2.18** Sectorized Array Antenna and Illustration of Sectorization

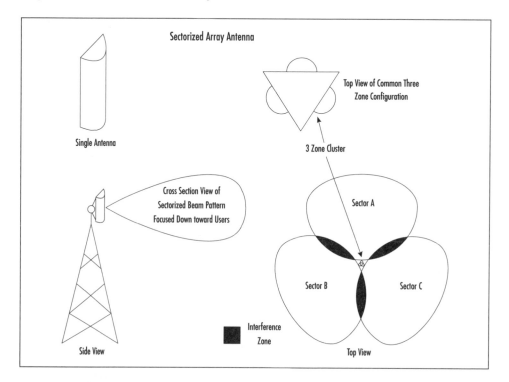

It is important to plan your zones carefully to minimize interference zones or to make interference zones reside in regions with no users.

## Parabolic Antennas

The most common examples of *parabolic* antennas are satellite dishes. Parabolic antennas have an emitter that is mounted so that it is aimed into a bowl-shaped reflector. Just as in a common flashlight, the reflector acts to focus the signal from the emitter into a very tight beam. On the receiving end, the dish reflector increases the area of the antenna, collecting a lot more of the transmitted signal and focusing that signal back onto the receiver. Figure 2.19 illustrates how parabolic antennas work.

**Figure 2.19** Parabolic Antenna and Focused Beam Pattern

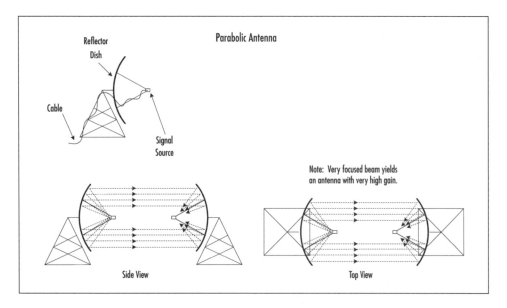

Parabolic antennas are used for terrestrial-to-stellar communication (ground-to-satellite) and for terrestrial-to-terrestrial point-to-point communication. Microwave long-distance telephone links use parabolic and cone antennas to carry phone conversations from one point to another. The number of microwave telephone links is rapidly diminishing with the advent of fiber optic cables; however, terrestrial point-to-point links using parabolic antennas could see new life in creating cheap alternatives to leased lines for short enterprise network connections.

# Base Stations and Mobile Stations

The terms *base station* and *mobile station* are very general terms. Base stations are usually fixed locations (such as a cellular telephone tower) that communicate to many mobile stations. In contrast to base stations, and as the name implies, mobile stations usually are not stationary. There are three basic scenarios for communications between mobile stations and base stations:

1.  Base Station to Base Station

2.  Base Station to Mobile

3.  Mobile to Mobile (that is, peer to peer)

Base stations are usually an aggregation point for many mobile stations. Also, the base station is usually a gateway for the mobile stations to reach a traditional wire-based network. Examples of base stations include:

-   **Cellular phone tower** Connects many mobile phones to the Public Switched Telephone Network (PSTN).

-   **Police dispatcher station** Coordinates and communicates with many mobile units.

-   **Access point for a wireless LAN** Connects various computers to a traditional wired Ethernet network.

Some mobile stations rely on a base station for all connectivity, such as mobile phones. Mobile phones cannot talk peer-to-peer. This is due partly to technology and partly to business. If mobile phones could recognize when another mobile phone was in range to engage in peer-to-peer communication, then the service provider could not bill for the air-time of that connection. Other mobile stations are designed to operate completely independent of any base station, such as the Motorola Talkabout Family Radio Service (FRS) handheld units. These units are designed for peer-to-peer communication. Still other mobile units, such as the IEEE 802.11 wireless LAN mobile units, can talk to a base station or can talk peer-to-peer.

## Access Points

*Access point* is another term that can be used very generally in reference to a point of access to a network. However, in the context of this book, access point most often refers to a base station for the IEEE 802.11 wireless LAN protocol. Access points provide computers that are equipped with a mobile radio card to access a LAN, usually via an Ethernet connection.

# Channelizing the Frequency Spectrum

Radio waves are just one of many electromagnetic bands that exist along the frequency spectrum. The range of frequency of EM waves goes from a few Hz, which is just above DC (Direct Current) all the way to cosmic radiation, which is above $10^{22}$ Hz. Figure 2.20 illustrates the entire EM spectrum. The spectrum is divided into the following broad categories:

1. **Radio Spectrum** 3 KHz–300 GHz
2. **Microwave Spectrum** 100 MHz–500 GHz
3. **Infrared Light** 500 GHz–400 THz (Terahertz, or $10^{12}$ Hz)
4. **Visible Light** 400 THz–750 THz
5. **Ultra Violet Light** 750 THz–30 PHz (Petahertz, or $10^{15}$ Hz)
6. **X-Ray** ~30 PHz – ~10 EHz (Exahertz, or $10^{18}$ Hz)
7. **Gamma** ~10 EHz – ~10 ZHz (Zettahertz, or $10^{21}$ Hz)
8. **Cosmic Rays** >$10^{22}$ Hz

**Figure 2.20** Entire EM Spectrum on Logarithmic Scale

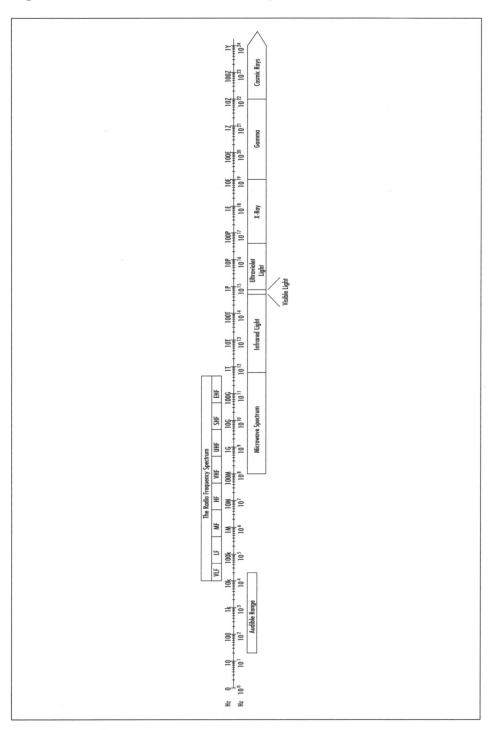

The most important part of the entire spectrum for wireless communication is the RF (Radio Frequency) spectrum, which includes a large chunk of the microwave spectrum. To prevent chaos and interruptions in wireless communications, government agencies regulate the use of frequencies. In the United States of America the Federal Communications Commission (FCC) and the National Telecommunications and Information Administration (NTIA) regulate the use of the RF spectrum and divide the RF spectrum into bands of frequencies that they assign for specific types of services, such as broadcast television or cellular phone use. These bands are then divided into blocks or individual channels that are allocated or sold to individual customers.

The other piece of the spectrum that is often used in wireless communication and worth briefly mentioning is the infrared band of frequencies. Infrared devices have a very short line-of-sight range.

# Channelizing

All RF communications require a little segment of the total RF spectrum to transmit their signal. These individual segments of the spectrum are called *channels*. In order to allow multiple simultaneous signals, different channels are assigned to different frequencies. This type of multiple access is called Frequency Division Multiple Accessing (FDMA). FDMA is the most common type of multiple accessing used in RF communications.

## Channel Bandwidth

Channels are named by their center frequency but they contain a range of frequencies both above and below the center frequency. This is referred to as *channel bandwidth*. The bandwidth of a channel depends on several factors, such as frequency and modulation technology, but in general, the more information you are trying to send over the channel, the wider the channel bandwidth.

By looking back at the FM example in Figure 2.3, you can see why a channel has a width. The carrier wave is the main determining factor for the frequency of the channel, yet clearly, the instantaneous frequency of the resulting signal varies from one point in time to the next based on the modulating wave frequency. Therefore the channel bandwidth is the maximum range that the signal fluctuates from the center frequency. An application of this can be seen on a digital display FM radio receiver. Most receivers jump in increments of 0.2 MHz, like from 94.1 MHz to 94.3 MHz, which includes the channel bandwidth plus a buffer zone between the channels called *channel spacing*.

## Channel Spacing and Buffer Zones

Theoretically, you could put the channels right next to each other to get the most number of channels in a certain band; to receive a channel, you would tune your receiver to that channel, and it would allow just that channel through and completely block all the others. However, in the real world, filters are not that precise. They require a buffer zone to attenuate other signals sufficiently to keep them from interfering with the desired channel. Figure 2.21 illustrates how a perfect passband filter would work, and how a real filter works.

**Figure 2.21** Channels and Channel Spacing

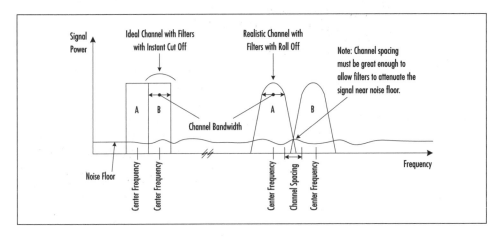

The requirements of channel spacing are part of the regulations that come out of the FCC and NTIA concerning the allocation of frequencies.

## Multichannel Systems and Channel Offsets

In a Citizen's Band (CB) radio, your radio is in listen mode or receive mode most of the time. When you want to talk, you push the transmit button and talk over the same channel to which you were previously listening. This type of communication is called *half-duplex* because you cannot send and transmit at the same time. In this example only one stream of information can utilize any given channel at one time.

There are many forms of communication in which you want multiple sources of information to be transmitted simultaneously. An example is wireless phone communications where you want a *full-duplex* connection. To accomplish this, there is a secondary channel assigned to the main channel, which allows two streams of information to propagate simultaneously (full duplex), or two receive channels such as the left and right audio channels for FM broadcast radio.

# Extending the Number of Channels (Frequency Reuse)

The RF spectrum is becoming a very valuable commodity. With more and more users demanding more and more different services, we are rapidly using all of the available channels. Frequency utilization is of growing concern for everyone in the wireless communications industry. One of the simplest ways to extend the number of channels is by reusing frequencies. As a signal propagates away from the transmitter, it is constantly losing power. At a great enough distance, the signal is little more than background noise. At this point, the frequency used to transmit that signal can be reused by a different transmitter.

A simple example of this is broadcast radio between distant cities. For example, Kansas City, MO has a country music station at 104.3 MHz. That same channel is used for a different station in Denver, CO. Since the stations are so distant from each other, their signals do not interfere. This type of frequency reuse is not designed specifically into the broadcast radio system. It happens almost naturally and therefore has been around almost as long as radios. However, the demand for wireless

phones has led to systems whose design is based on the reuse of frequencies. One of the first services to design a frequency reuse plan was
the Advanced Mobile Phone Service (AMPS), also known as a cellular
plan.

## Seven Cell Frequency Reuse

Before AMPS there were a limited number of channels available for
wireless phones; the towers to transmit and receive the signals from the
mobile units were designed to cover large geographic areas, so as to limit
the number of towers and lower costs. However, this resulted in very
low user density and crippled the systems in highly populated areas such
as New York City. AMPS was designed to allow frequencies to be reused
in a smaller geographical area, thereby increasing the available user density. Figure 2.22 illustrates how the AMPS or cellular telephones reuse
plan works.

**Figure 2.22** AMPS and Cellular Telephone Seven Cell Reuse Plan

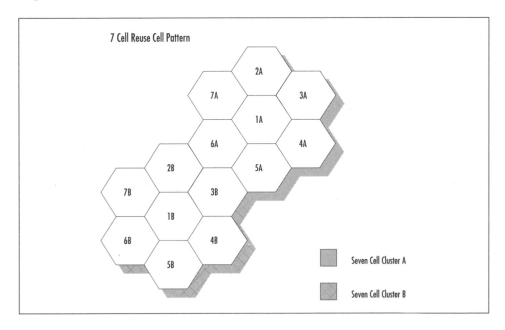

Each tower is made the center of its small coverage area, called a *cell*. Every cell is surrounded by six other cells, to form a honeycomb pattern. To prevent channel interference, the same channel cannot be used in adjacent cells. Once the signal has traveled the distance of 1.5 cells, it has been sufficiently attenuated so as not to cause interference to the main signals of that cell. Therefore, in every seventh cell, a channel could be reused.

# Multiple Accessing

*Multiple accessing* is a group of techniques that allows multiple users to access the network simultaneously. We have already looked at FDMA as a way of allocating channels with different frequencies for multiple users, but this technique alone falls well short of accommodating the demand. AMPS and its use of the Seven Cell Reuse Plan was a giant step forward for wireless communication, because it broke apart coverage areas into small cells that had fewer users in each cell. However, even the Seven Cell Reuse Plan is being saturated in dense population areas. This has lead to some other types of multiple access techniques that are being used, in addition to FDMA.

## Time Division Multiple Accessing

Time Division Multiple Accessing (TDMA) is used in addition to FDMA. Each channel is further divided into time slots. Each time slot is assigned to a different user. The transmitter transmits information for all time slots at the same frequency and the receivers receive all time slots but only listen to the time slot they have been allocated. The net affect is that the efficiency of the channel is increased by a multiple of the number of time slots that are being used. Most common second-generation TDMA phone systems use three time slots. Global System for Mobile Communication (GSM) is a type of TDMA that is common throughout much of the world.

## Code Division Multiple Access

Code Division Multiple Access (CDMA) is the newest of the multiple access technologies; it is not yet as widely used but is showing great promise. CDMA does not divide the allocated block of frequencies into individual channels. It assigns a unique code to each signal and then combines all the signals together in a single large channel. The receiver receives the integrated signal and uses the same code just to process the desired signal. CDMA is gaining popularity as a third-generation wireless phone technology because it is very efficient at utilizing bandwidth, plus it is natively very secure because all conversations are uniquely encoded.

# Regulating Wireless Communications

As the number of wireless devices dramatically increases, it is not difficult to see why there is a need for regulatory agencies. This section describes the regulatory agencies responsible for the development and operation of wireless systems. Although the Web sites provided by these agencies are the best source for the most current information, we will cover here some general operational and technical rules and regulations associated with domestic wireless broadband data networks. Remember, many rules and restrictions are based entirely on regulations proposed by federal, state, and local agencies in an evolving business and regulatory climate, so it is recommended to reference the regulations committees before designing a wireless network.

# Regulatory Agencies

The *International Telecommunication Union* (ITU) (www.itu.int/ITU-R), headquartered in Geneva, Switzerland, is an international organization that coordinates standards and regulations, and promotes the efficient use of the RF spectrum. The ITU established an international Table of Frequency Allocations that designates specific bands of frequencies for specific uses within different regions of the globe.

The ITU Radiocommunication Sector (ITU-R) was created in 1993 and comprises what once were the International Radio

Consultative Committee (CCIR) and the International Telephone Consultative Committee (CCIF). The ITU-R is responsible for all of the ITU's work in the field of radio communications.

In the United States of America , the Federal Communications Commission (FCC) and the National Telecommunications and Information Administration (NTIA) regulate the use of the RF spectrum, through the management of frequency allocations and the designation of specific bands of frequencies. The two agencies determine which portions of the spectrum are reserved for Federal use, for non-Federal use, and for shared use within the United States.

The FCC (www.fcc.gov) is an independent federal regulatory agency accountable directly to the United States Congress, established by the Communications Act of 1934. The FCC allocates frequency spectrums for commercial use including specific types of fixed, mobile, and broadcasting services such as broadcast television services, cellular telephone, paging, personal communications services, public safety, and other commercial and private radio services. Because the primary directive of the FCC is to govern the efficient use of the electromagnetic spectrum, it generally leaves the development of standards (such as the 802.11b standard) to the industries. Recently, the FCC has been associated with its additional objective of developing a domestic telecommunications infrastructure that provides services on national and global levels.

The NTIA, an agency of the U.S. Department of Commerce, is the Executive Branch's principal representative in domestic and international telecommunications and information technology issues, and frequently works with other Executive Branch agencies to develop and present the Administration's position on these issues. NTIA works to encourage innovation and competition, promote job creation, and provide consumers with more choices and the best quality telecommunications products and services at lower prices.

## The Need to Know

With the exception of a few unlicensed frequency bands, all transmitters in the private, commercial, and broadcast services require an FCC license prior to operation. An FCC fine for unlicensed operation varies from radio service to radio service, but penalties in the broadcast and commercial bands can be severe—for instance $5000 per day plus potential imprisonment. Unauthorized private systems are also subject to fines. Licensing and other legal requirements for operating any radio transmitter change periodically; consult the FCC regulations for the latest information.

## Regulations for Low Power, Unlicensed Transmitters

Three changes in FCC regulation contributed to the fast-paced growth of wireless communications. In 1985 the United States released the Industrial, Scientific, and Medical (ISM) frequency bands, provided that certain technical restrictions on transmitter power and modulation are met. The deregulation of this frequency spectrum eliminates the need for users and organizations to perform costly and time-consuming frequency planning to coordinate radio installations that avoid interference with existing radio systems. Successful introduction of new RF spectrum-dependent systems into congested frequency bands for worldwide use is difficult; however, requirements imposed by the regulations on unlicensed wireless networking equipment are relatively simple. First, the signal strength is limited, usually to less than 1 watt. Second, the signal must be transmitted using one of two spread-spectrum methods in which the signal is spread out over a certain range of frequencies, or hops, among a certain minimum number of narrow slots each second. Many devices operating in the ISM bands use these types of modulation; however the FCC does permit narrowband modulation techniques to be used, so all devices have to contend with interference from other unlicensed devices operating in the same frequency range.

The most specific restrictions imposed upon the ISM bands by the FCC is that the U.S. radio frequency systems must implement spread spectrum technology. Microwave systems are considered very low power systems and must operate at 500 milliwatts or less, but because of the interference avoidance characteristics of spread spectrum technology, these devices are permitted greater output power than transmitters not using spread spectrum technologies that operate in the same band. Again, although these restrictions may not generally apply to the consumer, for rules concerning eligibility for licensing, frequencies available, permissible communications and classes and number of stations, and any special requirements, the FCC remains the sole authority. If implementing a spread spectrum system outside the United States, it is important to investigate the local regulations, and as mentioned before, the regulatory bodies associated with the ITU would be considered an excellent point of reference. Since licensing is not required when operating under Part 47 Section 15.247 of the FCC Rules and Regulations, implementation of spread spectrum systems is simple and cost-effective.

# Summary

There is a tremendous amount of science, particularly physics, involved in understanding communication systems. Electromagnetic (EM) waves are the result of alternating current (AC) producing a change in the surrounding electric field, which in turn, creates a magnetic field. The oscillation from electric to magnetic fields creates electromagnetic waves. This physics phenomenon is the key facilitator of wireless technology. To optimize the transmission of waves, and to be able to use them for communication purposes, the signal must be modulated, which is the process of boosting the signal into the radio frequency (RF) range. This allows multiple signals to be transmitted simultaneously. Some inherent characteristics of RF waves need to be considered and remedied in the design of wireless networks, including the signal-to-noise ratio, attenuation, bouncing, refraction, and line of sight restrictions; these can be remedied with careful engineering with appropriate placement of wireless equipment.

Some of the components involved in wireless networking are the antennas, base stations, mobile stations, access points, and wireless PC cards. There is a wide selection of antennas, which can be categorized as omnidirectional and directional, depending on the application and terrain. Base stations have two primary functions: serving as aggregation points for multiple mobile stations and as gateways for mobile stations to access a wire-line network or backbone. Access points and PC wireless cards are used in wireless local area networks (WLANs). Access points function similar to base stations in a mobile wireless network.

The RF range is optimized for wireless communication by channelization. This is the process of dividing RF range into its constituent frequencies. The established frequency range indicated by the channel size binds the bandwidth of a channel, establishing the maximum range the signal can span. A major concern in designing wireless networks is the channel spacing—it is a delicate balance between allowing the maximum number of channels and avoiding interference between the channels. Two techniques for maximizing the use of frequencies are frequency reuse and multiple access.

As wireless regulations continually change, it is important to reference the activities of the regulatory committees before designing a wireless network. Nationally, this includes the Federal Communications Commission (FCC) and the National Telecommunications and Information Administration (NTIA), and internationally, the International Telecommunication Union (ITU).

# Solutions Fast Track

## Transmitting Radio Signals Over Electromagnetic Waves

- ☑ Electromagnetic waves are the result of applying alternating current (AC) to an electric field, which in turn, produces a magnetic field. Oscillating between the electric and magnetic fields produces an electromagnetic wave.

- ☑ Modulation of the signal is necessary in order for the signal to be transmitted.

- ☑ The benefits of modulation are two-fold. First, the frequency of the original signal is increased. Low-frequency voice signals, which inherently do not propagate well as EM waves, need to be increased to a higher frequency for better transmission. Secondly, modulation allows multiple signals to be transmitted simultaneously.

## Propagating a Strong Radio Signal

- ☑ Signal power is the most rudimentary requirement of wave propagation. The signal must be strong enough for the equipment to recognize it as a signal instead of noise.

- ☑ A high signal-to-noise ratio is another requirement. This is similar to signal power in that the signal must be stronger than the noise.

☑ Signal attenuation, where the signal degrades over the distance it has to travel to the destination, is also a consideration when designing a wireless network.

☑ There is equipment to combat the impedance of EM wave propagation. It is important to understand these potential complications in order to proactively design a successful network.

## Understanding the Network Elements

☑ Primarily, there are two truly "wireless" components: the antenna and the wireless device. It may seem oversimplified, but a wireless network typically is not a stand-alone network. It is a complementary portion of the wireline network infrastructure.

☑ There are antennas designed for every terrain and application.

## Channelizing the Frequency Spectrum

☑ To optimize the number of simultaneous signals in the RF range, the frequencies need to be channelized.

☑ The size of the channel is directly correlated with the bandwidth of the channel.

☑ Channel spacing is an important design consideration. The goal is to have as many channels possible without interference.

☑ Frequency reuse, as the name implies, is a method of reusing the frequencies. This is successful as long as there is adequate geographical space between the reused frequencies.

☑ Multiple accessing is a group of techniques that allows multiple users to access the network simultaneously. Examples of multiple access techniques are frequency division, time division, and code division.

## Regulating Wireless Communications

☑ The primary national wireless regulatory agencies are the Federal Communications Commission (FCC) and The National Telecommunications and Information Administration (NTIA).

# Frequently Asked Questions

The following Frequently Asked Questions, answered by the authors of this book, are designed to both measure your understanding of the concepts presented in this chapter and to assist you with real-life implementation of these concepts. To have your questions about this chapter answered by the author, browse to **www.syngress.com/solutions** and click on the **"Ask the Author"** form.

**Q:** What is the gain of an antenna and how is it different from one type to another?

**A:** Antenna gain is the measure of the amount of signal the antenna radiates or receives. It is given as a decibel ratio, compared to a theoretical omnidirectional antenna called an isotropic antenna. All other things being equal, a high-gain antenna will transmit and receive weaker signals farther than a low-gain antenna.
Omnidirectional antennas, such as dipole, will have lower gain than directional antennas because they distribute their power over a wider area. Parabolic antennas usually have the highest gain of any type of antenna. A half-wave dipole antenna will have a gain of near 1, or nearly equal the isotropic antenna.

**Q:** Why does the signal strength on my PCS phone drastically change when I move my head while talking?

**A:** PCS phones operate at high frequencies, meaning short wavelengths of a few inches. By slightly moving your phone, you are affecting the multipath scattering of the signals that are reaching your phone. At one phone position the signals are in phase and amplify each other, and at other positions the signals are out of phase and cancel each other.

# Chapter 3

# TCP/IP and the OSI Model

## Solutions in this chapter:

- Exploring the OSI and DoD Models
- Understanding the Network Access Layer
- Understanding the Internet Layer
- Understanding the Host-to-Host Layer
- Managing the Application Layer

- ☑ Summary
- ☑ Solutions Fast Track
- ☑ Frequently Asked Questions

# Introduction

With the explosion of the Internet, the Internet Protocol (IP) is the protocol of choice today. When you are designing an IP-based network, it is important to have a full understanding of Transmission Control Protocol/IP (TCP/IP) and how it relates to the conventions of the Open Systems Interconnection (OSI) Reference Model. In dealing with a strictly TCP/IP network, you can take a simplified approach. The Department of Defense (DoD) modeled such a network model in four layers and related it directly to the OSI model.

In addition to the relationship of IP and the OSI model, you must understand addressing methodologies, routing policies, and testing and troubleshooting tools. This chapter briefly explains each of these concepts in the DoD's four-layer model.

When you are designing a wireless network, whether it is an addition to an existing network or an autonomous network, the principles introduced in this chapter will be a part of your design process. The process of communication between network devices, regardless of the technology used for transmission (wireless, Ethernet, optical, and so on), adhere to the principles of the OSI and DoD reference models. These general networking models are independent of the protocols or applications characteristic of a particular network.

In addition, communications between networks via the Internet is accomplished using the TCP/IP suite. As a result, the success of your network depends on you understanding how the protocol suite functions and knowing the network design requirements, such as an IP addressing scheme and routing protocols.

# Exploring the OSI and DoD Models

The OSI Reference Model consists of seven layers: the physical layer (Layer 1), the data-link layer (Layer 2), the network layer (Layer 3), the transport layer (Layer 4), the session layer (Layer 5), the presentation layer (Layer 6), and the application layer (Layer 7). This convention has been developed to provide an initial framework to simplify network design and to provide a systematic approach to troubleshooting. Every network is unique; consequently, so are the characteristics of each layer. As our discussion progresses, the functionality of each layer and how these layers communicate will become increasingly clear. We cover the OSI model in detail first and then compare it to the DoD model.

In our discussion of how each layer functions, we look at the parallels between human communication and that of computer systems, breaking down the communication process into its components to allow more granular comparisons. Imagine yourself as a student in a classroom listening to an instructor's lecture. This constitutes our example of human communication; we then address how computer communications correspond to that example. Keep in mind that when we talk about computer systems communicating, we are really referring to one device talking to another.

# Layer 1: The Physical Layer

The *physical layer* is identified as the physical medium that facilitates communication. For instance, in our classroom example, air is considered the physical medium. It carries the sound waves produced by the instructor to the students. Both the air waves and the sound waves being transmitted are considered part of the physical layer. In the computer world, where wireless technology is implemented, air is also the primary mode of transmission. It carries a designated frequency to the other computers in the local network. Again, the radio frequency (RF) waves are a component of the physical layer. This layer is also responsible for specifying the frequency range of the RF waves and the type of modulation.

# Layer 2: The Data-Link Layer

The *data-link layer,* in our human analogy, formats thoughts passed from the instructor's brain into a simplified, organized structure. The structures at this phase are blocks of syllables. These syllables are the simplest elements of the message from the higher layers. In order to ensure that the instructor emits sound waves comprehensible to the audience, there is a "think before you speak" process, the human equivalent of error checking. This layer then hands these blocks of syllables, or *frames*, to the physical layer, which translates these messages into sounds that the students can understand. Lastly, sound waves are produced from the instructor and transmitted via air waves to the intended audience—the students in the class.

Another characteristic of communication at this layer is evidenced when a student has a question during a lecture. The instructor can either stop the lecture and address the question immediately or request that the student hold the question until the instructor is finished—that is, the instructor is managing the flow of the lecture. This function is important because it optimizes communication within the classroom. The instructor might think that the material needs to be presented in its entirety to maximize the level of understanding. On the other hand, the instructor could find that questions from the audience enhance the lecture. The flow of the class all depends on the instructor.

These same attributes are found in the computer world as well. Information (the instructor's thoughts) from higher-level layers (the instructor's brain) is formatted into frames (the syllables the instructor speaks). In addition to formatting, the intended destination (the students) and source identifier (their instructor) are attached. The destination and source information are represented as addresses, formally referred to as *media access control* (MAC) addresses. The Ethernet MAC address is a 48-bit number known as the hardware address, which is entirely unique and that is "burned into" the device. Also included in the frame created by the data-link layer is the *cyclical redundancy checksum* (CRC). The CRC provides a metric allowing the receiving device a way of determining whether or not the data is of acceptable quality upon receipt. This parallels the "think before you speak" process, making sure that what the data being transmitted is accurate. The frames are translated into bits and eventually radio waves that are sent by the physical layer for transmission.

The data-link layer is actually divided into two sublayers: the logical link control (LLC) and the MAC. The LLC is the liaison between the protocols within the network layer and the media access control sublayer. The media access controls access to the physical medium. An example of a protocol that works with MAC is the carrier sense multiple access/collision detect (CSMA/CD). This protocol performs a measure of flow control.

# Layer 3: The Network Layer

The primary function of the *network layer* is to determine the best known path for information to reach its intended destination. In our classroom example, the information is intended for everyone in the audience. This would be considered a broadcast. The instructor knows that all the students in the class are to hear the information in the lecture. The information is formatted, error checked, and translated into a message via the data-link layer. Subsequently, the frame is transmitted into the physical medium.

What if there is an emergency phone message for the instructor? The person taking the call knows the instructor and the location of the classroom and will deliver the information. The messenger knows the information in the message is important and needs to find the best—in this case, the fastest—way to the classroom. Perhaps the elevator is the fastest, but there are a lot of students in the building, which could cause delay. The stairs seem to be the most reliable and the fastest route. These decisions are similar to the decisions the network layer makes in order to deliver traffic as effectively as possible.

The network layer deals with *packets*, which are eventually encapsulated into frames by the data-link layer. The packets contain information from the layer above the network layer. This is also where the logical IP addresses reside. They are considered logical because, unlike the MAC address that is permanently "burned" into the network interface card (NIC), IP addressing provides a method of grouping devices regardless of their physical location. This is an important aspect of network design.

# Layer 4: The Transport Layer

The *transport layer* relates to our classroom scenario in that it establishes the way that the instructor presents the lecture. For instance, the instructor might look to the audience for an indication of whether or not they understand the lecture. The instructor could invite questions, look for body language indicating agreement, or perhaps even count sleeping students. The instructor attempts to give each student a chance to be involved in the lecture emulating one-on-one attention. On the other hand, it is also possible that the instructor does not desire feedback and will lecture regardless of audience reactions. This type of presentation could be necessary when there is an excessive amount of information and inadequate time to present the material. These two approaches are both appropriate for certain situations and audiences. You will see this type of communication in the computer world as well.

The transport layer can be categorized into *connection-oriented* and *connectionless* protocols. An example of a connection-oriented protocol is TCP. The term *connection-oriented* implies a level of reliability and guarantee of delivery of services, much like the first method of presentation in the classroom. The processes involved in the protocol function to provide a virtual one-on-one appearance. Connectionless protocols, like the User Datagram Protocol (UDP), do not provide these measures of reliability. This method is analogous to the second method in our classroom example, in which the instructor continues to lecture whether the students hear and understand everything or not.

# Layer 5: The Session Layer

The *session layer* establishes the parameters of any upcoming communication. The parameters include the language that will be used and the style of the lecture (whether or not questions are acceptable intermittently or need to be held until the end of the lecture), those being parameters that need to be predetermined. Another issue to resolve is setting time limits: when the lecture will conclude, for example, which could be at an established time or imply whenever all the topics and questions have been addressed. These parameters are established to set the expectations for everyone involved, a critical aspect of effective communication.

These types of parameters are also established prior to the exchange of data among computer systems. First, protocols need to be agreed on. Some examples of session-layer protocols are Network File System (NFS), Structured Query Language (SQL), and X Windows. Protocols are important because if the devices are not using the same protocols, they are essentially speaking different languages. Next, they decide on the communication flow. There are three types: *single mode, half-duplex mode*, and *full-duplex mode*. Single-mode communication occurs when only one device at a time transmits information, and it transmits until all the information has been completely sent. Half-duplex mode occurs when the devices take turns transmitting. This is comparable to a conversation between two people using walkie-talkies, in which only one person can talk at any given time. (If both people push the Talk button at the same time, neither person will hear anything.) Full-duplex mode occurs when the devices transmit and receive simultaneously. An example of full-duplex communication is when two people talk on a phone—both parties can talk at the same time.

Once the all the preliminary details have been established, data exchange can proceed. After the exchange is complete, the devices systematically disengage the session.

The session layer can be either *connection-oriented* or *connectionless*. A connection-oriented session contains checkpoints or activity management. This system provides a way to efficiently retransmit any data that is lost or is erroneous on receipt. It is efficient because only the data that needs to be transmitted is sent, rather than the entire session. Connectionless sessions, as with IP and UDP, are a best-effort delivery. As with the two other examples, in a connectionless session, the layer above (the presentation layer) is responsible for providing reliability.

# Layer 6: The Presentation Layer

The *presentation layer* establishes the way in which information is presented. The primary reason for someone to attend a class is that the presentation of information is designed to help that person learn. Students could, theoretically, pick up the literature and learn the material on their own; however, the value comes with the instructor's interpretation of the material. The instructor translates the information in such a way that students understand it. This is functionality that the presentation layer provides in computer systems.

The presentation layer translates information in a way that the application layer understands. Likewise, this layer translates information from the application layer to the session layer. This layer is responsible for encryption and decryption as well as compression and decompression. A few of the protocols associated with this layer are Joint Photographic Experts Group (JPEG), Motion Picture Experts Group (MPEG), and Tagged Image File Format (TIFF).

# Layer 7: The Application Layer

The *application layer* represents the overall point or concept of the instructor's lecture—this is what the student actually takes away from the course. All the layers of communication we have talked about to this point are transparent to the student, for the most part. However, the overall effectiveness of the course could depend on the way the material is communicated and how the class is structured. For instance, if the instructor is difficult to understand, for whatever reason, the content of the material is meaningless to the students. The same is true if the situation were reversed: The instructor could be a sensational communicator, but if the material being covered is inappropriate for the desired goal of the class, the content is worthless.

A parallel illustration of the application layer in relation to computer systems is found in looking at how the World Wide Web is used. The Web is something the end user employs to find value. The end user typically knows nothing of how the Internet actually works until something doesn't work correctly. It is apparent that the various layers of communication are complex and dependent on one another, but this interdependency goes unnoticed when everything functions properly. Some examples of application-layer protocols are the Hypertext Transfer

Protocol (HTTP), Simple Mail Transfer Protocol (SMTP), the Post Office Protocol (POP), and the File Transfer Protocol (FTP).

## OSI and DoD Correlation

The DoD reference model combines several layers of the OSI model. The DoD model consists of four layers rather than seven (some layers found in the OSI are combined in the DoD) and they are named differently. However, the functionality of the layers remains similar. The DoD chose the four-layer approach. For IP and the Internet, several of the OSI layers are functionally the same. The DoD model consists of a network access layer, an Internet layer, a host-to-host layer, and an application layer. Figure 3.1 shows a correlation between the OSI model and the DoD model.

**Figure 3.1** Comparison of the OSI Model and the DoD Model

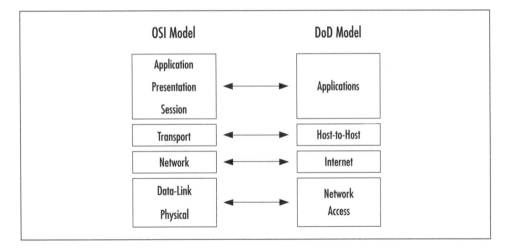

# Understanding the Network Access Layer

As shown in Figure 3.1, the network access layer of the DoD model is a combination of the physical and data-link layers. The functionality of the layer remains the same as in the OSI model. However, for simplicity, the DoD model does not recognize the two layers as being independent.

# Using Bridging

In this section, we focus on a commonly implemented device that resides in the network access layer: *bridges*, which are a way to move traffic without the complexity of routing and the associated routing protocols. Bridges are responsible for forwarding information, or *frames*, between two or more local area networks (LANs). A bridge switches frames based on the MAC addresses of the network nodes. There are two primary methods of bridging:

- Transparent bridging
- Source-route bridging

These two methods differ in the way that they learn switching routes. Furthermore, each is designed for different network access protocols.

*Transparent bridging* learns or associates node addresses with a particular port. The bridge "listens" to all the frames being sent on a LAN. When a bridge receives a frame, the source address of the frame and the port in which the bridge received the frame are put into a *bridge table*. Therefore, the bridge does not know exactly where the node is located within the network; rather, it knows the first step of where to send a frame and the general direction of a potential destination node. Each bridge makes these associations individually and develops and maintains its own bridge table. This method of bridging is designed for Ethernet environments, as illustrated in Figure 3.2.

The bridge serves to extend the distance limitations imposed by the 802.3 standard. It does this by connecting multiple Ethernet segments. However, the devices in the network are unaware of the existence of multiple segments. The LAN appears to be one segment. In addition, the devices on a segment or domain are unaware of the existence of a bridge. True to its name, these bridges are *transparent*. You might be wondering how collisions are avoided—if a device on one segment is sending information, then a device on another segment would not know about the activity and would try to send information at the same time. The solution is that a bridge operates in a *store-and-forward mode*, which means that the bridge will store the frame(s) and check for any activity before forwarding.

**Figure 3.2** Transparent Bridging

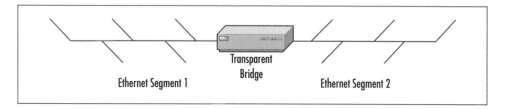

*Source-route bridging* (SRB) operates differently from the transparent method. SRB devices are not silent partners of a network. The end users in a SRB network share the responsibilities frame switching. When a node intends to send a frame, it sends what is called an *explorer frame*. The bridge receives the explorer frame and provides a path from the source node to the desired destination. This path is appended to the explorer frame and is sent to the source node. The source node sends the frame, now containing the path information, to the destination node. The bridge ensures that the frame reaches the destination.

How does a bridge know the difference between an explorer frame and a frame that already contains path information? A field within the frame, called the *routing information indicator* (RII), is set to 1 if it contains path information; if this information is absent, the field is set to 0. The value (0 or 1) is determined by the source node. This is how the bridge distinguishes whether it is an explorer frame, in which case it adds the path information, or a frame that needs to be switched to the destination node. The SRB does not maintain a table the way a transparent bridge does. Instead, it stores path information in the form of a routing infor- mation (RIF) cache. This method of bridging, as shown in Figure 3.3, is used to join two Token Ring networks.

There are also hybrids of these two bridging methods: *source-route transparent bridging* (SRT) and *source-route translational bridging* (SR/TLB).

SRT also exists in a Token Ring environment. Figure 3.4 shows that this type of bridge can function as either an SRB or a transparent bridge. SR/TLB allows communication between Ethernet and Token Ring networks.

**Figure 3.3** Source-Route Bridging

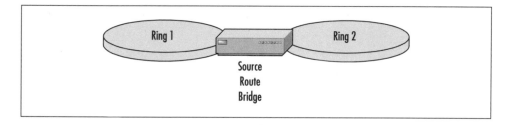

**Figure 3.4** Source-Route Translational Bridging

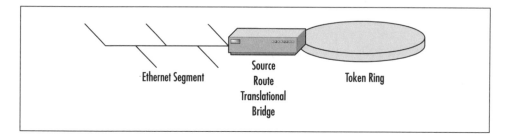

What if a LAN has multiple bridges? As you can imagine, the potential complications of multiple devices, in charge of forwarding frames, which are not communicating with one another or are even oblivious of each other's the existence, are a concern. As always, a protocol has been developed to save the day—the *Spanning Tree Protocol* (STP).

Essentially, STP prevents network loops by establishing how multiple switches or bridges talk to one another. This protocol is designed so that the bridges in an environment of many connected LANs can automatically discover each other. However, they actually learn about only a portion of the entire network topology. This is to ensure that looped paths are not created.

The first step in the discovery process is the election of a single root bridge. This bridge functions as the centralized device from which all the other bridges base their path calculations. Subsequently, each bridge must find the shortest path to the root. Next, one *designated bridge* is elected for each individual LAN. Typically, the designated bridge is the one closest to the root on a particular LAN. Lastly, each bridge elects the ports that will participate in the spanning tree. The ports that are selected provide a loop-free but fully connected topology.

# The Ethernet Protocol

Ethernet, the 802.3 standard, is a key part of local area networking. This protocol has survived the test of the ever-changing technological environment. It has evolved from transmission rates of 10/100Mbps to 10Gbps. Ethernet is even used within wireless networks.

Looking at the structure of an Ethernet frame is important to better understand the functions this layer provides. Figure 3.5 examines an Ethernet frame.

**Figure 3.5** An Ethernet Frame

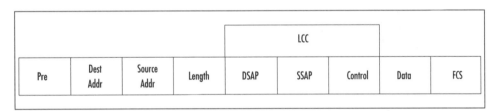

The frame format of the Ethernet packet includes the following fields:

- **Preamble** Distinguishes the beginning of a new frame.

- **Destination** and **Source Addresses** These are MAC addresses.

- **Length** Indicates how many bytes of data the receiving device should expect to receive within the particular frame.

- **LLC header** Contains the Destination Service Access Point (DSAP) and Source Service Access Point (SSAP) and a Control field.

- **Frame Check Sequence (FCS)** Provides a metric to determine the health of the information contained in the frame. The CRC is responsible for providing this measurement. This is important since data can become erroneous in the process of transmission.

## Understanding the ARP Process

The *Address Resolution Protocol* (ARP) defines a process by which the MAC address of a device is discovered. Because the information flow is top-down for the sender and bottom-up for the receiver, the information from the network layer, in the form of a packet, is sent to the data-link layer. This is where more information, such as the MAC address, is appended. If the MAC address of the destination device is unknown, it must be discovered before the information is handed down to the physical layer for transmission. This is where ARP comes into play. The process is initiated with an ARP request. The request is a packet comprising the sender's IP and MAC address and the IP address of the device of interest. In the request process, the data-link layer appends a broadcast MAC address to the destination MAC address so that every device on the data link will receive the request.

All the devices receive the ARP request via the physical layer. The request is examined by the data-link layers of all devices on the link, and since it is a broadcast MAC address, the device thinks the request is information destined for it. The network layer looks at the IP address to determine if the request is intended for that particular device. If the addresses do not match, the packet is discarded. The destination device of interest sends back a reply containing its MAC address. Consequently, the original sending device makes an association between the IP and MAC address it has just discovered. This process is commonly referred to as *address mapping*.

# Wireless Protocols

Wireless technology is similar to Ethernet in that they both reside in the network access layer, which implies that they are responsible for physical specifications (for example, frequency band and transmission speed), flow control, and so on. In fact, Ethernet coexists with wireless protocols such as 802.11 in a wireless network. This relationship between wireless technology and "wired" technology factors into the hardware components within a wireless network; one of these hardware components is an *access point* (AP), which functions as a transparent bridge. When a network has more than one AP, a wired connection between them uses Ethernet for transmission. However, transmission from an AP to a wireless node or user involves a wireless protocol.

One of the most significant differences between wireless protocols and Ethernet is the way in which they handle flow control. As you know, Ethernet uses CSMA/CD. However, a node using RF is not always able to "hear" any other user or node activity. This is because its own signal masks that of any other node on the network. Another possible problem occurs if two nodes are communicating and a third node is too far from the node transmitting but within the reach of the receiving node; the third node will be oblivious of the existing session. The third node, unable to hear the signal of the transmitting node, could cause excessive collisions. As a result, another type of collision avoidance protocol called *request to send/clear to send* (RTS/CTS) is used. When a node would like to transmit information to another node, a request-to-send message is sent. If the destination node is not sending or receiving, it responds with a clear-to-send message.

Another difference between wireless (RF) protocols and Ethernet is the need for modulation. There are two types of modulation: Frequency Hopping Spread Spectrum (FHSS) and Direct Sequence Spread Spectrum (DSSS). Transmission rates with DSSS modulation can be up to 11Mbps; in contrast, FHSS is limited to between 1Mbps and 2Mbps.

There are basically two types of design for wireless LANs (WLANs), referred to as *infrastructure* and *ad hoc*. Infrastructure is similar to a traditional LAN, with APs bridging traffic. Ad hoc is typically a temporary network with limited users that does not use APs. Within the group of users, a master is dynamically designated, and the remaining nodes are slaves. An application of an ad hoc network occurs when users gather in a conference room for a meeting in which data is exchanged among the users. It is worth mentioning that within the 802.11 standards, there is infrared (IR) and RF transmission; currently, however, RF is most typically implemented in WLANs because it has higher-bandwidth capabilities and wider area of coverage. (IR requires direct line of sight, meaning that it cannot penetrate solid surfaces such as walls.)

## Other Network Access Protocols

Some additional network access protocols are Frame Relay, Asynchronous Transfer Mode (ATM), and Synchronous Optical Networking (SONET). Frame Relay is a wide area network (WAN) technology. This allows communication between LANs that interconnect. ATM, on the other hand, is primarily used in the high-speed core or backbone of a network. Typically, this technology provides the switching functionality in carrier-class networks. SONET is another core switching technology. However, as the name indicates, SONET is an optical technology, whereas ATM is mostly electrical. Optical transmission is becoming increasingly more popular than the traditional electrical signaling, due to the increasing demand in transmission speed or bandwidth.

# Understanding the Internet Layer

The Internet layer, or the network layer, is responsible for determining the network path for computer data. The major devices that operate at this layer are *routers*. Routers make the Internet possible. They connect thousands of networks, creating a single global WAN (the Internet) used by millions of people. This section explains the various protocols that make up this layer and how they operate.

# The Internet Protocol

The *Internet Protocol* (IP) is one of the most important protocols for communication among computer systems. IP is a network layer protocol. Because each layer provides services for the layer above it, IP facilitates the communication of information from the transport layer protocols, such as TCP and UDP.

With all the responsibility this protocol carries, it functions as a best-effort delivery system. Like UDP, it is a connectionless protocol, and with that comes unreliability. (The term *connectionless* refers to the fact that there are no record-keeping responsibilities within this layer.) However, this does not imply that the system is ineffective—rather, it relies on the upper layers to provide reliability. TCP is most commonly the transport protocol of choice for data that requires guaranteed delivery to its destination. The packets might not all reach the destination in order, but TCP ensures that they are all received. Keep in mind that transmission of data takes place in milliseconds, so if the receiving device has to reorganize the packets into sequential order, that is usually not perceived by the end user. The contents of the IP header are illustrated in Figure 3.6.

**Figure 3.6** IP Header

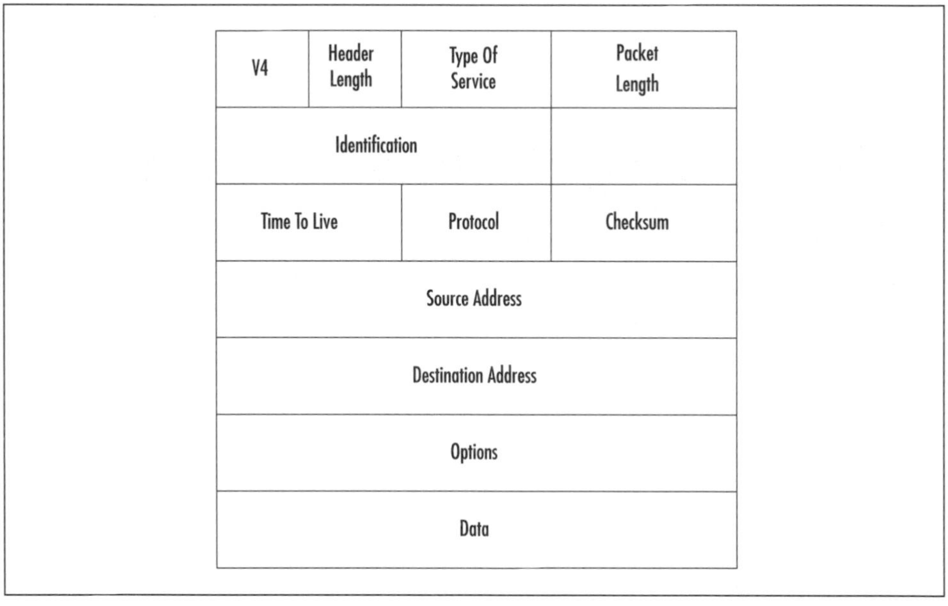

| V4 | Header Length | Type Of Service | Packet Length |
|----|----|----|----|
| Identification | | | |
| Time To Live | | Protocol | Checksum |
| Source Address | | | |
| Destination Address | | | |
| Options | | | |
| Data | | | |

The IP header includes the following fields:

- **V4** The version of the Internet Protocol being used (IPv4).

- **Header length (HL)** The number in bits that the header occupies.

- **Type of service (TOS)** Consists of four bits representing minimization of delay, maximization of throughput, maximization of reliability, and minimization of cost. Only one of these priorities can be active. The most beneficial priority depends on the application: A Simple Network Management Protocol (SNMP) packet containing information about a link failure would benefit from a maximization of reliability.

- **Packet length** This field is included because some network access protocols pad, or add stuff bits to, a small packet in order to meet the minimum size requirement.

- **Identification** Assigned to each packet to provide a unique identity. This field is important with fragmentation, because the identifier is duplicated in each fragment of the packet. Flags are also used to identify fragments. Fragment offset identifies the sequence of a particular fragment in relation to the beginning of the original packet.

- **Time to live (TTL)** The number of hops a packet can travel before being discarded. This is a way of preventing routing loops.

- **Protocol** This field identifies the protocol that generated the data in the packet.

- **Checksum** A metric used by the receiving device to ensure that the information in the header is not corrupted on receipt.

- **Source address** The sender's IP address.

- **Destination address** Indicates the address of the intended recipient.

- **Options** This field can be used to provide information about the routers, such as addresses and timestamps, that the packet encounters in its path to the destination.

# IP Addressing

IP addresses identify both a specific network and a specific device. The network identifier is the same for all devices on the same network. However, the device identifier is unique.

The entire IP address consists of 32 bits, which appear as one large binary number to computer devices. However, in order to simplify this massive number, we break it into four *octets*. Each octet is eight bits long. To further simplify IP addresses, we represent them in decimal format. In decimal, each octet ranges from 0 to 255. It is important to understand how to count in binary to design an IP architecture. This is a totally different way of counting and requires practice. Table 3.1 shows how to count in binary.

**Table 3.1** How to Count in Binary

| Binary | Equivalent |
| --- | --- |
| 00000000 | 0 |
| 00000001 | 1 |
| 00000010 | 2 |
| 00000011 | 3 |
| 00000100 | 4 |
| 00000101 | 5 |
| 00000110 | 6 |
| 00000111 | 7 |
| 00001000 | 8 |
| 00001001 | 9 |
| 00001010 | 10 |
| 00001011 | 11 |
| 00001100 | 12 |
| 00001101 | 13 |
| 00001110 | 14 |
| 00001111 | 15 |
| 00010000 | 16 |
| 00100000 | 32 |

**Continued**

**Table 3.1** How to Count in Binary

| Binary | Equivalent |
| --- | --- |
| 01000000 | 64 |
| 10000000 | 128 |
| … | … |

You can continue with the counting until you reach the binary number of all 1s or eight consecutive 1s: 11111111. This number is equivalent to 255, which is the largest number any octet can be. If you wanted to increase the number to 256, it would require an additional digit (for a total of nine digits), which is larger than allowed. Once you understand how to count in binary, you can begin to work with IP addresses.

As stated earlier, an IP address is a 32-bit number, broken down into octets. The way we write an IP address is in the form *X.X.X.X,* where *X* is a number between 0 and 255. Remember that an IP address identifies both a network and a host; the network portion of the address is divided into three classes, to accommodate the number of hosts on a particular network:

> **Class A** Designed for large networks. The network portion is contained within the first octet. Consequently, the host portion of the address consists of the remaining three octets. In other words, there is a possibility for 128 autonomous or unique networks, each having the potential of 16,777,216 devices.
>
> **Class B** Designed for medium-sized networks. The network portion is contained with the first two octets. As a result, there are two remaining octets for the devices attached to the network. As you might have already guessed, there is a potential of 16,384 different networks, each with 65,536 devices.
>
> **Class C** Designed for small networks. The network portion is three octets, and the host identifier is within the last octet. This is the most abundant group of networks, totaling 2,097,152. Networks of this class comprise no more than 256 devices.

To quickly identify the class to which an IP address belongs, you can follow an easy rule. It is known as the *first octet rule* and is illustrated in Table 3.2.

**Table 3.2** Quick and Easy Rule of the First Octet

| Class | First Octet Rule | Decimal | Binary |
|-------|------------------|---------|--------|
| A | First bit 0 | 0–127 | 00000000–01111111 |
| B | First two bits 10 | 128–191 | 10000000–10111111 |
| C | First three bits 110 | 192–223 | 11000000–11011111 |
| D* | First four bits 1110 | 224–239 | 11100000–11101111 |
| E* | First four bits 1111 | 240–255 | 11110000–11111111 |

Furthermore, within each class is an address range reserved for private addresses. The private addresses are as follows: 10.0.0.0–10.255.255.255, 172.16.0.0–172.31.255.255, and 192.168.0.0–192.168.255.255. In many cases, these addresses are designated for devices that will not be sending or receiving traffic outside their own networks. Another possible application for private addresses is a situation in which only a limited number of people would be communicating outside their network at any one time. In this case, an address pool would be established in which addresses are dynamically assigned to a device for a limited time. This is a measure to help conserve address space. These few private address ranges, along with a few others, are the only addresses that are not permitted on the Internet. For a complete list of all the Internet addresses, go to www.isi.edu/in-notes/iana/assignments/ipv4-address-space.

## Conserving Address Space with VLSM

It was identified early in the development of the Internet that the limited number of IP addresses would eventually run out, so a method of splitting classes into smaller blocks needed to be developed. Conservation efforts are absolutely necessary. Let's think about why this is important. Imagine that you are the owner of a large telecommunications company. You support voice and data, which means that you might have a Frame Relay network, an ATM network, an IP network, and so on. Not only do you need addresses for your equipment, but you must supply your customers Internet services along with address space for their equipment. Remember, you are only one of the many companies in this business. It quickly becomes apparent how address space is rapidly being depleted.

One measure to conserve address space is called *Variable Length Subnet Mask* (VLSM). What is an address mask? The default address mask is represented in Table 3.3. (Remember that a Class A address uses the first octet for the network portion, Class B the first two octets, and Class C the first three octets.)

**Table 3.3** Default Address Masks

| Class | Address | Default Mask |
| --- | --- | --- |
| Class A | 11111111.00000000.00000000.00000000 | 255.0.0.0 |
| Class B | 11111111.11111111.00000000.00000000 | 255.255.0.0 |
| Class C | 11111111.11111111.11111111.00000000 | 255.255.255.0 |

You can tell that an address of 192.168.1.1 is a Class C address, since it falls between the range of 192 and 223. Given Table 3.3, you can see that the mask for this address is 255.255.255.0. This is also noted as a */24*, which represents the number of 1 bits in the mask. You can also see that there are three entire octets containing one bit (8 x 3 = 24).

VLSM allows you to make the address mask a value other than the default ones. If we relied on the default address masks for our Internet addressing, only 2,113,664 networks would be allowed on the Internet. Two million networks might sound like a lot, but with standard address masks, most would be networks with only 254 devices. With VLSM we can extend the number of networks on the Internet and allow for several different network sizes.

If you see an address of 192.168.0.0/26, what would the mask be in binary format? There will be 26 one bits:

11111111.11111111.11111111.11 000000 = mask

11000000.10101000.00000000.00 000000 = address

Now, how do you know which part of the address is the network portion and which is reserved for hosts? Draw a line after the last 1 bit in the mask and carry it through the address. This line will show you how many hosts are available for the network. We know the first two bits in the last octet are 1s, so they are part of the network. We also know the maximum for one octet is 255 and the first two bits are equal to 192. Therefore, 255 − 192 = 63, and that gives us the maximum number of hosts on this /26 network.

How is this information useful? Let's say that you are given an address such as the preceding example and you are asked to figure out the broadcast address for the network. We know that the network portion is 192.168.0.x and, as far as we know, the available hosts are 192.168.0.0-192.168.0.63. In order to tell what the broadcast address is for this particular network, we have to do the following:

11111111.11111111.11111111.11 000000 = mask

11000000.10101000.00000000.00 000000 = network address

00000000.00000000.00000000.00 111111 = broadcast address

As illustrated, the network broadcast address is at the top of the range for network hosts. In our example, the broadcast address is 192.168.0.63. Furthermore, it is general practice to assign the default gateway to the first available host address. Continuing with our example, the default gateway would be 192.168.0.1. The ability to identify the network and host range of an address is useful in troubleshooting.

# Routing

*Routing* is responsible for moving information along an optimal path through a network. The router determines the best path using *routing algorithms*, which calculate the path based on certain metrics. The types of metrics used in calculating the path depend on the algorithm, and each protocol uses a different algorithm. This allows the network designer some choices in designing a network to fit the needs of the users. For instance, in banking, money transactions need to be error-free upon delivery, so speed is of a lesser priority than reliability. Another situation with totally different needs is video streaming. Speed is the number-one priority here. Reliability is, of course, desirable, but *error-free* doesn't mean a lot when delay dominates the show. Now the question is, how do we know which type of protocol or algorithm is right for the applications of a particular network?

## *Static and Dynamic Routing*

The first decision in choosing a routing protocol is based on the complexity of the network. A small, simplistic network might be best suited for a statically routed network. Static routing is configured by a network administrator; its rules do not change unless the administrator chooses to change them. No algorithm is associated with static routing because path determination is the responsibility of the administrator. The strength of static routing is in its reliability. For example, the amount of traffic on a link can be somewhat controlled by the administrator. This is possible because if there are relatively few users, traffic flow is more predictable.

In a situation in which the demands of users, and subsequently the traffic flow, are continually changing, *dynamic routing* is the best solution. A dynamically routed network utilizes algorithmic calculations to adjust to network changes. A possible network change could occur when a financial officer is putting together a quarterly report. Perhaps he or she is downloading large files from various sources. This process might consume a considerable amount of bandwidth. Consequently, the traffic from other network users might need to be routed to a different link. A dynamically routed network is capable of facilitating these types of changes.

How is an algorithm aware that the network has changed? Remember that an algorithm is just one component of a routing protocol. There are also routing tables, which contain the information from routing update messages. The update messages are sent either periodically or when a network change occurs, depending on the protocol. The algorithm uses the information in the routing table for path determination. In conjunction with the routing table, the algorithm uses metrics such as path length, throughput speed of the link, and amount of traffic on a link.

In order to statically route the entire network in Figure 3.7, the administrator needs to configure and maintain 54 routes for full connectivity.

**Figure 3.7** Static Routing in a Multihop, Multipath Network

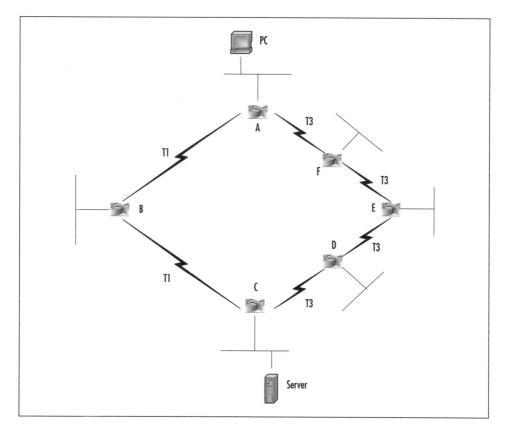

Let's look at the logistics of how this network would be configured. How many routes will be on each router? Router A is directly connected to the local LAN, Router B, and Router F. Since each router is already connected to three of the 12 networks within this architecture, that leaves nine routes to be statically configured. That doesn't seem like

an overwhelming amount until there is a link failure. In the event of a
link failure between Router A and Router B, any router using A to get
to B and vice versa must be changed. Let's say that Router F needs to
forward a packet to Router B, intended for the LAN directly connected
to B. Normally, it would go through A to get to B. However, due to the
failure, the packet now has to travel through E, D, and C to finally reach
B, but only after the new routes have been manually reconfigured.

   Static routing is fine for a small, simple network. However, it
becomes increasingly difficult to manage as the network grows, especially when problems arise.

## Designing & Planning…

### Serial Links /30 Networks

Each serial link is considered an autonomous network. It requires
only a /30, four host addresses—one address for each of the interfaces between the link and the router. The remaining two
addresses comprise the network and broadcast addresses.

## Distance Vector and Link State Routing

There are basically two groups of routing protocols, *distance vector* and
*link state*. The distinguishing properties are how the two groups learn
about a network (specifically, the routes within a network), the algorithms that are used, and the associated metrics.

   Distance vector routing learns by the rumor method. In other
words, an adjacent router sends its routing table to its neighbor. The
neighbor accepts the received table as trustworthy and merely adds its
information to the table. In essence, routers running this type of protocol
learn only about the relative distances, in terms of hop count, of their
neighbors to the nodes in a network. (*Hop count* refers to the number of
routers a packet must encounter on the way to its destination.) The

router does not know anything about the other routers in the network beyond its adjacent neighbors. The primary concern of the router is to route a packet to the next hop. It looks up the destination address in its routing table and decides which neighbor is closer to the destination.

These types of protocols run Bellman-Ford algorithms. The metrics used to calculate the optimal path are generally less complex than the metrics used in link-state routing. For example, Routing Information Protocol (RIP) calculates the best path based solely on hop count. A potential problem with this method is when the connections or links between the routers are of differing bandwidths. A router chooses the path with the least number of hops, but this path might also have the slowest links. In a case like this, the best route could actually be more hops away, but the information flow is actually faster. In Figure 3.7, using RIP, traffic from Router A to Router C would have a path from A to B to C. This is a total of three hops, but the bandwidth of a T1 is 1/28 the speed of a T3.

How does this type of routing protocol inform the routers of a network change? Periodically, each router broadcasts its routing table to its neighbors. The broadcast tables are compared with the existing tables for any changes that occur. Since each router communicates only with its neighbors, any changes that occur are also learned by the rumor method. This can potentially be a problematic situation without certain configurable remedies. Routing loops, for instance, can occur without preventative measures such as split horizon and poison reverse.

Another consideration with distance vector protocols such as RIP is IP addressing limitations. Some distance vector protocols such as RIP Version 1 do not support VLSM, so the default masks are the boundaries for the addressing ranges. This means that each network has a minimum of 255 host addresses. Remember, each serial link is considered its own network. A network requiring two host addresses will waste the remaining 252.

Routers using a *link-state protocol* build a topological database containing information about every link in the entire network. In fact, the network topology database is the resource all the routers on a network use to build their routing tables. The database obtains network information through the use of *link-state advertisements* (LSA). There are several different types of LSAs, each containing information on a particular aspect of the network.

A link-state routing protocol uses a shortest-path-first algorithm, sometimes referred to as the *Dijkstra algorithm*. The most commonly implemented type of link-state protocol is Open Shortest Path First (OSPF). The metrics used by this algorithm to determine the optimal path include considerations such as path distance, load, link bandwidth, delay, and reliability. Metrics with such granularity provide a more accurate evaluation of available paths than simple hop count. These metrics are configurable, allowing the network designer or administrator options, depending on network users' demands. In addition, the router calculates alternative paths in the event that the primary route deteriorates.

For example, in Figure 3.7, data exchange from the workstation behind Router A to the server behind Router C would travel from A to F to E to D and finally to C, based on the link bandwidths. Although the information must travel more hops than if the path were from A to B to C, it will undoubtedly get to its destination more quickly.

Network updates are sent when the network changes; this is performed by the IP Multicasting protocol. During times when the network does not change, there is no need to update the network—the routing tables remain in a current state. Due to the nature of how the network updates, the routers are able to quickly adapt to the changes. This quick convergence time eliminates some of the problems encountered in distance vector routing, such as routing loops.

As you know, each type of routing provides a different set of characteristics. A classic saying in network design is "It depends," which again applies to decisions regarding which type of routing protocols are appropriate for a particular network. It is best to keep things as simple as possible but with enough functionality to be effective. Attention to the current or anticipated applications, number of users, and forecast network growth will be good indicators of what protocols are appropriate.

# The Internet Control Message Protocol

*Internet Control Message Protocol* (ICMP) is designed to provide diagnostic and troubleshooting information and tools in order to manage an IP network. A variety of messages are provided by this protocol, indicating errors as well as query and response. A complete listing can be found in Request for Comments (RFC) 792. Examples of common triggers for ICMP messages are when a destination is unreachable or when a request has timed out. Two tools in particular that are useful for troubleshooting are ping and traceroute.

*Ping* is used to check the end-to-end connectivity of a host to a remote device. An echo message is sent to the remote device. If there is connectivity, the device sends back echo reply messages. If at least one echo reply is sent, the remote device is considered still "alive." The health of the connection is also indicated by the ratio of echo messages to echo replies. If the ratio is not one to one, the echo messages are timing out due to excessive delay in the connection or packet loss. This process is equivalent to sonar for computer systems.

*Traceroute* provides a packet-tracking system. This tool allows the user to see every hop, or IP address, along the path to the packet's destination address. If there are connectivity problems, this tool will show where the packet is being dropped. This tool also shows the time lapse between hops, which is helpful in detecting network congestion and the resulting delay.

# Understanding the Host-to-Host Layer

The host-to-host layer is identical to the transport layer in terms of functionality and the protocols that reside in this layer. In order to avoid redundancy, we discuss in greater detail two of the most commonly implemented protocols, UDP and TCP.

# User Datagram Protocol

UDP is preferred for dealing with time-sensitive applications. For example, imagine having a conversation with someone when all of a sudden he or she tells you some fragment of information just remembered from a previous topic—and then he or she continues with the current topic. The information from the past topic has now confused the current topic. This event does not occur in UDP, because the sender assumes that all the packets are received and will not retransmit information. In addition to having time sensitivity, an advantage of UDP is reduced overhead in both the packet header and the absence of acknowledgments. As illustrated in Figure 3.8, the UDP header is quite simple.

**Figure 3.8** UDP Header

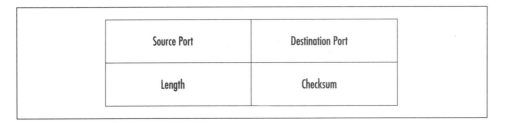

| Source Port | Destination Port |
|:---:|:---:|
| Length | Checksum |

The IP header includes the following fields:

- **Source port number** Indicates the sending application.
- **Destination port number** Indicates the receiving application.
- **Length** The size of the header and attached data, if any.
- **Checksum (optional)** Includes a metric for both the header and any data.

# Transmission Control Protocol

TCP uses three primary mechanisms to achieve reliable transmission of information: packet numbering, acknowledgments, and windowing. The importance of these attributes are evident when you look at the header, shown in Figure 3.9, where each has a dedicated field. *Packet numbering* ensures sequential delivery of packets to the destination. *Acknowledgments* provide a method of record keeping. When a packet is received, the receiver sends an acknowledgment back to the sender. If the packets are received out of sequence, implying a loss of packet(s), or if errors are detected, an acknowledgment is not sent. In this case, the sender will retransmit the packet(s). *Windowing* is a measure of flow control. In other words, the sender and receiver agree on the number of packets the sender will transmit before waiting for an acknowledgment. This system provides reliability without compromising the amount of throughput by acknowledging every single packet.

**Figure 3.9** TCP Header

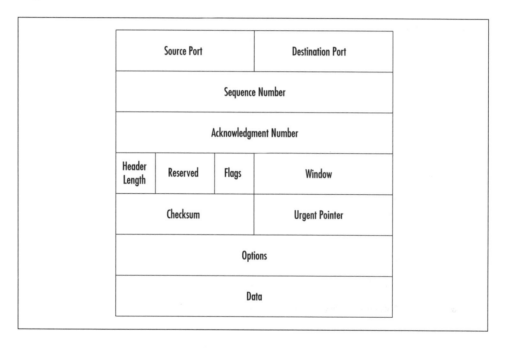

As you can see, there is constant communication between the sender and the audience, thus creating a virtual point-to-point connection. This method of transport is advantageous in a data environment, where each piece of data is vital.

Since this protocol is connection-oriented, a connection must be established among the devices that want to exchange data. The establishment of this connection is often referred to as a *handshake* process. Once the device has established a TCP session with the remote device, the devices establish certain parameters such as windowing size, and information is exchanged. Once the session is complete, the two devices must terminate the session.

As mentioned earlier, the overhead in the header alone is greater for TCP than UDP:

- **Source port number** Identifies the sending application.

- **Destination port number** Identifies the receiving application.

- **Sequence number** Identifies where a particular packet fits in the data stream. This field provides information similar to the fragment offset field in an IP header.

- **Acknowledgment number** Provides the receiving device with the sequence number of the following packet the device should be expecting.

- **Header length** This field indicates the size of the header in bits. Since there might or might not be information in the options field, it provides the media access protocol a value to compare with the minimum required size and determine if there is a need for filler bits.

- **Flags bits** Provides additional information about the header or the session itself.

- **Window size** Indicates the number of bytes the receiving device should expect before sending an acknowledgement message. This is a key field for flow control.

- **Checksum** Provides information to the receiver to verify the validity of the information in the TCP portion of a packet.

- **Urgent pointer** This is valid only if the flag field turns it on. When it is activated, it provides a way of interrupting the original data stream to send urgent information. The pointer tells the receiver where in the data stream the urgent information resides.

- **Options** An example of this field is time stamping.

# Managing the Application Layer

The DoD summarized the top three layers of the OSI model into a single application layer. If you look at the operation and function of the session, presentation, and application layers together, you can also conclude that they perform different pieces of the same function: providing the link between the host-to–host layer and providing the link to the end user. This section briefly discusses some of the networking functions and protocols that operate at this level.

## Monitoring Tools: SNMP

SNMP is a protocol within the IP suite that manages network events and monitors the overall heath of a network. Events such as link failure, router failure, or anything causing loss of connectivity are reported to the network administrator. Monitoring the volume of traffic on a link is one way to manage events. SNMP facilitates the evaluation of network health. Any device that uses TCP/IP can be managed using this protocol.

SNMP communication occurs between network devices and management stations, which display the information for the administrator. The network devices are commonly referred to as *agents* in this context. Numerous variables are configured on the agents to provide tailored information about the overall network.

## Assigning Addresses with DHCP

*Dynamic Host Configuration Protocol* (DHCP) is a server-based application that dynamically assigns IP addresses to network devices. This application eliminates at least two difficulties for a network administrator. First, it eliminates the need to statically address all the network devices. A static method implies constant updating as devices are moved within the network or even between networks. (For example, when there is a meeting between employees from different buildings and all employees bring laptops because they need to exchange data during the meeting, the laptops will require IP addresses. Imagine the administrator scurrying around the meeting assigning addresses manually!) The second difficulty that DHCP eliminates is keeping track of a dynamic network with static addressing. DHCP maintains a database of all addresses and to what device they are assigned, as well as which addresses are available.

Let's talk about the process of *address assignment*. When a device running TCP/IP is initially logging on to the network, it sends out a DHCP discover message. The DHCP server receives the message and sends a message to the hardware or MAC address of the device, containing an IP address with the subnet mask, the time limit on the address lease, and IP address of the server. The device broadcasts a message of acceptance. The final step occurs when the address is actually assigned and the device implements its new identity. Once the process is complete, the device is capable of having TCP/IP sessions, and it operates as though the address were a permanent configuration. Once the address lease period expires, it is put back into the pool of addresses and becomes available for reallocation.

Another benefit of using DHCP is that there can be more users than addresses due to the fact that the addresses are leased for a limited amount of time. This would be appropriate if some network users did not frequently communicate with other services and devices, such as e-mail and the Internet. Setting the ratio of users to addresses is a judgment call on the part of the administrator.

# Conserving with Network Address Translation

*Network address translation* (NAT) is a method of IP address conservation. As discussed in the IP addressing section of this chapter, it is apparent that addresses are rapidly being depleted. This depletion is due to the fact that resources on the Internet are being used by far more people than initially expected. The way that the address space has been divided into classes is not optimized for the current and ever-growing number of users. VLSM is an attempt to alleviate some of the impact of wasted address space, but it is not a long-term solution. Using NAT in addition to VLSM is a way to extend the life (in terms of the address space) of the current version of IP (IPv4). Development of a new version, IPv6, is under way and should theoretically combat the problematic shortage of address space. However, in the meantime, measures such as NAT are a good intermediate solution.

NAT gives networks that have private addresses the ability to access public networks (that is, the Internet). Typically, networks that have private addressing schemes, usually referred to as *internal networks*, are designed that way because a majority of the traffic on that network is local traffic, meaning that it does not leave the network. However, when a user needs access to the Internet, NAT translates the private address into a unique, public address. The public address comes from a pool of addresses reserved for that particular network. The number of addresses in the pool depends on the number of network users and the way NAT is configured.

The specifications and desired version of NAT are typically configured on a router. The router is responsible for the actual translation or mapping of internal and external addresses. In addition to address conservation, another benefit of NAT is security. The router configured with NAT enables anonymity. The external environment does not know the real identity of the user in the private network.

We will discuss three ways in which to configure NAT. The appropriate version of NAT depends on the demands of the users on a particular network. The three types are:

- Static NAT

- Dynamic NAT

- Overloading (PAT)

*Static NAT* refers to a configuration in which individual private addresses are assigned their own public addresses. This is useful when a limited number of users on the network frequently need to send and receive traffic outside the internal network. This configuration is not optimized when numerous users sporadically use the resources of an external network.

*Dynamic NAT* is a better-suited solution for numerous, sporadic external network users. This form of NAT operates by mapping an internal address with an address from an external address pool. Address mapping is illustrated in Figure 3.10. A unique address range is assigned to a particular network making up the address pool. As the name indicates, the process of mapping addresses is dynamic. Once a user is finished using the external address, the address enters into the pool and is available again.

**Figure 3.10** Network Address Translation

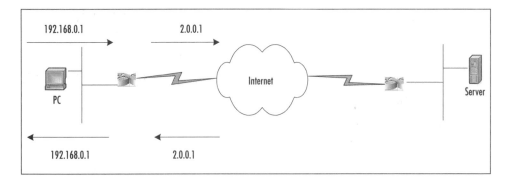

*Overloading*, or *port address translation* (PAT), extends the functionality of dynamic NAT. This configuration is the most effective method of address conservation. PAT operates by mapping one external address to many internal addresses. What about the criteria of being a unique address for Internet use? To an external network, the users on the internal network appear as one user. The external network does not care, since the single address for the internal network is indeed unique, and that is all that matters.

Let's look at an example of a user who wants to surf the Web. A TCP session is initiated and the HTTP port identifier is added to the packet. When the router receives the packet, it contains the port identifier for HTTP set by the transport protocol and the internal address of the user's device. The router adds an external address translation and a session port identifier. This process is shown in Figure 3.11. The router keeps a record of the translated IP addresses and the associated ports.

**Figure 3.11** Simultaneous PAT Sessions

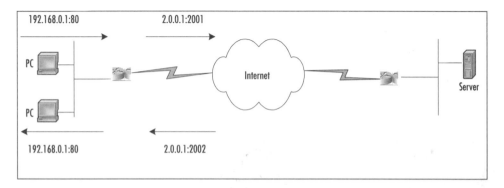

## Designing & Planning...

## TCP/UDP Port Assignments

The port number that is assigned in the TCP/UDP header to a session is a *logical port*. This is not a port on an actual piece of physical hardware. Port numbers 1–1024 are reserved for protocols such as HTTP, FTP, POP, and so on. Port numbers 1025 to approximately 65000 are available for sessions. This means that a router could perform over 60,000 port address translations simultaneously, provided that it has adequate processing power. That amounts to a tremendous saving of registered external IP addresses!

# Summary

As the Internet becomes a ubiquitous entity, our networks grow more dependent on the protocol suite that facilitates its existence. The Internet Protocol (IP) suite includes IP addressing, routing protocols, and troubleshooting tools. This chapter focuses on IP because an understanding of its components is important for network design. Along with an understanding of IP, you must have an understanding of the process of communication among computer systems. Through the examination of the OSI and DoD reference models, we broke this process into its functional components.

The OSI model is comprised of seven layers, consisting of the physical, data-link, network, transport, session, presentation, and application layers. The DoD chose to use four layers and applied it specifically to IP and the Internet. The DoD model consists of the network access layer, Internet layer, host-to-host layer, and the applications layer. Understanding these two models and how they interact is the basis for understanding TCP/IP.

The network access layer defines technologies that computer systems use to interact with one another. Some of the more widely used network access layer technologies include Ethernet, Token Ring, Frame Relay, ATM, and, of course, wireless. Bridges and switches deal with frames of data at this layer and locally send the data to its destination.

The Internet layer is mainly where IP comes into the picture. This layer is responsible for the addressing of all devices and is the basis for the global network known as the Internet. Routers operate at this layer and are responsible for determining the path that packets of data need to take. There are several different methods of routing the data. Static, distance vector, and link-state routing are the most common methods, in order of complexity and functionality. TCP and UDP are the two IP-based host-to-host protocols in use today. Both protocols run on top of IP and identify themselves by port numbers. TCP and UDP both have port values between 1 and approximately 65000. UDP is primarily used for time-sensitive, low-priority traffic. It is a very simple protocol that has no reliability and operates in a connectionless environment. Video, voice, and other multimedia applications normally operate over UDP. TCP is a connection-oriented protocol that supports reliable data transfer. Most traditional Internet traffic such as e-mail, FTP, and certain Web uses operate over TCP connections.

A growing number of applications operate over the Internet. This chapter focused on the applications that help support and maintain the Internet and IP. DHCP is a protocol that operates between a server and clients. It dynamically allocates IP addresses to computers to simplify administration functions. Another application is NAT. NAT and its variations are helping solve the shortage of IP addresses. NAT allows a company to conserve public IP addresses by translating private IP addresses to public IP addresses. The concept is based on the assumption that not all computers in a private network will access the Internet at the same time. The smaller the ratio of nonactive Internet computer sessions to active Internet computer session, the farther NAT can go. PAT is an addition to NAT and not only allows for IP address translations but for TCP and UDP port translations as well. This means that dozens, even hundreds, of computers can share the same IP address.

All these protocols make up the suite known as TCP/IP. Although TCP/IP is a fully implemented and robust technology, enhancements and modifications are still under way, attempting to make it even better than it is today. IPv6 is expected to provide a new suite of additions to the existing ones.

# Solution Fast Track

## Exploring the OSI and DoD Models

☑ Open System Interconnection (OSI) and the Department of Defense (DoD) reference models are a way to systematically approach the communication process among computer systems.

☑ The OSI and DoD models differ in the granularity of each layer. The layers in the OSI model consist of physical, data-link, network, transport, session, and application layers. The DoD model condenses these layers into network access, Internet, host-to-host, and application layers.

☑ Each layer of the models provides a piece of the communications puzzle. Each layer provides functions that, as a whole, facilitate communication.

# Understanding the Network Access Layer

☑ The network access layer comprises physical protocols such as 802.11, which is used in wireless networking.

☑ Bridging is a method that resides in the network access layer and provides a method of forwarding traffic based on MAC addressing.

☑ Bridging types include transparent bridging for Ethernet LANs, source-route bridging (SRB) used in Token Ring environments, and source-route translational bridging (SR/TLB) for a hybrid Ethernet/Token Ring network.

# Understanding the Internet Layer

☑ IP is a driving force of the Internet layer. It provides a logical addressing scheme that facilitates packet forwarding by routing devices.

☑ Routing protocols are responsible for calculating optimal paths within and between networks.

# Understanding the Host-to-Host Layer

☑ Transmission Control Protocol (TCP) and User Datagram Protocol (UDP) are the primary protocols within the host-to-host layer.

## Managing the Application Layer

☑ The applications within the application layer are the resources computer users actually see and use.

☑ The DoD summarized the top three layers of the OSI model into a single application layer. These layers perform different pieces of the same function: providing the link between the host-to-host layer and providing the link to the end user.

☑ Network management tools are a component of this layer as well.

# Frequently Asked Questions

The following Frequently Asked Questions, answered by the authors of this book, are designed to both measure your understanding of the concepts presented in this chapter and to assist you with real-life implementation of these concepts. To have your questions about this chapter answered by the author, browse to **www.syngress.com/solutions** and click on the **"Ask the Author"** form.

**Q:** In an Ethernet environment, how is it determined when to bridge and when to route?

**A:** There is a saying in network design: "Bridge where you can, route when you must." This saying implies that simplicity without compromising functionality is the best solution. However, accompanying a good solution is a good evolution plan. It is important to consider and prepare for future demands on a network.

**Q:** Is an access point (AP) a bridge or a router?

**A:** Most APs can function as either bridge or a router, depending on the needs of the network.

**Q:** What is involved in obtaining an IP address range?

**A:** Basically, if you consult the organization responsible for maintaining IP addresses, you can get the details necessary to obtain a range. In North America, South America, the Caribbean, and sub-Saharan Africa, the organization responsible is the Address Registry for Internet Numbers (ARIN), which can be found at www.arin.net. In Europe, the Middle East, and parts of Africa, the organization responsible is Reseaux IP Europeens (RIPE), which can be found at www.ripe.net. Lastly, for the Asia/Pacific region, the organization is the Asia/Pacific Network Information Centre (APNIC), which can be found at www.apnic.net.

**Q:** When using PAT, how can I accommodate all the necessary ports?

**A:** Approximately 60,000 logical port numbers can be associated with one external IP address. That means 60,000 different TCP sessions occurring simultaneously! If port numbers become limited, all you need is an additional address to provide double the capacity in terms of potential sessions.

# Chapter 4

# Identifying Evolving Wireless Technologies and Standards

## Solutions in this chapter:

- Fixed Wireless Technologies
- Developing WLANs through the 802.11 Architecture
- Developing WPANs through the 802.15 Architecture
- Mobile Wireless Technologies
- Optical Wireless Technologies

☑ Summary

☑ Solutions Fast Track

☑ Frequently Asked Questions

# Introduction

The wireless industry, like many other sectors of Information Technology, is advancing at a rapid pace. Driving forces of this advancement are the protocols and standards that provide more and more bandwidth, as well as the convergence of data, voice, and video within a network. This chapter will present the various forms of emerging wireless communication from a service provider perspective, all the way down to the home networking environment. In covering wireless technology from the perspective of the service provider, we'll be discussing Multichannel Multipoint Distribution Service (MMDS), Local Multipoint Distribution Service (LMDS), and Wireless Local Loop (WLL); in covering wireless technologies for the home and enterprise network, we will discuss wireless local area networks (WLANs) and the 802.11 protocol suite. The three primary areas of discussion are *fixed wireless*, *mobile wireless*, and *optical wireless* technology.

We have provided generic architectures under each of these wireless technologies to help you understand their evolution. We also provide a brief overview of why these technologies were developed (that is, the market that they serve), and what new capabilities they will provide. The intention is to provide an overview of the direction of wireless technology. When designing a network, you need to know what functionality is available currently and in the future to make longer term plans.

However, before we dive into emerging technologies, let's define what *wireless* means in the context of this chapter. In earlier chapters, a basic understanding of wireless technology was introduced in the context of using radio frequencies to transmit data over the medium of air instead of the traditional wireline copper and fiber transports. The term *wireless*, however, is used in so many more contexts that it would be beneficial to you now to provide a brief description of the various types of wireless technologies. For example, to a voice engineer the term *wireless* would refer to the mobile phone technologies. To a data network engineer the term *wireless* would refer to wireless LANs. These two wireless applications are the most commonly implemented.

# Fixed Wireless Technologies

The basic definition of a fixed wireless technology is any wireless technology where the transmitter and the receiver are at a fixed location such as a home or office, as opposed to mobile devices such as cellular phones. Fixed wireless devices normally use utility main power supplies (AC power), which will be discussed later in more detail. The technologies under fixed wireless can be MMDS connectivity models, LMDS, encompassing WLL, Point-to-Point Microwave, or WLAN.

Fixed wireless technologies provide advantages to service providers in several areas. First, just by nature of the wireless technology, fixed wireless systems provide the ability to connect to remote users without having to install costly copper cable or optical fiber over long distances. The service provider can deploy a fixed wireless offering much quicker and at a much lower cost than traditional wireline services. Also, the service provider can provide services via fixed wireless access without having to use the local service provider's last mile infrastructure. The disadvantages to fixed wireless vary, depending on which technology is being used, but some of the issues include line-of-sight and weather issues as well as interference from various sources, and licensing issues. After we discuss service provider implementations of fixed wireless, we will discuss how fixed wireless benefits the home and enterprise users.

# Multichannel Multipoint Distribution Service

Allocated by the Federal Communications Commission (FCC) in 1983 and enhanced with two-way capabilities in 1998, *Multichannel Multipoint Distribution Service* (MMDS) is a licensed spectrum technology operating in the 2.5 to 2.7 GHz range, giving it 200 MHz of spectrum to construct cell clusters. Service providers consider MMDS a complementary technology to their existing digital subscriber line (DSL) and cable modem offerings by providing access to customers not reachable via these wireline technologies (see Figure 4.1 for an example of a service provider MMDS architecture).

**Figure 4.1** MMDS Architecture

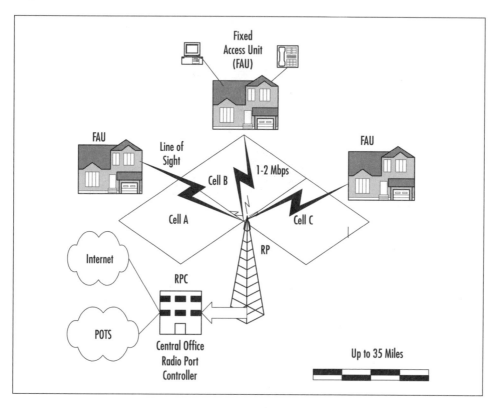

MMDS provides from 1 to 2 Mbps of throughput and has a relative range of 35 miles from the radio port controller (RPC) based on signal power levels. It generally requires a clear line of sight between the radio port (RP) antenna and the customer premise antenna, although several vendors are working on MMDS offerings that don't require a clear line of sight. The *fresnel* zone of the signal (the zone around the signal path that must be clear of reflective surfaces) must be clear from obstruction as to avoid absorption and reduction of the signal energy. MMDS is also susceptible to a condition known as *multipath reflection*. Multipath reflection or interference happens when radio signals reflect off surfaces such as water or buildings in the fresnel zone, creating a condition where the same signal arrives at different times. Figure 4.2 depicts the fresnel zone and the concept of absorption and multipath interference.

**Figure 4.2** Fresnel Zone: Absorption and Multipath Issues

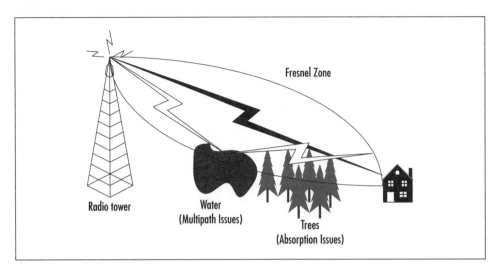

# Local Multipoint Distribution Services

*Local Multipoint Distribution Service* (LMDS) is a broadband wireless point-to-multipoint microwave communication system operating above 20 GHz (28–38 GHz in the US). It is similar in its architecture to MMDS with a couple of exceptions. LMDS provides very high-speed bandwidth (upwards of 500 Mbps) but is currently limited to a relative maximum range of 3 to 5 miles of coverage. It has the same line-of-sight issues that MMDS experiences, and can be affected by weather conditions, as is common among line-of-sight technologies.

LMDS is ideal for short-range campus environments requiring large amounts of bandwidth, or highly concentrated urban centers with large data/voice/video bandwidth requirements in a relatively small area. LMDS provides a complementary wireless architecture for the wireless service providers to use for markets that are not suited for MMDS deployments. Figure 4.3 illustrates a generic LMDS architecture.

**Figure 4.3** Local Multipoint Distribution Services (LMDS) Architecture

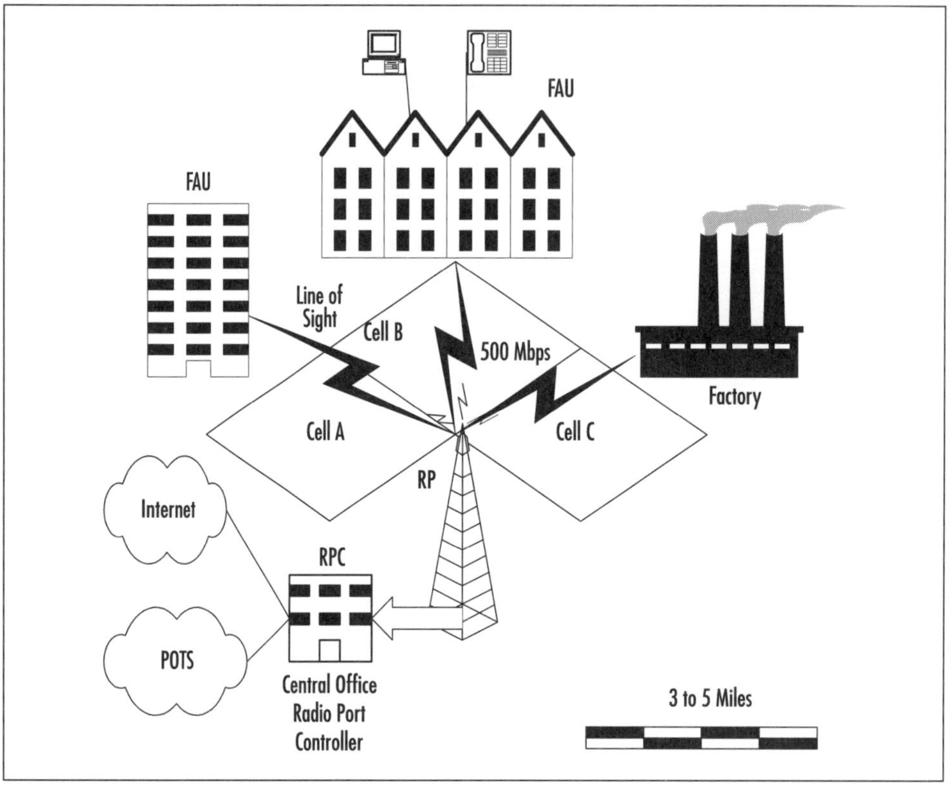

# Wireless Local Loop

*Wireless Local Loop* (WLL) refers to a fixed wireless class of technology aimed at providing last-mile services normally provided by the local service provider over a wireless medium. This includes Plain Old Telephone Service (POTS) as well as broadband offerings such as DSL service. As stated earlier, this technology provides service without the laying of cable or use of the Incumbent Local Exchange Carrier (ILEC), which in layman's terms is the Southwestern Bells of the world.

The generic layout involves a point-to-multipoint architecture with a central radio or radio port controller located at the local exchange (LE). The RPC connects to a series of base stations called radio ports (RPs) via fixed access back to the LE. The RPs are mounted on antennas and arranged to create coverage areas or sectored cells. The radios located at the customer premise, or fixed access unit (FAU), connects to an external antenna optimized to transmit and receive voice/data from the RPs. The coverage areas and bandwidth provided vary depending on the technology used, and coverage areas can be extended through the use of repeaters between the FAU and the RPs. Figure 4.4 provides a generic depiction of a wireless local loop architecture.

**Figure 4.4** Wireless Local Loop Architecture

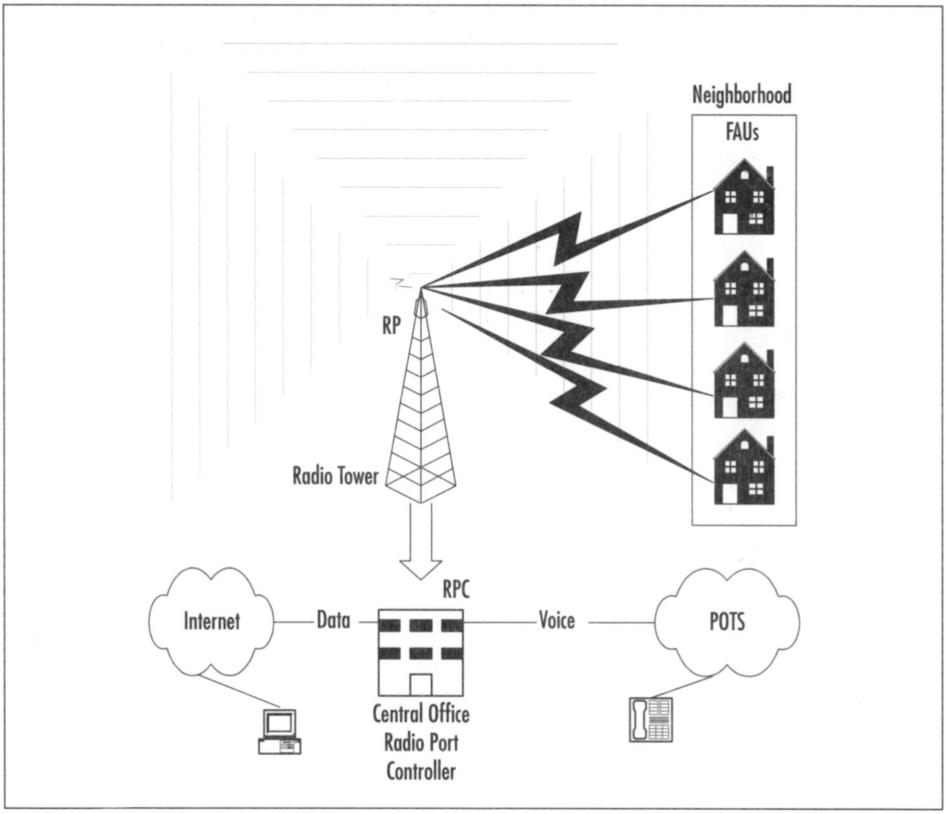

## Point-to-Point Microwave

*Point-to-Point (PTP) Microwave* is a line-of-sight technology, which is affected by multipath and absorption much like MMDS and LMDS. PTP Microwave falls into two categories: licensed and unlicensed, or spread spectrum. The FCC issues licenses for individuals to use specific frequencies for the licensed version. The advantage with the licensed PTP Microwave is that the chance of interference or noise sources in the frequency range is remote. This is critical if the integrity of the traffic on that link needs to be maintained. Also, if the link is going to span a long distance or is in a heavily populated area, the licensed version is a much safer bet since the probability of interference is greater in those cases. The drawback to licensed PTP Microwave is that it may take a considerable amount of time for the FCC to issue the licenses, and there are fees associated with those licenses. Unlicensed PTP Microwave links can be used when a licensed PTP Microwave is not necessary and expediency is an issue.

Since PTP can span long distances, determined mostly by the power of the transmitter and the sensitivity of the receiver, as well as by traditional weather conditions, many different aspects need to be considered in designing a PTP Microwave link. First, a site survey and path analysis need to be conducted. Obstructions and curvature of the earth (for links over six miles) determine the height of the towers or the building required to build the link in a line-of-sight environment. As stated earlier, the fresnel zone must be clear of obstructions and reflective surfaces to avoid absorption and multipath issues. Predominant weather conditions can limit the distance of the PTP Microwave link since the signal is susceptible to a condition called *rain fade*. The designers must take the predicted amount of signal degradation in a projected area and factor that into the design based on reliability requirements for the PTP Microwave link. Figure 4.5 gives a basic depiction of a PTP Microwave link.

# Wireless Local Area Networks

Benefits of fixed wireless can also provide value to the enterprise and home networks. This is where wireless capabilities get exciting for the end user. The benefits are literally at your fingertips. Imagine sitting at your desk when your boss calls announcing an emergency meeting immediately—there is a document on its way to you via e-mail that will be the focus of the meeting. Before wireless, you would first have to

**Figure 4.5** Point-to-Point Microwave

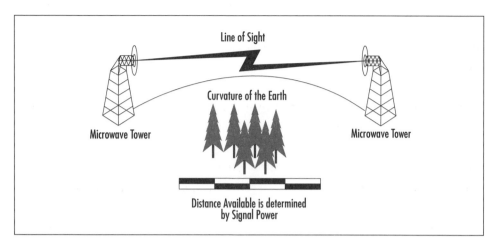

wait for your computer to receive the e-mail, then perhaps print the document before traveling to the meeting; with a laptop, you would have to consider cords, batteries, and connections. After the meeting, you would go back to your desk for any document changes or further correspondence by e-mail. In a wireless environment, you can receive the e-mail and read the document while you are on your way to the meeting, and make changes to the document and correspond with other attendees real-time during the meeting.

# Why the Need for a Wireless LAN Standard?

Prior to the adoption of the 802.11 standard, wireless data-networking vendors made equipment that was based on proprietary technology. Wary of being locked into a relationship with a specific vendor, potential wireless customers instead turned to more standards-based wired technologies. As a result, deployment of wireless networks did not happen on a large scale, and remained a luxury item for large companies with large budgets.

The only way Wireless Local Area Networks (WLANs) would be generally accepted would be if the wireless hardware involved had a low cost and had become commodity items like routers and switches.

Recognizing that the only way for this to happen would be if there were a wireless data–networking standard, the Institute of Electrical and Electronics Engineers' (IEEE's) 802 Group took on their eleventh challenge. Since many of the members of the 802.11 Working Group were employees of vendors making wireless technologies, there were many pushes to include certain functions in the final specification. Although this slowed down the progress of finalizing 802.11, it also provided momentum for delivery of a feature–rich standard left open for future expansion.

On June 26, 1997, the IEEE announced the ratification of the 802.11 standard for wireless local area networks. Since that time, costs associated with deploying an 802.11-based network have dropped, and WLANs rapidly are being deployed in schools, businesses, and homes.

In this section, we will discuss the evolution of the standard in terms of bandwidth and services. Also, we will discuss the WLAN standards that are offshoots of the 802.11 standard.

## NOTE

The IEEE (www.ieee.org) is an association that develops standards for almost anything electronic and /or electric. Far from being limited to computer-related topics, IEEE societies cover just about any technical practice, from automobiles to maritime, from neural networks to superconductors. With 36 Technical Societies covering broad interest areas, more specific topics are handled by special committees. These other committees form Working Groups (WGs) and Technical Advisory Groups (TAGs) to create operational models that enable different vendors to develop and sell products that will be compatible. The membership of these committees and groups are professionals who work for companies that develop, create, or manufacture with their technical practice. These groups meet several times a year to discuss new trends within their industry, or to continue the process of refining a current standard.

# What Exactly Does the 802.11 Standard Define?

As in all 802.x standards, the 802.11 specification covers the operation of the media access control (MAC) and physical layers. As you can see in Figure 4.6, 802.11 defines a MAC sublayer, MAC services and protocols, and three physical (PHY) layers.

**Figure 4.6** 802.11 Frame Format

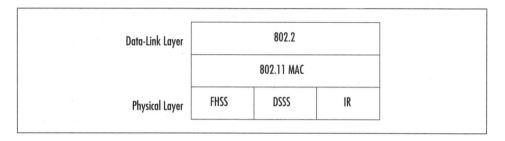

The three physical layer options for 802.11 are infrared (IR) baseband PHY and two radio frequency (RF) PHYs. Due to line-of-sight limitations, very little development has occurred with the Infrared PHY. The RF physical layer is composed of Frequency Hopping Spread Spectrum (FHSS) and Direct Sequence Spread Spectrum (DSSS) in the 2.4 GHz band. All three physical layers operate at either 1 or 2 Mbps. The majority of 802.11 implementations utilize the DSSS method.

FHSS works by sending bursts of data over numerous frequencies. As the name implies, it hops between frequencies. Typically, the devices use up to four frequencies simultaneously to send information and only for a short period of time before hopping to new frequencies. The devices using FHSS agree upon the frequencies being used. In fact, due to the short time period of frequency use and device agreement of these frequencies, many autonomous networks can coexist in the same physical space.

DSSS functions by dividing the data into several pieces and simultaneously sending the pieces on as many different frequencies as possible, unlike FHSS, which sends on a limited number of frequencies. This process allows for greater transmission rates than FHSS, but is vulnerable to greater occurrences of interference. This is because the data is spanning a larger portion of the spectrum at any given time than FHSS. In essence, DHSS floods the spectrum all at one time, whereas FHSS selectively transmits over certain frequencies.

## Designing & Planning...

## Additional Initiatives of the 802 Standards Committee

**802.1 LAN/MAN Bridging and Management** 802.1 is the base standard for LAN/MAN Bridging, LAN architecture, LAN management, and protocol layers above the MAC and LLC layers. Some examples would include 802.1q, the standard for virtual LANs, and 802.1d, the Spanning Tree Protocol.

**802.2 Logical Link Control** Since Logical Link Control is now a part of all 802 standards, this Working Group is currently in hibernation (inactive) with no ongoing projects.

**802.3 CSMA/CD Access Method (Ethernet)** 802.3 defines that an Ethernet network can operate at 10 Mbps, 100 Mbps, 1 Gbps, or even 10 Gbps. It also defines that category 5 twisted pair cabling and fiber optic cabling are valid cable types. This group identifies how to make vendors' equipment interoperate despite the various speeds and cable types.

**802.4 Token-Passing Bus** This Working Group is also in hibernation with no ongoing projects.

**802.5 Token Ring** Token Ring networks operate at 4 mps or 16 Mbps. Currently, there are Working Groups proposing 100 mb Token Ring (802.5t) and Gigabit Token Ring (802.5v). Examples of other 802.5 specs would be 802.5c, Dual Ring Wrapping, and 802.5j, fiber optic station attachment.

**Continued**

**802.6 Metropolitan Area Network (MAN)** Since Metropolitan Area Networks are created and managed with current internetworking standards, the 802.6 Working Group is in hibernation.

**802.7 Broadband LAN** In 1989, this Working Group recommended practices for broadband LANs, which were reaffirmed in 1997. This group is inactive with no ongoing projects. The maintenance effort for 802.7 is now supported by 802.14.

**802.8 Fiber Optics** Many of this Working Group's recommended practices for fiber optics get wrapped into other Standards at the Physical Layer.

**802.9 Isochronous Services LAN (ISLAN)** Isochronous Services refer to processes where data must be delivered within certain time constraints. Streaming media and voice calls are examples of traffic that requires an isochronous transport system.

**802.10 Standard for Interoperable LAN Security (SILS)** This Working Group provided some standards for Data Security in the form of 802.10a, Security Architecture Framework, and 802.10c, Key Management. This Working Group is currently in hibernation with no ongoing projects.

**802.11 Wireless LAN (WLAN)** This Working Group is developing standards for Wireless data delivery in the 2.4 GHz and 5.1 GHz radio spectrum.

**802.12 Demand Priority Access Method** This Working Group provided two Physical Layer and Repeater specifications for the development of 100 Mbps Demand Priority MACs. Although they were accepted as ISO standards and patents were received for their operation, widespread acceptance was overshadowed by Ethernet. 802.12 is currently in the process of being withdrawn.

Continued

**802.13** This standard was intentionally left blank.

**802.14 Cable-TV Based Broadband Comm Network**

This Working Group developed specifications for the Physical and Media Access Control Layers for Cable Televisions and Cable Modems. Believing their work to be done, this Working Group has no ongoing projects.

**802.15 Wireless Personal Area Network (WPAN)** The vision of Personal Area Networks is to create a wireless interconnection between portable and mobile computing devices such as PCs, peripherals, cell phones, Personal Digital Assistants (PDAs), pagers, and consumer electronics, allowing these devices to communicate and interoperate with one another without interfering with other wireless communications.

**802.16 Broadband Wireless Access** The goal of the 802.16 Working Group is to develop standards for fixed broadband wireless access systems. These standards are key to solving "last-mile" local-loop issues. 802.16 is similar to 802.11a in that it uses unlicensed frequencies in the unlicensed national information infrastructure (U-NII) spectrum. 802.16 is different from 802.11a in that Quality of Service for voice/video/data issues are being addressed from the start in order to present a standard that will support true wireless network backhauling.

# Does the 802.11 Standard Guarantee Compatibility across Different Vendors?

As mentioned earlier, the primary reason WLANs were not widely accepted was the lack of standardization. It is logical to question whether vendors would accept a nonproprietary operating standard, since vendors compete to make unique and distinguishing products. Although 802.11 standardized the PHY, MAC, the frequencies to send/receive on, transmission rates and more, it did not absolutely guarantee that differing vendors' products would be 100 percent compatible. In fact, some vendors built in backward-compatibility features into their 802.11 products in order to support their legacy customers. Other vendors have introduced proprietary extensions (for example, bit-rate adaptation and stronger encryption) to their 802.11 offerings.

To ensure that consumers can build interoperating 802.11 wireless networks, an organization called the Wireless Ethernet Compatibility Alliance (WECA) tests and certifies 802.11 devices. Their symbol of approval means that the consumer can be assured that the particular device has passed a thorough test of interoperations with devices from other vendors. This is important when considering devices to be implemented into your existing network, because if the devices cannot communicate, it complicates the management of the network—in fact, essentially you will have to deal with two autonomous networks. It is also important when building a new network because you may be limited to a single vendor.

Since the first 802.11 standard was approved in 1997, there have been several initiatives to make improvements. As you will see in the following sections, there is an evolution unfolding with the 802.11 standard. The introduction of the standard came with 802.11 followed by 802.11b. Then along came 802.11a, which provides up to five times the bandwidth capacity of 802.11b. Now, accompanying the ever-growing demand for multimedia services, is the development of 802.11e. Each task group, outlined next, is endeavoring to speed up the 802.11 standard, making it globally accessible, while not having to reinvent the MAC layer of 802.11:

- **The 802.11d Working Group** is concentrating on the development of 802.11 WLAN equipment to operate in markets not served by the current standard (the current 802.11 standard defines WLAN operation in only a few countries).

- **The 802.11f Working Group** is developing an *Inter-Access Point Protocol*, due to the current limitation prohibiting roaming between access points made by different vendors. This protocol would allow wireless devices to roam across access points made by competing vendors.

- **The 802.11g Working Group** is working on furthering higher data rates in the 2.4 GHz radio band.

- **The 802.11h Working Group** is busy developing Spectrum and Power Management Extensions for the IEEE 802.11a standard for use in Europe.

# 802.11b

Ignoring the FHSS and IR physical mediums, the 802.11b PHY uses DSSS to broadcast in any one of 14 center-frequency channels in the 2.4 GHz Industrial, Scientific, and Medical (ISM) radio band. As Table 4.1 shows, North America allows 11 channels; Europe allows 13, the most channels allowed. Japan has only one channel reserved for 802.11, at 2.483 GHz.

**Table 4.1** 802.11b Channels and Participating Countries

| Channel Number | Frequency GHz | North America | Europe | Spain | France | Japan |
|---|---|---|---|---|---|---|
| 1 | 2.412 | X | X | | | |
| 2 | 2.417 | X | X | | | |
| 3 | 2.422 | X | X | | | |
| 4 | 2.427 | X | X | | | |
| 5 | 2.432 | X | X | | | |
| 6 | 2.437 | X | X | | | |
| 7 | 2.442 | X | X | | | |
| 8 | 2.447 | X | X | | | |
| 9 | 2.452 | X | X | | | |
| 10 | 2.457 | X | X | X | X | |
| 11 | 2.462 | X | X | X | X | |
| 12 | 2.467 | | X | | X | |
| 13 | 2.472 | | X | | X | |
| 14 | 2.483 | | | | | X |

There are many different devices competing for airspace in the 2.4 GHz radio spectrum. Unfortunately, most of the devices that cause interference are especially common in the home environment, such as microwaves and cordless phones. As you can imagine, the viability of an 802.11b network depends on how many of these products are near the network devices.

One of the more recent entrants to the 802.11b airspace comes in the form of the emerging Bluetooth wireless standard. Though designed for short-range transmissions, Bluetooth devices utilize FHSS to communicate with each other. Cycling through thousands of frequencies a second, this looks as if it poses the greatest chance of creating interference for 802.11. Further research will determine exactly what—if any—interference Bluetooth will cause to 802.11b networks. Many companies are concerned with oversaturating the 2.4 GHz spectrum, and are taking steps to ensure that their devices "play nicely" with others in this arena.

These forms of interference will directly impact the home user who wishes to set up a wireless LAN, especially if neighbors operate interfering devices. Only time will tell if 802.11b will be able to stand up against these adversaries and hold on to the marketplace.

# 802.11a

Due to the overwhelming demand for more bandwidth and the growing number of technologies operating in the 2.4 GHz band, the 802.11a standard was created for WLAN use in North America as an upgrade from the 802.11b standard. 802.11a provides 25 to 54 Mbps bandwidth in the 5 GHz spectrum (the unlicensed national information infrastructure [U-NII] spectrum). Since the 5 GHz band is currently mostly clear, chance of interference is reduced. However, that could change since it is still an unlicensed portion of the spectrum. 802.11a still is designed mainly for the enterprise, providing Ethernet capability.

802.11a is one of the physical layer extensions to the 802.11 standard. Abandoning spread spectrum completely, 802.11a uses an encoding technique called Orthogonal Frequency Division Multiplexing (OFDM). Although this encoding technique is similar to the European

5-GHz HiperLAN physical layer specification, which will be explained in greater detail later in the chapter, 802.11a currently is specific to the United States.

As shown in Table 4.2, three 5-GHz spectrums have been defined for use with 802.11a. Each of these three center-frequency bands covers 100 MHz.

**Table 4.2** 802.11a Channels Usable in the 5-GHz U-NII Radio Spectrum

| Regulatory Area | Frequency Band | Channel Number | Center Frequencies |
|---|---|---|---|
| USA | U-NII Lower Band 5.15 - 5.25 GHz | 36 | 5.180 GHz |
| | | 40 | 5.200 GHz |
| | | 44 | 5.220 GHz |
| | | 48 | 5.240 GHz |
| USA | U-NII Middle Band 5.25 - 5.35 GHz | 52 | 5.260 GHz |
| | | 56 | 5.280 GHz |
| | | 60 | 5.300 GHz |
| | | 64 | 5.320 GHz |
| USA | U-NII Upper Band 5.725 - 5.825 GHz | 149 | 5.745 GHz |
| | | 153 | 5.765 GHz |
| | | 157 | 5.785 GHz |
| | | 161 | 5.805 GHz |

# 802.11e

The IEEE 802.11e is providing enhancements to the 802.11 standard while retaining compatibility with 802.11b and 802.11a. The enhancements include multimedia capability made possible with the adoption of quality of service (QoS) functionality as well as security improvements. What does this mean for a service provider? It means the ability to offer video on demand, audio on demand, high-speed Internet access and Voice over IP (VoIP) services. What does this mean for the home or business user? It allows high-fidelity multimedia in the form of MPEG2 video and CD quality sound, and redefinition of the traditional phone use with VoIP.

QoS is the key to the added functionality with 802.11e. It provides the functionality required to accommodate time-sensitive applications such as video and audio. QoS includes queuing, traffic shaping tools, and scheduling. These characteristics allow priority of traffic. For example, data traffic is not time sensitive and therefore has a lower priority than applications like streaming video. With these enhancements, wireless networking has evolved to meet the demands of today's users.

# Developing WLANs through the 802.11 Architecture

The 802.11 architecture can best be described as a series of interconnected cells, and consists of the following: the wireless device or station, the access point (AP), the wireless medium, the distribution system (DS), the basic service set (BSS), the extended service set (ESS), and station and distribution services. All of these working together providing a seamless mesh gives wireless devices the ability to roam around the WLAN looking for all intents and purposes like a wired device.

## The Basic Service Set

The core of the IEEE 802.11 standard is the basic service set (BSS). As you can see in Figure 4.7, this model is made up of one or more wireless devices communicating with a single Access Point (AP) in a

**Figure 4.7** Basic Service Set

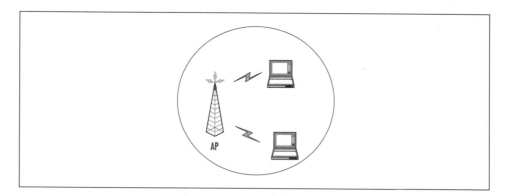

single radio cell. If there are no connections back to a wired network, this is called an *independent basic service set*.

If there is no access point in the wireless network, it is referred to as an *ad-hoc network*. This means that all wireless communications is transmitted directly between the members of the ad-hoc network. Figure 4.8 describes a basic ad-hoc network.

**Figure 4.8** Ad-Hoc Network

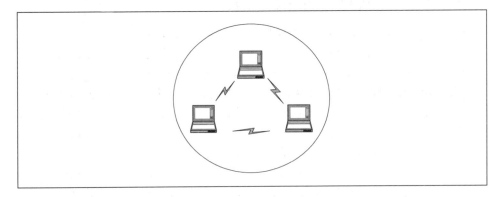

When the BSS has a connection to the wired network via an AP, it is called an *infrastructure BSS*. As you can see in the model shown in Figure 4.9, the AP bridges the gap between the wireless device and the wired network.

**Figure 4.9** 802.11 Infrastructure Architecture

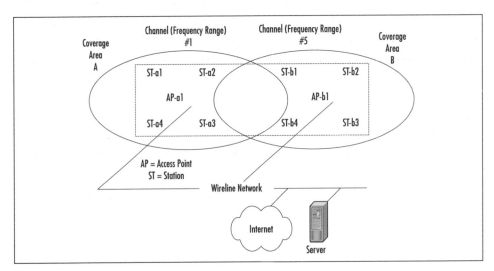

Since multiple Access Points exist in this model, the wireless devices no longer communicate in a peer-to-peer fashion. Instead, all traffic from one device destined for another device is relayed through the AP. Even though it would look like this would double the amount of traffic on the WLAN, this also provides for traffic buffering on the AP when a device is operating in a low-power mode.

# The Extended Service Set

The compelling force behind WLAN deployment is the fact that with 802.11, users are free to move about without having to worry about switching network connections manually. If we were operating with a single infrastructure BSS, this moving about would be limited to the signal range of our one AP. Through the extended service set (ESS), the IEEE 802.11 architecture allows users to move between multiple infrastructure BSSs. In an ESS, the APs talk amongst themselves forwarding traffic from one BSS to another, as well as switch the roaming devices from one BSS to another. They do this using a medium called the distribution system (DS). The distribution system forms the spine of the WLAN, making the decisions whether to forward traffic from one BSS to the wired network or back out to another AP or BSS.

What makes the WLAN so unique, though, are the invisible interactions between the various parts of the extended service set. Pieces of equipment on the wired network have no idea they are communicating with a mobile WLAN device, nor do they see the switching that occurs when the wireless device changes from one AP to another. To the wired network, all it sees is a consistent MAC address to talk to, just as if the MAC was another node on the wire.

# Services to the 802.11 Architecture

There are nine different services that provide behind-the-scenes support to the 802.11 architecture. Of these nine, four belong to the *station services* group and the remaining five to the *distribution services* group.

## Station Services

The four station services (*authentication, de-authentication, data delivery,* and *privacy*) provide functionality equal to what standard 802.3 wired networks would have.

The authentication service defines the identity of the wireless device. Without this distinct identity, the device is not allowed access to the WLAN. Authentication can also be made against a list of MACs allowed to use the network. This list of allowable MAC addresses may be on the AP or on a database somewhere on the wired network. A wireless device can authenticate itself to more than one AP at a time. This sort of "pre-authentication" allows the device to prepare other APs for its entry into their airspace.

The de-authentication service is used to destroy a previously known station identity. Once the de-authentication service has been started, the wireless device can no longer access the WLAN. This service is invoked when a wireless device shuts down, or when it is roaming out of the range of the access point. This frees up resources on the AP for other devices.

Just like its wired counterparts, the 802.11 standard specifies a data delivery service to ensure that data frames are transferred reliably from one MAC to another. This data delivery will be discussed in greater detail in following sections.

The privacy service is used to protect the data as it crosses the WLAN. Even though the service utilizes an RC4-based encryption scheme, it is not intended for end-to-end encryption or as a sole method of securing data. Its design was to provide a level of protection equivalent to that provided on a wired network—hence its moniker Wireless Equivalency Privacy (WEP).

## Distribution Services

Between the Logical Link Control (LLC) sublayer and the MAC, five distribution services make the decisions as to where the 802.11 data frames should be sent. As we will see, these distribution services make the roaming handoffs when the wireless device is in motion. The five services are *association, reassociation, disassociation, integration,* and *distribution.*

The wireless device uses the association service as soon as it connects to an AP. This service establishes a logical connection between the devices, and determines the path the distribution system needs to take in order to reach the wireless device. If the wireless device does not have an association made with an access point, the DS will not know where that device is or how to get data frames to it. As you can see in Figure 4.10, the wireless device can be authenticated to more than one AP at a time, but it will never be associated with more than one AP.

**Figure 4.10** Wireless Authentication through the Association Service

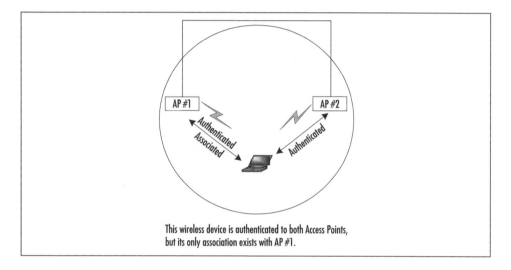

This wireless device is authenticated to both Access Points, but its only association exists with AP #1.

As we will see in later sections dealing with roaming and low-power situations, sometimes the wireless device will not be linked continuously to the same AP. To keep from losing whatever network session information the wireless device has, the reassociation service is used. This service is similar to the association service, but includes current information about the wireless device. In the case of roaming, this information tells the current AP who the last AP was. This allows the current AP to contact the previous AP to pick up any data frames waiting for the wireless device and forward them to their destination.

The disassociation service is used to tear down the association between the AP and the wireless device. This could be because the device is roaming out of the AP's area, the AP is shutting down, or any one of a number of other reasons. To keep communicating to the network, the wireless device will have to use the association service to find a new AP.

The distribution service is used by APs when determining whether to send the data frame to another AP and possibly another wireless device, or if the frame is destined to head out of the WLAN into the wired network.

The integration service resides on the APs as well. This service does the data translation from the 802.11 frame format into the framing format of the wired network. It also does the reverse, taking data destined for the WLAN, and framing it within the 802.11 frame format.

# The CSMA-CA Mechanism

The basic access mechanism for 802.11 is carrier sense multiple access collision avoidance (CSMA-CA) with binary exponential backoff. This is very similar to the carrier sense multiple access collision detect (CSMA-CD) that we are familiar with when dealing with standard 802.3 (Ethernet), but with a couple of major differences.

Unlike Ethernet, which sends out a signal until a collision is detected, CSMA-CA takes great care to not transmit unless it has the attention of the receiving unit, and no other unit is talking. This is called *listening before talking* (LBT).

Before a packet is transmitted, the wireless device will listen to hear if any other device is transmitting. If a transmission is occurring, the device will wait for a randomly determined period of time, and then listen again. If no one else is using the medium, the device will begin transmitting. Otherwise, it will wait again for a random time before listening once more.

## The RTS/CTS Mechanism

To minimize the risk of the wireless device transmitting at the same time as another wireless device (and thus causing a collision), the designers of 802.11 employed a mechanism called Request To Send/ Clear To Send (RTS/CTS).

For example, if data arrived at the AP destined for a wireless node, the AP would send a RTS frame to the wireless node requesting a certain amount of time to deliver data to it. The wireless node would respond with a CTS frame saying that it would hold off any other communications until the AP was done sending the data. Other wireless nodes would hear the transaction taking place, and delay their transmissions for that period of time as well. In this manner, data is passed between nodes with a minimal possibility of a device causing a collision on the medium.

This also gets rid of a well-documented WLAN issue called *the hidden node*. In a network with multiple devices, the possibility exists that one wireless node might not know all the other nodes that are out on the WLAN. Thanks to RST/CTS, each node hears the requests to transmit data to the other nodes, and thus learns what other devices are operating in that BSS.

## Acknowledging the Data

When sending data across a radio signal with the inherent risk of interference, the odds of a packet getting lost between the transmitting radio and the destination unit are much greater than in a wired network model. To make sure that data transmissions would not get lost in the ether, *acknowledgment* (ACK) was introduced. The acknowledgement portion of CSMA-CA means that when a destination host receives a packet, it sends back a notification to the sending unit. If the sender does not receive an ACK, it will know that this packet was not received and will transmit it again.

All this takes place at the MAC layer. Noticing that an ACK has not been received, the sending unit is able to grab the radio medium before any other unit can and it resends the packet. This allows recovery from interference without the end user being aware that a communications error has occurred.

# Configuring Fragmentation

In an environment prone to interference, the possibility exists that one or more bits in a packet will get corrupted during transmission. No matter the number of corrupted bits, the packet will need to be re-sent.

When operating in an area where interference is not a possibility, but a reality, it makes sense to transmit smaller packets than those traditionally found in wired networks. This allows for a faster retransmission of the packet to be accomplished.

The disadvantage to doing this is that in the case of no corrupted packets, the cost of sending many short packets is greater than the cost of sending the same information in a couple of large packets. Thankfully, the 802.11 standard has made this a configurable feature. This way, a network administrator can specify short packets in some areas and longer packets in more open, noninterfering areas.

# Using Power Management Options

Because the whole premise of wireless LANs is mobility, having sufficient battery power to power the communications channel is of prime concern. The IEEE recognized this and included a power management service that allows the mobile client to go into a sleep mode to save power without losing connectivity to the wireless infrastructure.

Utilizing a 20-byte Power Save Poll (PS-Poll) frame, the wireless device sends a message to its AP letting it know that is going into power-save mode, and the AP needs to buffer all packets destined for the device until it comes back online. Periodically, the wireless device will wake up and see if there are any packets waiting for it on the AP. If there aren't, another PS-Poll frame is sent, and the unit goes into a sleep mode again. The real benefit here is that the mobile user is able to use the WLAN for longer periods of time without severely impacting the battery life.

# Multicell Roaming

Another benefit to wireless LANs is being able to move from wireless cell to cell as you go around the office, campus, or home without the need to modify your network services. Roaming between access points in your ESS is a very important portion of the 802.11 standard. Roaming is based on the ability of the wireless device to determine the quality of the wireless signal to any AP within reach, and decide to switch communications to a different AP if it has a stronger or cleaner signal. This is based primarily upon an entity called the signal-to-noise (S/N) ratio. In order for wireless devices to determine the S/N ratio for each AP in the network, access points send out *beacon* messages that contain information about the AP as well as link measurement data. The wireless device listens to these beacons and determines which AP has the clearest and cleanest signal. After making this determination, the wireless device sends authentication information and attempts to reassociate with the new AP. The reassociation process tells the new AP which AP the device just came from. The new AP picks up whatever data frames that might be left at the old AP, and notifies the old AP that it no longer needs to accept messages for that wireless device. This frees up resources on the old AP for its other clients.

Even though the 802.11 standard covers the concepts behind the communications between the AP and the DS, it doesn't define exactly how this communication should take place. This is because there are many different ways this communication can be implemented. Although this gives a vendor a good deal of flexibility in AP/DS design, there could be situations where APs from different vendors might not be able to interoperate across a distribution system due to the differences in how those vendors implemented the AP/DS interaction. Currently, there is an 802.11 Working Group (802.11f) developing an Inter-Access Point Protocol. This protocol will be of great help in the future as companies who have invested in one vendor's products can integrate APs and devices from other vendors into their ESSs.

## Security in the WLAN

One of the biggest concerns facing network administrators when implementing a WLAN is data security. In a wired environment, the lack of access to the physical wire can prevent someone from wandering into your building and connecting to your internal network. In a WLAN scenario, it is impossible for the AP to know if the person operating the wireless device is sitting inside your building, passing time in your lobby, or if they are seated in a parked car just outside your office. Acknowledging that passing data across an unreliable radio link could lead to possible snooping, the IEEE 802.11 standard provides three ways to provide a greater amount of security for the data that travels over the WLAN. Adopting any (or all three) of these mechanisms will decrease the likelihood of an accidental security exposure.

The first method makes use of the 802.11 Service Set Identifier (SSID). This SSID can be associated with one or more APs to create multiple WLAN segments within the infrastructure BSS. These segments can be related to floors of a building, business units, or other data-definition sets. Since the SSID is presented during the authentication process, it acts as a crude password. Since most end-users set up their wireless devices, these SSIDs could be shared among users, thus limiting their effectiveness. Another downside to using SSIDs as a sole form of authentication is that if the SSID were to be changed (due to an employee termination or other event), all wireless devices and APs would have to reflect this change. On a medium-sized WLAN, rotating SSIDs on even a biannual basis could prove to be a daunting and time-consuming task.

As mentioned earlier in the station services section, the AP also can authenticate a wireless device against a list of MAC addresses. This list could reside locally on the AP, or the authentication could be checked against a database of allowed MACs located on the wired network. This typically provides a good level of security, and is best used with small WLAN networks. With larger WLAN networks, administering the list of allowable MAC addresses will require some back-end services to reduce the amount of time needed to make an addition or subtraction from the list.

The third mechanism 802.11 offers to protect data traversing the WLAN was also mentioned earlier in the section on station services. The *privacy* service uses a RC-4 based encryption scheme to encapsulate the payload of the 802.11 data frames, called Wired Equivalent Privacy (WEP). WEP specifies a 40-bit encryption key, although some vendors have implemented a 104-bit key. As mentioned previously, WEP is not meant to be an end-to-end encryption solution. WEP keys on the APs and wireless devices can be rotated, but since the 802.11 standard does not specify a key-management protocol, all key rotation must be done manually. Like the SSID, rotating the WEP key would affect all APs and wireless users and take significant effort from the network administrator.

Some network designers consider WLANs to be in the same crowd as Remote Access Service (RAS) devices, and claim the best protection is to place the WLAN architecture behind a firewall or Virtual Private Network (VPN) device. This would make the wireless client authenticate to the VPN or firewall using third-party software (on top of WEP). The benefit here is that the bulk of the authenticating would be up to a non-WLAN device, and would not require additional AP maintenance.

The uses of 802.11 networks can range from homes to public areas like schools and libraries, to businesses and corporate campuses. The ability to deploy a low-cost network without the need to have wires everywhere is allowing wireless networks to spring up in areas where wired networks would be cost prohibitive. The 802.11 services allow the wireless device the same kind of functionality as a wired network, yet giving the user the ability to roam throughout the WLAN.

Next, we will discuss another wireless technology breakthrough, appealing to the truly free-spirited. This emerging technology is capable of providing a personal network that moves along with you wherever you go. Let's say you receive a text message on your cellular and personal communications services (PCS) phone and would like to transfer the contents into your PDA. No problem—with the 802.15 standard, this is possible no matter where you are. And if you happen to be in a public place and someone near you is using the same technology, there is no need to worry, because your information is encrypted.

# Developing WPANs through the 802.15 Architecture

*Wireless personal area networks* (WPANs) are networks that occupy the space surrounding an individual or device, typically involving a 10m radius. This is referred to as a personal operating space (POS). This type of network adheres to an ad-hoc system requiring little configuration. The devices in a WPAN find each other and communicate with little effort by the end user.

WPANs generally fall under the watchful eyes of the IEEE 802.15 working group (technically, 802.15 networks are defined as *short-distance wireless networks*). The growing trend toward more "smart" devices in the home and the increasing number of telecommuters and small office/home office (SOHO) users is driving the demand for this section of the wireless industry. Another driving requirement for this segment is the need for simplistic configuration of such a network. As this segment grows, the end users involved are not the technically elite, early technology adopters, but the average consumer. The success of this segment is rooted in its ability to simplify its use while maintaining lower costs. In addition, various efforts are under way to converge the 802.11 and 802.15 standards for interoperability and the reduction of interference in the 2.4 GHz space. Since this is the same unlicensed range shared by numerous wireless devices such as garage door openers, baby monitors, and cordless phones, 802.15 devices must be able to coexist. They fall under two categories. The first is the collaborative model where both standards not only will coexist with interference mitigated, but also will interoperate. The second is the noncollaborative model, where the interference is mitigated but the two standards do not interoperate.

# Bluetooth

*Bluetooth* technology was named after Harold Blaatand (Bluetoothe) II, who was the King of Denmark from 940–981 and was generally considered a "unifying figurehead" in Europe during that period. The unification of Europe and the unification of PDAs and computing devices is the parallelism that the founders of this technology sought to create when they chose the name *Bluetooth*. Bluetooth began in 1994 when Ericsson was looking for inexpensive radio interfaces between cell phones and accessories such as PDAs. In 1998, Ericsson, IBM, Intel, Nokia, and Toshiba formed the Bluetooth Special Interest Group (SIG) and expanded to over 1000 members by 1999, including Microsoft. However, the Bluetooth technology is currently behind schedule and the projected cost of $5 per transceiver is not being realized. This combined with the expansion and success of the 802.11 standard may threaten the survivability of this technology.

Bluetooth is primarily a cable replacement WPAN technology that operates in the 2.4 GHz range using FHSS. One of the main drivers for the success of the Bluetooth technology is the proposition of low-cost implementation and size of the wireless radios. Bluetooth networks are made up of *piconets*, which are loosely fashioned or *ad-hoc* networks. Piconets are made up of one master node and seven simultaneously active slaves or an almost limitless number of virtually attached but not active (standby) nodes. Master nodes communicate with slaves in a hopping pattern determined by a 3-bit Active Member Address (AMA). Parked nodes are addressed with an 8-bit Parked Member Address, (PMA). Up to ten piconets can be colocated and linked into what is called *scatternets*. A node can be both a master in one piconet and a slave in another piconet at the same time, or a slave in both piconets at the same time. The range of a Bluetooth standard piconet is 10 meters, relative to the location of the master. Bluetooth signals pass through walls, people, and furniture, so it is not a line-of-sight technology. The maximum capacity of Bluetooth is 740 Kbps per piconet (actual bit rate) with a raw bit rate of 1 Mbps. Figure 4.11 provides a logical depiction of several piconets linked together as a scatternet.

Since Bluetooth shares the 2.4 GHz frequency range with 802.11b, there is a possibility for interference between the two technologies if a Bluetooth network is within ten meters of an 802.11b network. Bluetooth was designed to be a complementary technology to the 802.11 standard and the IEEE Task Group f (TGf) is chartered with proposing interoperability standards between the two technologies. Bluetooth has also been working with the FCC and FAA to provide safe operation on aircraft and ships. Figure 4.12 gives a broad view of the envisioned uses of Bluetooth as a technology (more information on Bluetooth can be obtained at www.bluetooth.com).

**Figure 4.11** Bluetooth Piconet and Scatternet Configuration

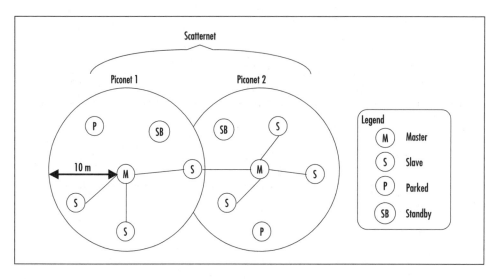

**Figure 4.12** Bluetooth Uses

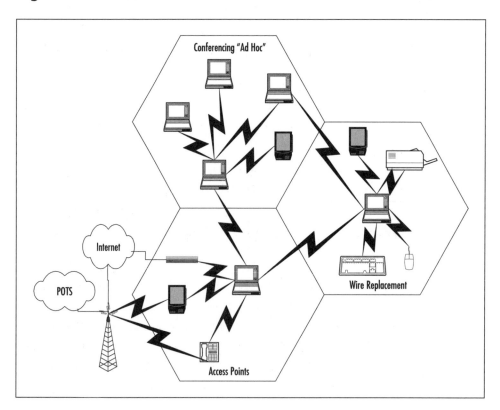

## HomeRF

*HomeRF* is similar to Bluetooth since it operates in the 2.4 GHz spectrum range and provides up to 1.6 Mbps bandwidth with user throughput of about 650 Kb/s. HomeRF has a relative range of about 150 feet as well. Home RF uses FHSS as its physical layer transmission capability. It also can be assembled in an ad hoc architecture or be controlled by a central connection point like Bluetooth. Differences between the two are that HomeRF is targeted solely towards the residential market—the inclusion of the Standard Wireless Access Protocol (SWAP) within HomeRF gives it a capability to handle multimedia applications much more efficiently.

SWAP combines the data beneficial characteristics of 802.11's CSMA-CA with the QoS characteristics of the Digital Enhanced Cordless Telecommunications (DECT) protocol to provide a converged network technology for the home. SWAP 1.0 provides support for four DECT toll quality handsets within a single ad-hoc network. SWAP 1.0 also provides 40-bit encryption at the MAC layer for security purposes.

SWAP 2.0 will extend the bandwidth capabilities to 10 Mbps and provide roaming capabilities for public access. It also provides upward scalability for support of up to eight toll quality voice handsets based on the DECT protocol within the same ad-hoc network. The QOS features are enhanced by the addition of up to eight prioritized streams supporting multimedia applications such as video. SWAP 2.0 extends the security features of SWAP 1.0 to 128 bits encryption. For more information on HomeRF, go to www.homerf.com.

## High Performance Radio LAN

*High Performance Radio LAN* (HiperLAN) is the European equivalent of the 802.11 standard. HiperLAN Type 1 supports 20 Mbps of bandwidth in the 5 GHz range. HiperLAN Type 2 (HiperLAN2) also operates in the 5 GHz range but offers up to 54 Mbps bandwidth. It also offers many more QoS features and thus currently supports many more multimedia applications that its 802.11a counterpart. HiPerLAN2 is also a connection-oriented technology, which, combined with its QoS and bandwidth, gives it applications outside the normal enterprise networks.

# Mobile Wireless Technologies

The best way to describe *mobile wireless* is to call it your basic cellular phone service. The cell phone communications industry has migrated along two paths; the United States has generally progressed along the Code Division Multiple Access (CDMA) path, with Europe following the Global System for Mobile Communications (GSM) path. However, both areas' cellular growth has progressed from analog communications to digital technologies, and both continents had an early focus on the voice communication technology known as 1G and 2G (the G stands for *generations*). Emerging technologies are focused on bringing both voice and data as well as video over the handheld phones/devices. The newer technologies are referred to as 2.5G and 3G categorically. A linear description of the evolution of these two technologies is presented in the following sections.

Figure 4.13 illustrates a generic cellular architecture. A geographic area is divided into cells; the adjacent cells always operate on different frequencies to avoid interference—this is referred to as *frequency reuse*. The exact shape of the cells actually vary quite a bit due to several factors, including the topography of the land, the anticipated number of calls in a particular area, the number of man-made objects (such as the buildings in a downtown area), and the traffic patterns of the mobile users. This maximizes the number of mobile users.

A lower powered antenna is placed at a strategic place, but it is not in the center of the cell, as you might think. Instead, the transmitter is located at a common point between adjacent cells. For example, in Figure 4.13, a base station is built at the intersection of cells A, B, C, and D. The tower then uses directional antennas that point inward to each of the adjacent cells. Other transmitters subsequently are placed at other locations through the area. By using the appropriately sized transmitter, frequencies in one particular cell are also used in nearby cells. The key to success is making sure cells using the same frequency cannot be situated right next to each other, which would result in adverse effects. The benefit is that a service provider is able to reuse the frequencies allotted to them continually so long as the system is carefully engineered. By doing so, more simultaneous callers are supported, in turn increasing revenue.

**Figure 4.13** Basic Cell Architecture

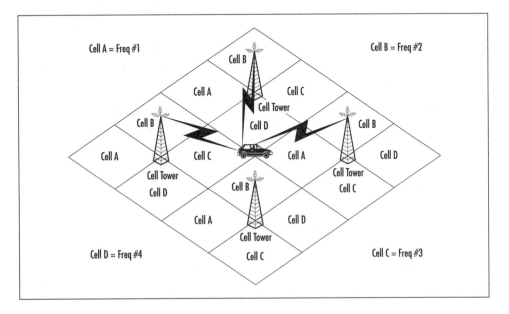

As a cell phone moves through the cells, in a car for example, the cell switching equipment keeps track of the relative strength of signal and performs a handoff when the signal becomes more powerful to an adjacent cell site. If a particular cell becomes too congested, operators have the ability to subdivide cells even further. For example, in a very busy network, the operator may have to subdivide each of the cells shown in Figure 4.12 into an even smaller cluster of cells. Due to the lower powered transmitters, the signals do not radiate as far, and as we mentioned, the frequencies are reused as much as we desire as long as the cells are spaced apart appropriately.

Mobile technology has developed with various protocols associated with each generation. These protocols will be explained in greater detail in the following sections, after we introduce the migration scheme.

# First Generation Technologies

The introduction of semiconductor technology and the smaller micro-processors made more sophisticated mobile cellular technology a reality in the late 1970s and early 1980s. The *First Generation* (1G) technologies started the rapid growth of the mobile cellular industry. The most pre-dominant systems are the Advanced Mobile Phone System (AMPS), Total Access Communication System (TACS), and the Nordic Mobile Telephone (NMT) system. However, analog systems didn't provide the signal quality desired for a voice system. These systems provided the foundation for the growth of the industry into the digital systems characterized by 2G.

# Second Generation Technologies

The need for better transmission quality and capacity drove the development of the *Second Generation* (2G) systems and brought about the deployment of digital systems in the mobile industry. The U.S. companies like Sprint PCS predominantly gravitated towards the CDMA systems; most of the rest of the world embraced the GSM systems. Dual band mobile phones were created to allow roaming between digital 2G coverage areas through analog 1G areas. The CDMA and GSM 2G technologies are currently incompatible. The globalization of the world economy and the market for mobile data capabilities fueled the development of the 2.5G and 3G technologies. Both provide a migration path towards convergence of the two standards (GSM and CDMA) toward a globally interoperable mobile system. Both 2.5G and 3G also provide a migration path for a fully converged mobile voice/data/video system.

# 2.5G Technology

With the beginning of convergence came the development of new protocols created to optimize the limited bandwidth of mobile systems. The Wireless Access Protocol (WAP) was one of the first specifications for protocols created to meet these challenges by creating more efficient applications for the mobile wireless environment. The General Packet

Radio Service (GPRS) was created to provide a packet-switched element (classical data) to the existing GSM voice circuit-switched architecture. In addition, GPRS seeks to increase the relative throughput of the GSM system fourfold, using a permanent IP connection from the handset to the Internet. Enhanced Data Rates for GSM Evolution (EDGE) was created as a further extension to the GSM data rates but is not limited to the time division multiple access (TDMA)-based GSM systems. EDGE uses the same TDMA frame structure, logic channel and 200 kHz carrier bandwidth as today's GSM networks. EDGE's acceptance in the market to date is limited, and as with any technology, may be affected by the low acceptance rate. Many mobile service providers may migrate directly from existing GSM/GPRS systems directly to 3G systems.

# Third Generation Technologies

The promise of the *Third Generation* (3G) mobile wireless technologies is the ability to support applications such as full motion video that require much larger amounts of bandwidth. This capability is known as Broadband and generally refers to bandwidths in excess of 1 Mbps. Wideband CDMA and cdma2000 are two versions of systems designed to meet this demand; however, they still are not globally compatible. A global group of standards boards called the Third-Generation Partnership Project (3GPP) has been created to develop a globally compatible 3G standard so the global interoperability of mobile systems can be a reality. The standard this group has developed is named the Universal Mobile Telecommunications System (UMTS). For more information on 3G and UMTS, go to www.umts.com. Figure 4.14 illustrates the progression of the mobile wireless industry.

# Wireless Application Protocol

The *Wireless Application Protocol* (WAP) has been implemented by many of the carriers today as the specification for wireless content delivery. WAP is an open specification that offers a standard method to access Internet-based content and services from wireless devices such as mobile

**Figure 4.14** Mobile Wireless Progression

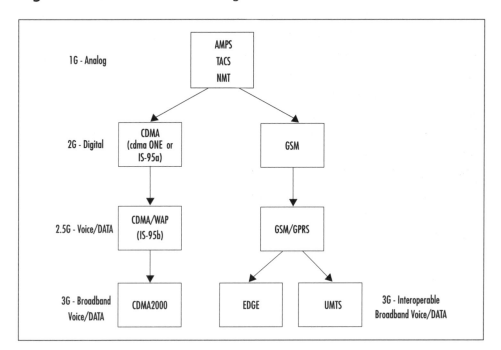

phones and PDAs. Just like the OSI reference model, WAP is non-proprietary. This means anyone with a WAP-capable device can utilize this specification to access Internet content and services. WAP is also not dependent on the network, meaning that WAP works with current network architectures as well as future ones.

WAP as it is known today is based on the work of several companies that got together in 1997 to research wireless content delivery: Nokia, Ericsson, Phone.com, and Motorola. It was their belief at that time that the success of the wireless Web relied upon such a standard. Today, the WAP Forum consists of a vast number of members including handset manufacturers and software developers.

WAP uses a model of accessing the Internet very similar in nature to the standard desktop PC using Internet Explorer. In WAP, a browser is embedded in the software of the mobile unit. When the mobile device wants to access the Internet, it first needs to access a WAP gateway. This gateway, which is actually a piece of software and not a physical device, optimizes the content for wireless applications. In the desktop model, the browser makes requests from Web servers; it is the same in wireless. The Web servers respond to URLs, just like the desktop model, but the difference is in the formatting of the content. Because Internet-enabled phones have limited bandwidth and processing power, it makes sense to scale down the resource-hungry applications to more manageable ones. This is achieved using the Wireless Markup Language (WML). A WML script is used for client-side intelligence.

# Global System for Mobile Communications

The *Global System for Mobile Communications* (GSM) is an international standard for voice and data transmission over a wireless phone. Utilizing three separate components of the GSM network, this type of communication is truly portable. A user can place an identification card called a Subscriber Identity Module (SIM) in the wireless device, and the device will take on the personal configurations and information of that user. This includes telephone number, home system, and billing information. Although the United States has migrated toward the PCS mode of wireless communication, in large part the rest of the world uses GSM.

The architecture used by GSM consists of three main components: a *mobile station*, a *base station subsystem*, and a *network subsystem*. These components work in tandem to allow a user to travel seamlessly without interruption of service, while offering the flexibility of having any device used permanently or temporarily by any user.

The mobile station has two components: mobile equipment and a SIM. The SIM, as mentioned, is a small removable card that contains identification and connection information, and the mobile equipment is the GSM wireless device. The SIM is the component within the mobile station that provides the ultimate in mobility. This is achieved because you can insert it into any GSM compatible device and, using the identification information it contains, you can make and receive calls and use other subscribed services. This means that if you travel from one country to another with a SIM, and take the SIM and place it into a rented mobile equipment device, the SIM will provide the subscriber intelligence back to the network via the mobile GSM compatible device. All services to which you have subscribed will continue through this new device, based on the information contained on the SIM. For security and billing purposes, SIM and the terminal each have internationally unique identification numbers for independence and identification on the network. The SIM's identifier is called the International Mobile Subscriber Identity (IMSI). The mobile unit has what is called an International Mobile Equipment Identifier (IMEI). In this way a user's identity is matched with the SIM via the IMSI, and the position of the mobile unit is matched with the IMEI. This offers some security, in that a suspected stolen SIM card can be identified and flagged within a database for services to be stopped and to prevent charges by unauthorized individuals.

The base station subsystem, like the mobile station, also has two components: the base transceiver station and the base station controller. The base transceiver station contains the necessary components that define a cell and the protocols associated with the communication to the mobile units. The base station controller is the part of the base station subsystem that manages resources for the transceiver units, as well as the communication with the mobile switching center (MSC). These two components integrate to provide service from the mobile station to the MSC.

The network subsystem is, in effect, the networking component of the mobile communications portion of the GSM network. It acts as a typical class 5 switching central office. It combines the switching services of the core network with added functionality and services as requested by the customer. The main component of this subsystem is the MSC. The MSC coordinates the access to the POTS network, and acts similarly to any other switching node on a POTS network. It has the added ability to support authentication and user registration. It coordinates call hand-off with the Base Station Controller, call routing, as well as coordination with other subscribed services. It utilizes Signaling System 7

(SS7) network architecture to take advantage of the efficient switching methods. There are other components to the network subsystem called *registers*: visitor location register (VLR) and home location register (HLR). Each of these registers handles call routing and services for mobility when a mobile customer is in their local or roaming calling state. The VLR is a database consisting of visitor devices in a given system's area of operation. The HLR is the database of registered users to the home network system.

# General Packet Radio Service

*General Packet Radio Service* (GPRS), also called GSM-IP, sits on top of the GSM networking architecture offering speeds between 56 and 170 Kbps. GPRS describes the bursty packet-type transmissions that will allow users to connect to the Internet from their mobile devices. GPRS is nonvoice. It offers the transport of information across the mobile telephone network. Although the users are always on like many broadband communications methodologies in use today, users pay only for usage. This provides a great deal of flexibility and efficiency. This type of connection, coupled with the nature of packet-switched delivery methods, truly offers efficient uses of network resources along with the speeds consumers are looking for. The data rates offered by GPRS will make it possible for users to partake in streaming video applications and interact with Web sites that offer multimedia, using compatible mobile handheld devices. GPRS is based on Global System for Mobile (GSM) communication and as such will augment existing services such as circuit-switched wireless phone connections and the Short Message Service (SMS).

# Short Message Service

*Short Message Service* (SMS) is a wireless service that allows users to send and receive short (usually 160 characters or less) messages to SMS-compatible phones. SMS, as noted earlier, is integrated with the GSM standard. SMS is used either from a computer by browsing to an SMS site, entering the message and the recipient's number, and clicking **Send**, or directly from a wireless phone.

# Optical Wireless Technologies

The third wireless technology we'll cover in this chapter is *optical*, which marries optical spectrum technology with wireless transmissions.

An optical wireless system basically is defined as any system that uses modulated light to transmit information in open space or air using a high-powered beam in the optical spectrum. It is also referred to as *free space optics* (FSO), *open air photonics*, or *infrared broadband*. FSO systems use low-powered infrared lasers and a series of lenses and mirrors (known as a telescope) to direct and focus different wavelengths of light towards an optical receiver/telescope. FSO is a line-of-sight technology and the only condition affecting its performance besides obstruction is fog, and to a lesser degree, rain. This is due to the visibility requirements of the technology. Fog presents a larger problem than rain because the small dense water particles deflect the light waves much more than rain does. The technology communicates bi-directionally (that is, it is full duplex) and does not require spectrum licensing. Figure 4.15 represents a common FSO implementation between buildings within a close proximity, which is generally within 1000 feet, depending on visibility conditions and reliability requirements. Some FSO vendors claim data rates in the 10Mbps to 155Mbps range with a maximum distance of 3.75 kilometers, as well as systems in the 1.25 Gbps data rate range with a maximum distance of 350 meters. The optical sector is growing in capability at a rapid rate, so expect these data rates and distance limits to continue to increase.

**Figure 4.15** Free Space Optical Implementation

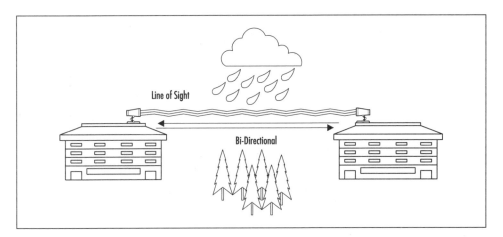

# Summary

This chapter provides an overview of differences and purposes of the emerging technologies in the wireless sector. The three primary areas of discussion are *fixed wireless*, *mobile wireless*, and *optical wireless* technology.

We began with a discussion of the fixed wireless technologies that include Multichannel Multipoint Distribution Service (MMDS), Local Multipoint Distribution Service (LMDS), Wireless Local Loop (WLL) technologies, and the Point-to-Point Microwave technology. The primary definition of a fixed wireless technology is that the transmitter and receiver are both in a fixed location. Service providers consider MMDS a complementary technology to their existing digital subscriber line (DSL) and cable modem offerings; LMDS is similar, but provides very high-speed bandwidth (it is currently limited in range of coverage). Wireless Local Loop refers to a fixed wireless class of technology aimed at providing last mile services normally provided by the local service provider over a wireless medium. Point-to-Point (PTP) Microwave is a line-of-sight technology that can span long distances. Some of the hindrances of these technologies include line of sight, weather, and licensing issues.

In 1997, the Institute of Electrical and Electronics Engineers (IEEE) announced the ratification of the 802.11 standard for wireless local area networks. The 802.11 specification covers the operation of the media access control (MAC) and physical layers; the majority of 802.11 implementations utilize the DSSS method that comprises the physical layer. The introduction of the standard came with 802.11 followed by 802.11b. Then along came 802.11a, which provides up to five times the bandwidth capacity of 802.11b. Now, accompanying the ever-growing demand for multimedia services is the development of 802.11e.

The 802.11 architecture can be best described as a series of interconnected cells, and consists of the following: the wireless device or station, the access point (AP), the wireless medium, the distribution system (DS), the basic service set (BSS), the extended service set (ESS), and station and distribution services. All these working together providing a seamless mesh allows wireless devices the ability to roam around the WLAN looking for all intents and purposes like a wired device.

High Performance Radio LAN (HiperLAN) is the European equivalent of the 802.11 standard. Wireless personal area networks (WPANs) are networks that occupy the space surrounding an individual or device, typically involving a 10m radius. This is referred to as a personal operating space (POS). This type of network adheres to an ad-hoc system requiring little configuration. Various efforts are under way to converge the 802.11 and 802.15 standards for interoperability and the reduction of interference in the 2.4 GHz space.

Bluetooth is primarily a cable replacement WPAN technology that operates in the 2.4 GHz range using FHSS. One of the main drivers for the success of the Bluetooth technology is the proposition of low-cost implementation and size of the wireless radios. HomeRF is similar to Bluetooth but is targeted solely toward the residential market.

The second category of wireless technology covered in the chapter is *mobile wireless*, which is basically your cell phone service. In this section we described the evolution of this technology from the analog voice (1G) to the digital voice (2G) phases. We continued with a discussion of the next generation technologies including the digital voice and limited data phase (2.5G) to the broadband multimedia (3G) phase, which supports high data rate voice, video, and data in a converged environment.

Finally, an *optical wireless* system basically is defined as any system that uses modulated light to transmit information in open space or air using a high-powered beam in the optical spectrum. It is also referred to as free space optics (FSO); it has growing capabilities in the infrared arena for bi-directional communication. It does not require licensing.

Hopefully this chapter has provided you with enough basic understanding of the emerging wireless technologies to be able to differentiate between them. The information in this chapter affords you the ability to understand which technology is the best solution for your network design. Evaluate the advancements in these technologies and see how they may impact your organization.

# Solutions Fast Track

## Fixed Wireless Technologies

☑ In a fixed wireless network, both transmitter and receiver are at fixed locations, as opposed to mobile. The network uses utility power (AC). It can be point-to-point or point-to-multipoint, and may use licensed or unlicensed spectrums.

☑ Fixed wireless usually involves line-of-sight technology, which can be a disadvantage.

☑ The *fresnel* zone of a signal is the zone around the signal path that must be clear of reflective surfaces and clear from obstruction, to avoid absorption and reduction of the signal energy. *Multipath reflection* or interference happens when radio signals reflect off surfaces such as water or buildings in the fresnel zone, creating a condition where the same signal arrives at different times.

☑ Fixed wireless includes Wireless Local Loop technologies, Multichannel Multipoint Distribution Service (MMDS) and Local Multipoint Distribution Service (LMDS), and also Point-to-Point Microwave.

## Developing WLANs through the 802.11 Architecture

☑ The North American wireless local area network (WLAN) standard is 802.11, set by the Institute of Electrical and Electronics Engineers (IEEE); HiperLAN is the European WLAN standard.

☑ The three physical layer options for 802.11 are infrared (IR) baseband PHY and two radio frequency (RF) PHYs. The RF physical layer is comprised of Frequency Hopping Spread

Spectrum (FHSS) and Direct Sequence Spread Spectrum (DSSS) in the 2.4 GHz band.

☑ WLAN technologies are not line-of-sight technologies.

☑ The standard has evolved through various initiatives from 802.11b, to 802.11a, which provides up to five times the bandwidth capacity of 802.11b—now, accompanying the ever growing demand for multimedia services is the development of 802.11e.

☑ 802.11b provides 11 Mbps raw data rate in the 2.4 GHz transmission spectrum.

☑ 802.11a provides 25 to 54 Mbps raw data rate in the 5 GHz transmission spectrum.

☑ HiperLAN type 1 provides up to 20 Mbps raw data rate in the 5 GHz transmission spectrum.

☑ HiperLAN type 2 provides up to 54 Mbps raw data rate and QOS in the 5 GHz spectrum.

☑ The IEEE 802.11 standard provides three ways to provide a greater amount of security for the data that travels over the WLAN: use of the 802.11 Service Set Identifier (SSID); authentication by the access point (AP) against a list of MAC addresses; use of Wired Equivalent Privacy (WEP) encryption.

# Developing WPANs through the 802.15 Architecture

☑ Wireless personal area networks (WPANs) are networks that occupy the space surrounding an individual or device, typically involving a 10m radius. This is referred to as a personal operating space (POS). WPANs relate to the 802.15 standard.

☑ WPANs are characterized by short transmission ranges.

☑ Bluetooth is a WPAN technology that operates in the 2.4 GHz spectrum with a raw bit rate of 1 Mbps at a range of 10 meters. It is not a line-of-sight technology. Bluetooth may interfere with existing 802.11 technologies in that spectrum.

☑ HomeRF is similar to Bluetooth but targeted exclusively at the home market. HomeRF provides up to 10 Mbps raw data rate with SWAP 2.0.

## Mobile Wireless Technologies

☑ Mobile wireless technology is basic cell phone technology; it is not a line-of-sight technology. The United States has generally progressed along the Code Division Multiple Access (CDMA) path, with Europe following the Global System for Mobile Communications (GSM) path.

☑ Emerging technologies are known in terms of *generations*: 1G refers to analog transmission of voice; 2G refers to digital transmission of voice; 2.5G refers to digital transmission of voice and limited bandwidth data; 3G refers to digital transmission of multimedia at broadband speeds (voice, video, and data).

☑ The Wireless Application Protocol (WAP) has been implemented by many of the carriers today as the specification for wireless content delivery. WAP is a nonproprietary specification that offers a standard method to access Internet-based content and services from wireless devices such as mobile phones and PDAs.

☑ The Global System for Mobile Communications (GSM) is an international standard for voice and data transmission over a wireless phone. A user can place an identification card called a Subscriber Identity Module (SIM) in the wireless device, and the device will take on the personal configurations and information of that user (telephone number, home system, and billing information).

# Optical Wireless Technologies

☑ Optical wireless is a line-of-sight technology in the infrared (optical) portion of the spread spectrum. It is also referred to as free space optics (FSO), open air photonics, or infrared broadband.

☑ Optical wireless data rates and maximum distance capabilities are affected by visibility conditions, and by weather conditions such as fog and rain.

☑ Optical wireless has very high data rates over short distances (1.25 Gbps to 350 meters). Full duplex transmission provides additional bandwidth capabilities. The raw data rate available is up to a 3.75 kilometer distance with 10 Mbps.

☑ There are no interference or licensing issues with optical wireless, and its data rate and distance capabilities are continuously expanding with technology advances.

# Frequently Asked Questions

The following Frequently Asked Questions, answered by the authors of this book, are designed to both measure your understanding of the concepts presented in this chapter and to assist you with real-life implementation of these concepts. To have your questions about this chapter answered by the author, browse to **www.syngress.com/solutions** and click on the **"Ask the Author"** form.

**Q:** What does the G stand for in 1G, 2G, 2.5G, and 3G mobile wireless technologies?

**A:** It stands for *generation* and the use of it implies the evolutionary process that mobile wireless is going through.

**Q:** What are the primary reasons that service providers use a Wireless Local Loop (WLL)?

**A:** The primary reasons are speed of deployment, deployment where wireline technologies are not practical, and finally, for the avoidance of the local exchange carrier's network and assets.

**Q:** Why is digital transmission better than analog in mobile wireless technologies?

**A:** Digital transmissions can be reconstructed and amplified easily, thus making it a cleaner or clearer signal. Analog signals cannot be reconstructed to their original state.

**Q:** Why does fog and rain affect optical links so much?

**A:** The tiny water particles act as tiny prisms that fracture the light beam and minimize the power of the signal.

**Q:** What is the difference between an ad-hoc network and an infrastructure network?

**A:** Ad-hoc networks are a peer-to-peer group of network nodes that communicate wirelessly directly with each other; they do not access the wired network, nor an access point. An infrastructure network serves the same purpose but also provides connectivity to infrastructure such as printers and Internet access via a connection to the wired network through an access point.

**Q:** What is a fresnel zone?

**A:** A fresnel zone is the energy lobe created by a radiated wireless signal. In line-of-sight technologies, objects such as trees may absorb some of the signal's energy if they are in the fresnel zone. If reflective objects such as lakes or glass buildings are in the fresnel zone, a condition known as multipath reflection may occur, causing duplications of the signal to arrive at the receiver at different times from the original signal. This creates errors in the signal and reduces the amount of data throughput.

# Chapter 5

# Designing a Wireless Network

## Solutions in this chapter:

- **Exploring the Design Process**
- **Identifying the Design Methodology**
- **Understanding Wireless Network Attributes from a Design Perspective**

☑ **Summary**

☑ **Solutions Fast Track**

☑ **Frequently Asked Questions**

# Introduction

Up to this point in the book, we've explained the technologies behind wireless networking, as well as some of the essential components used to support a wireless network. Now it's time to begin applying what you have learned thus far to network design. This chapter outlines the framework necessary to design a wireless network. We will also discuss the *process* associated with bringing a network design to fruition.

Initially, we will evaluate the design process with a high-level overview, which will discuss the preliminary investigation and design, followed by implementation considerations and documentation. The goal is to provide the big picture first, and then delve into the details of each step in the process. There are numerous steps—diligently planning the design according to these steps will result in fewer complications during the implementation process. This planning is invaluable because often, a network infrastructure already exists, and changing or enhancing the existing network usually impacts the functionality during the migration period. As you may know, there is nothing worse than the stress of bringing a network to a halt to integrate new services—and especially in the case of introducing wireless capabilities, you may encounter unforeseen complications due to a lack of information, incomplete planning, or faulty hardware or software. The intention of this chapter is to provide you with design considerations to help avoid potential network disasters.

The final portion of this chapter will discuss some design considerations and applications specific to a wireless network. These include signal budgeting, importance of operating system efficiency, signal-to-noise ratios, and security.

# Exploring the Design Process

For years, countless network design and consulting engineers have struggled to streamline the design and implementation process. Millions of dollars are spent defining and developing the steps in the design process in order to make more effective and efficient use of time. Many companies, such as Accenture (www.accenture.com), for example, are hired specifically for the purpose of providing processes.

For the network recipient or end user, the cost of designing the end product or the network can sometimes outweigh the benefit of its use. As a result, it is vital that wireless network designers and implementers pay close attention to the details associated with designing a wireless network in order to avoid costly mistakes and forego undue processes. This section will introduce you to the six phases that a sound design methodology will encompass—conducting a preliminary investigation regarding the changes necessary, performing an analysis of the existing network environment, creating a design, finalizing it, implementing that design, and creating the necessary documentation that will act as a crucial tool as you troubleshoot.

# Conducting the Preliminary Investigation

Like a surgeon preparing to perform a major operation, so must the network design engineer take all available precautionary measures to ensure the lifeline of the network. Going into the design process, we must not overlook the network that is already in place. In many cases, the design process will require working with an existing legacy network with pre-existing idiosyncrasies or conditions. Moreover, the network most likely will be a traditional 10/100BaseT wired network. For these reasons, the first step, conducting a preliminary investigation of the existing system as well as future needs, is vital to the health and longevity of your network.

In this phase of the design process, the primary objective is to learn as much about the network as necessary in order to understand and uncover the problem or opportunity that exists. What is the impetus for change? Almost inevitably this will require walking through the existing site and asking questions of those within the given environment. Interviewees may range from network support personnel to top-level business executives. However, information gathering may also take the form of confidential questionnaires submitted to the users of the network themselves.

It is in this phase of the process that you'll want to gather floor-plan blueprints, understand anticipated personnel moves, and note scheduled structural remodeling efforts. In essence, you are investigating anything that will help you to identify the *who, what, when, where,* and *why* that has compelled the network recipient to seek a change from the current network and associated application processes.

In this phase, keep in mind that with a wireless network, you're dealing with three-dimensional network design impacts, not just two-dimensional impacts that commonly are associated with wireline networks. So you'll want to pay close attention to the *environment* that you're dealing with.

# Performing Analysis of the Existing Environment

Although you've performed the preliminary investigation, oftentimes it is impossible to understand the intricacies of the network in the initial site visit. Analyzing the existing requirement, the second phase of the process, is a critical phase to understanding the inner workings of the network environment.

The major tasks in this phase are to understand and document all network and system dependencies that exist within the given environment in order to formulate your approach to the problem or opportunity. It's in this phase of the process that you'll begin to outline your planned strategy to counter the problem or exploit the opportunity and assess the feasibility of your approach. Are there critical interdependencies between network elements, security and management systems, or billing and accounting systems? Where are they located physically and how are they interconnected logically?

Although wireless systems primarily deal with the physical and data-link layers (Layers 1 and 2 of the OSI model), remember that, unlike a traditional wired network, access to your wireless network takes place "over the air" between the client PC and the wireless access point (AP). The point of entry for a wireless network segment is critical in order to maintain the integrity of the overall network. As a result, you'll want to ensure that users gain access at the appropriate place in your network.

# Creating a Preliminary Design

Once you've investigated the network and identified the problem or opportunity that exists, and then established the general approach in the previous phase, it now becomes necessary to create a preliminary design of your network and network processes. All of the information gathering that you have done so far will prove vital to your design.

In this phase of the process, you are actually transferring your approach to paper. Your preliminary design document should restate the problem or opportunity, report any new findings uncovered in the analysis phase, and define your approach to the situation. Beyond this, it is useful to create a network topology map, which identifies the location of the proposed or existing equipment, as well as the user groups to be supported from the network. A good network topology will give the reader a thorough understanding of all physical element locations and their connection types and line speeds, along with physical room or landscape references. A data flow diagram (DFD) can also help explain new process flows and amendments made to the existing network or system processes.

It is not uncommon to disclose associated costs of your proposal at this stage. However, it would be wise to communicate that these are estimated costs only and are subject to change. When you've completed your design, count on explaining your approach before the appropriate decision-makers, for it is at this point that a deeper level of commitment to the design is required from both you and your client.

It is important to note that, with a wireless network environment, terminal or PC mobility should be factored into your design as well as your network costs. Unlike a wired network, users may require network access from multiple locations, or continuous presence on the network between locations. Therefore, additional hardware or software, including PC docking stations, peripherals, or applications software may be required.

# Finalizing the Detailed Design

Having completed the preliminary design and received customer feedback and acceptance to proceed, your solution is close to being implemented. However, one last phase in the design process, the detailed design phase, must be performed prior to implementing your design.

In the detailed design phase, all changes referenced in the preliminary design review are taken into account and incorporated into the detailed design accordingly. The objective in this phase is to finalize your approach and capture all supporting software and requisite equipment on the final Bill Of Materials (BOM). It is in this phase that you'll want to ensure that any functional changes made in the preliminary design review do not affect the overall approach to your design. Do the requested number of additional network users overload my planned network capacity? Do the supporting network elements need to be upgraded to support the additional number of users? Is the requested feature or functionality supported through the existing design?

Although wireless networking technology is rapidly being embraced in many different user environments, commercial off-the-shelf (COTS) software is on the heels of wireless deployment and is still in development for broad applications. As a result, you may find limitations, particularly in the consumer environment, as to what can readily be supported from an applications perspective.

## Executing the Implementation

Up to this point, it may have felt like an uphill battle; however, once that you've received sign-off approval on your detailed design and associated costs, you are now ready to begin the next phase of the design process—implementing your design. This is where the vitality of your design quickly becomes evident and the value of all your preplanning is realized.

As you might have already suspected, this phase involves installing, configuring, and testing all supporting hardware and software that you have called for in your network design. Although this may be an exhilarating time, where concept enters the realm of reality, it is vital that you manage this transition in an effective and efficient manner. Do not assume that the implementation is always handled by the network design engineer. In fact, in many large-scale implementations, this is rarely the case.

The key in this phase of the process is minimizing impact on the existing network and its users, while maximizing effective installation efforts required by the new network design. However, if your design calls for large-scale implementation efforts or integration with an existing real-time network or critical system process, I would highly recommend that you utilize skilled professionals trained in executing this phase of the project. In doing so, you'll ensure network survivability and reduce the potential for loss in the event of network or systems failure.

There are many good books written specifically on the subject of project management and implementation processes that outline several different approaches to this key phase and may prove useful to you at this point. At a minimum, from a wireless network perspective, you'll want to build and test your wireless infrastructure as an independent and isolated network, whenever possible, prior to integrating this segment with your existing network. This will aid you in isolating problems inherent to your design and will correct the outstanding issue(s) so that you may complete this phase of the process. Similarly, all nodes within the wireless network should be tested independently and added to the wireless network in building-block fashion, so that service characteristics of the wireless network can be monitored and maintained.

# Capturing the Documentation

Although the last phase of this process, capturing the documentation, has been reserved for last mention, it is by no means a process to be conducted solely in the final stages of the overall design process. Rather, it is an iterative process that actually is initiated at the onset of the design process. From the preliminary investigation phase to the implementation phase, the network design engineer has captured important details of the existing network and its behavior, along with a hardened view of a new network design and the anomalies that were associated with its deployment.

In this process phase, capturing the documentation, the primary focus is to preserve the vitality and functionality of the network by assembling all relevant network and system information for future reference. Much of the information you've gathered along the way will find its way into either a user's manual, an instructional and training guide, or troubleshooting reference material. Although previous documentation and deliverables may require some modification, much can be gleaned from the history of the network design and implementation process. Moreover, revisiting previous documentation or painstakingly attempting to replicate the problem itself may result in many significant findings.

For these reasons, it is crucial to your success to ensure that the documentation procedures are rigorously adhered to throughout the design and implementation process. Beyond network topology maps and process flow diagrams, strongly consider using wire logs and channel plans wherever possible. Wire logs provide a simple description of the network elements, along with the associated cable types, and entry and exit ports on either a patch panel or junction box. Channel plans outline radio frequency (RF) channel occupancy between wireless access points. Trouble logs are also invaluable tools for addressing network issues during troubleshooting exercises. In all cases, the information that you have captured along the way will serve to strengthen your operational support and system administration teams, as well as serve as an accurate reference guide for future network enhancements.

# Identifying the Design Methodology

There are many ways to create a network design, and each method must be modified for the type of network being created. At the beginning of this chapter, we outlined the necessary phases for a sound design methodology (preliminary investigation, analysis, preliminary design, detailed design, implementation, and documentation). Nevertheless, network types can vary from service provider to enterprise, to security, and so on. As wireless networking becomes more commonplace, new design methodologies tuned specifically for the wireless environment will be created.

In this chapter, we give you an overview of the piece of the engagement methodology that provides Lucent consultants a framework for applying their technical expertise during the various stages of the net-work lifecycle. Referred to as the Network Engagement Methodology (NEM), it is a tool developed by the consultants of Lucent ESS and pro-vides best practices, procedures, and tools from their most successful pro-jects. What you will see in this chapter is the basis for what makes up the final network design (the other phases of NEM include business development, initiation and definition, planning, execution and control, and finally, closeout. This section provides information on the execution and control phase, specifically tuned for *a service provider network*. The execution and control phase has been broken down into five stages: *plan*, *architect*, *design*, *implement*, and *operate*. The next several sections provide a high-level description of what makes up the plan, architect, and design stages of NEM.

# Creating the Network Plan

Every good network design begins with a well thought out plan. The *network plan* is the first step in creating a network design. It is where information regarding desired services, number of users, types of applica-tions, and so forth is gathered. This phase is the brainstorming phase during which the initial ideas are put together. The planning stage can be one of the longest segments of a network design, because it is depen-dent on several factors that can be very time consuming. However, if each planning step is thoroughly completed, the architecture and design stages move along much more quickly.

## Gathering the Requirements

The first and most important step in creating a network plan is to gather the requirements. The requirements will be the basis for formulating the architecture and design. If a requirement is not identified at the begin-ning of the project, the entire design can miss the intended goal of the network. The requirements include:

- **Business Requirements** A few examples of possible business requirements are budget, time frame for completion, the impact of a network outage, and the desired maintenance window to minimize the negative effects of an outage.

- **Regulatory Issues** Certain types of wireless networks (such as MMDS) require licenses from the FCC. If the wireless network is going to operate outside of the public RF bands, the regulatory issues need to be identified.

- **Service Offerings** This is the primary justification for the design of a new network or migration of an existing network. Simply, these are services or functionality the network will provide to the end users.

- **Service Levels** Committed information rate (CIR) is an example of a service level agreement (SLA). This involves the customer's expectation of what the service provider guarantees to provide.

- **Customer Base** This establishes who the anticipated end users are, and what their anticipated applications and traffic patterns are.

- **Operations, Management, Provisioning, and Administration Requirements** This identifies how the new network will impact the individuals performing these job functions, and whether there will be a need to train these individuals.

- **Technical Requirements** This can vary from a preferred equipment vendor to management system requirements.

- **Additional Information** Any additional information that can affect the outcome of the design.

Once all of the requirements have been collected, it is recommended that a meeting be set up with the client to ensure that no key information is missing. This is important because it not only keeps the client involved, but also allows both the client and network architect to establish and understand the expectations of the other. Once you get client buy-off on the goals and requirements of the network, you can proceed with baselining the existing network.

# Baselining the Existing Network

The reason you need to baseline the existing network is to provide an accurate picture of the current network environment. This information will be used later on to identify how the new design will incorporate/interface with the existing network. When conducting the baseline, be sure to include the following considerations:

- Business processes

- Network architecture

- IP addressing

- Network equipment

- Utilization

- Bandwidth

- Growth

- Performance

- Traffic patterns

- Applications

- Site identification/Surveys

- Cost analysis

With proper identification of these items, you will gain a good understanding of both the existing network and get an idea of any potential issues or design constraints. In the case of utilization—that is, *overutilization*—unless kept under a watchful eye, it can contribute to a less-than-optimized network. Therefore, by evaluating the health of the existing network, you can either eliminate or compensate for potential risks of the new network. In addition to monitoring network conditions, it is also a good idea to perform site surveys in this step, to identify any possible problems that are not identified in either the requirements collection or the baseline monitoring.

## Analyzing the Competitive Practices

When you compare the client's business and technology plan to the competitors' in the same industry, you can learn what has and hasn't worked and why. Once you have evaluated and understand the industry practices, you can identify what not to do as well. This is a potential opportunity for a network architect to influence the functionality, in terms of services and choice of technology, that will facilitate the desired network. The primary reason the architect is involved is because of his or her knowledge of the technology—not only how it works, but also how it is evolving.

## Beginning the Operations Planning

The operations systems support daily activities of telecommunications infrastructures. The purpose of this step is to identify all of the elements required for the operations system. Depending on the needs of the client, any or all of the following processes need to be identified:

- Pre-order
- Order management
- Provisioning
- Billing
- Maintenance
- Repair
- Customer care

If your client is not planning on offering any services with the new design, then this step can be skipped. Once the operations planning step is complete, you can move on to the *gap analysis*.

## Performing a Gap Analysis

The *gap analysis* will be a comparison of the existing network to the future requirements. The information obtained through the gathering of requirements and baselining of the current network provide the data needed to develop a gap analysis. The gap analysis is a method of developing a plan to improve the existing network, and integrate the new requirements. The documented result should include the following items:

- Baseline
- Future requirements
- Gap analysis
- Alternative technology options
- Plan of action

Once the client reviews and accepts the requirements' definition document and gap analysis, the time frame required to complete the project becomes more evident. At this point, the client should have a good understanding of what the current network entails and what it will take to evolve into their future network. Once this step is complete, the next task is to create a *technology plan*.

## Creating a Technology Plan

This step involves identifying the technology that will enable the business goals to be accomplished. There can be several different technology plans—a primary plan and any number of alternatives. The alternative plans can be in anticipation of constraints not uncovered yet, such as budget. Being able to provide alternatives allows the client some options; it provides them with a choice regarding the direction of their network and the particular features that are of top priority. Oftentimes, until a plan is devised and on paper, the "big picture" (the process from ideas to a functioning network) can be somewhat difficult to realize fully.

The *technology plan* should identify what types of equipment, transport, protocols, and so on will be used in the network. Make sure that the plan has both a short-term focus (usually up to a year), and a long-term outlook (typically a 3 to 5 year plan). Creating a good technology plan requires that you understand the existing technology, migration paths, and future technology plans. There are several steps you can take when creating a technology plan. Some of the more important steps include:

- Business assessment
- Future requirements analysis
- Current network assessment
- Identifying technology trends and options
- Mapping technology to client needs

The technology plan will not contain specific details about how the new network will operate—it will identify the technologies that will enable the network.

## Creating an Integration Plan

Whenever a new service, application, network component, or network is added to an existing network, an integration plan needs to be created. The *integration plan* will specify what systems will be integrated, where, and how. The plan should also include details as to what level of testing will be done prior to the integration. Most importantly, the integration plan must include the steps required to complete the integration. This is where the information from the gap analysis is utilized. As you may recall, the gap analysis provides information on what the network is lacking, and the integration plan provides the information on how the gaps will be resolved.

## Beginning the Collocation Planning

If the network needs to locate some of its equipment off the premises of the client, collocation agreements will need to be made. Specifically with wireless networks, if you plan on connecting buildings together and you lease the buildings, you will need to collocate the equipment on the rooftops. Depending on the amount of collocation required, this step can be skipped or it can be a significantly large portion of the plan phase.

# Performing a Risk Analysis

It is important to identify any risks that the client could be facing or offering its perspective customers. Once the risks have been identified, you will need to document and present them to the client. The way to identify risks is by relating them to the return they will provide (such as cost savings, increased customer satisfaction, increased revenue, and so on). An easy way to present the various risks is in a matrix form, where you place risk on the horizontal axis and return on the vertical axis. Assign the zero value of the matrix (lower left corner) a low setting for both risk and return, and assign the max value (upper right corner) a high setting. This provides a visual representation of the potential risks. Once the matrix is created, each service can be put in the matrix based on where they fit. An example of this would be providing e-mail service, which would be put in the lower left corner of the matrix (low risk, low return).

This is important because you are empowering the client to make certain decisions based on industry and technological information. For example, if the client is planning on offering a service and is unaware that the service is high risk with low return, the client will need to offset or eliminate the risk. Perhaps the client could offer a service package pairing the high risk, low return with a low risk, high return service. After all, the goal is to help make your client successful. Once the client accepts the risk analysis, the *action plan* can be created.

# Creating an Action Plan

Once all of the previous planning steps have been completed, an action plan needs to be created. The *action plan* identifies the recommended "next steps." The recommended next steps can either identify what needs to be done to prepare for the architecture phase (such as a project plan), or what action needs to be taken to clarify/correct any problems encountered during the planning phase. For example, with a situation as indicated in the risk analysis section previously, the action plan may need to provide a solution to a particular risk. Basically, the action plan functions to address any open issues from the information gathering stages.

This step is to ensure all of the required information has been obtained in order to provide the best solution for the client. As soon as the action plan is created and approved, the planning deliverables can be prepared.

## Preparing the Planning Deliverables

The last step in the plan phase is to gather all information and documentation created throughout the plan and put them into a deliverable document. This is somewhat of a sanity checkpoint, in terms of making the client fully aware of the plans you have devised and what to expect for the remainder of the project. Some of the items to include in the document are:

- Requirements document
- Current environment analysis
- Industry practices analysis
- Operations plan
- Gap analysis
- Technology plan
- Collocation plan
- Risk analysis
- Action plan

Once the planning deliverable document is complete and has been presented to the client, the next phase of the network design can begin.

# Developing the Network Architecture

The *network architecture* is also referred to as a *high-level* design. It is a phase where all of the planning information is used to begin a conceptual design of the new network. It does not include specific details to the design, nor does it provide enough information to begin implementation. (This will be explained in greater detail in the following sections.) The architecture phase is responsible for marrying the results of the planning phase with the client's expectations and requirements for the network.

## Reviewing and Validating the Planning Phase

The first step in developing a network architecture is to review and validate the results of the planning phase. Once you have thoroughly gone through the results of the planning phase, and you understand and agree to them, you are finished with this step and can move on to creating a high level topology. The reason that this step is included here is that many times teams on large projects will be assembled but the architecture team can consist of people that were *not* in the plan team. This step is to get everyone familiar with what was completed prior to his or her participation.

## Creating a High-Level Topology

A *high-level topology* describes the logical architecture of a network. The logical architecture should describe the functions required to implement a network and the relationship between the functions. The logical architecture can be used to describe how different components of the network will interoperate, such as how a network verifies the authentication of users. The high-level topology will not include such granularity as specific hardware, for example; rather, it illustrates the desired functionality of the network. Some of the components to include in the high-level topology are:

- Logical network diagrams
- Functional network diagrams
- Radio frequency topology
- Call/Data flows
- Functional connectivity to resources
- Wireless network topology

# Creating a Collocation Architecture

Once the *collocation plan* has been complete, a more detailed architecture needs to be created. The architecture should include information that will be used as part of the requirements package that you give to vendors for bids on locations. Information to include in the requirements includes:

- Power requirements in Watts
- Amperage requirements
- Voltage (both AC and DC) values
- BTU dissipated by the equipment
- Equipment and cabinet quantity and dimensions
- Equipment weight
- Equipment drawings (front, side, top, and back views)
- Environmental requirements

The intention of this type of architecture is to provide information to assist in issuing either a request for information (RFI) or a request for proposal (RFP) to a vendor(s). It is in the best interest of the client to include enough information about the network requirements to evoke an adequate response from the vendor, but not give away information that potentially could be used for competitive intelligence.

# Defining the High-Level Services

The services that the client plans on offering their customers will usually help determine what the necessary equipment requirements will be. These services should match up with the services identified in the risk portion of the plan phase. Once the services have been identified, they need to be documented and compared against the risk matrix to determine what services will be offered. The client typically will already have identified the types of services they are interested in providing, but this is an opportunity to double-check the client's intentions. Any services that will not be offered need to be removed from the architecture. Once you have presented the documented services and get the client's service offering list, you can move on to creating a high-level physical design.

## Creating a High-Level Physical Design

The *high-level physical design* is the most important step in the architecture phase and is usually the most complicated and time consuming. A lot of work, thought, and intelligence go into this step. It defines the physical location and types of equipment needed throughout the network to accomplish its intended operation. It does not identify specific brands or models of equipment, but rather functional components such as routers, switches, access points, etc. The high-level physical design takes the RF topology, for example, completed in the high-level topology step, and converts that to physical equipment locations. Due to the many unknowns with RF engineering, several modifications and redesigns may be necessary before this step is complete. Upon acceptance of the high-level physical design, the operations services needs to be defined.

## Defining the Operations Services

The purpose of defining the *operations services* is to identify the functionality required within each operations discipline. Some of the more common operations disciplines include:

- Pre-order
- Order management
- Provisioning
- Billing
- Maintenance
- Repair
- Customer care

Once the functionality for each discipline has been defined, documented, and accepted, you are ready to create a high-level operations model.

## Creating a High-Level Operating Model

If a network can't be properly maintained once built, then its success and even its life can be in jeopardy. The purpose of creating a *high-level operating model* is to describe how the network will be managed. Certainly a consideration here is how the new network management system will interoperate with the existing management system. Some of the steps that need to be considered when creating a high-level operating model include:

- Leveraging technical abilities to optimize delivery of management information

- Providing an easily managed network that is high quality and easy to troubleshoot

- Identifying all expectations and responsibilities

The high-level operating model will be used later to create a detailed operating model. Once the high-level operating model has been developed and accepted by the client, you can proceed with evaluating the products for the network.

## Evaluating the Products

In some cases, the step of evaluating the products can be a very lengthy process. Depending on the functionality required, level of technology maturity, and vendor availability/competition, this can take several months to complete. When evaluating products, it is important to identify the needs of the client and make sure that the products meet all technical requirements. This is where the responses from the RFI/RFP will be evaluated. However, if the project is not of a large scale, it may be the responsibility of the design engineer to research the products available on the market. Once the list of products has been identified, an evaluation needs to be performed to determine which vendor will best fit the client. There are several factors that affect the decision process including:

- Requirement satisfaction
- Cost
- Vendor relationship
- Vendor stability
- Support options
- Interoperability with other devices
- Product availability
- Manufacturing lag time

The result of this step should leave you with each product identified to the model level for the entire network. Once the products have been identified, an action plan can be created.

## Creating an Action Plan

The *action plan* will identify what is necessary to move on to the design phase. The action plan's function is to bridge any gaps between the architectural phase and the actual design of the network. Some of the items for which an action plan can be given are:

- Create a project plan for the design phase
- Rectify any problems or issues identified during the architecture phase
- Establish equipment and/or circuit delivery dates

This is another checkpoint in which the network architect/design engineer will verify the progression and development direction of the network with the client. Once the action plan is complete and approved by the client, the network architecture deliverables can be created.

## Creating the Network Architecture Deliverable

During this step, all of the documents and information created and collected during the architecture phase will be gathered and put into a single location. There are several different options for the location of the deliverable, such as:

- Master document
- CD-ROM
- Web page

Any and all of the methods listed can be used for creating the architecture deliverable. One thing to include in this step is the deliverables from the plan phase as well. This lets the client reference any of the material up this point. Also, as new documents and deliverables are developed, they should be added. Once the architecture deliverable has been completed and it has been presented to the client, the detailed design phase can begin.

# Formalizing the Detailed Design Phase

The *detailed design phase* of the NEM is the last step before implementation begins on the network. This phase builds on the architecture phase and fills in the details of each of the high-level documents. This is the shortest and easiest phase of the design (assuming the plan and architecture phase was completed thoroughly and with accurate information). Basically, the detail design is a compilation of the entire planning process. This is absolutely where the rewards of the prior arduous tasks are fully realized.

## Reviewing and Validating the Network Architecture

The first step of a detailed design phase is to review and validate the network architecture. The network architecture is the basis for the design, and there must be a sanity check to ensure that the architecture is on track. This involves making sure all of the functionality is included. As you did at the beginning of the architecture phase, you may be validating work done by other people. Once the network architecture has been validated, you begin the detailed design by creating a detailed topology.

## Creating the Detailed Topology

The *detailed topology* builds on the high-level topology, adding information specific to the network topology, such as:

- Devices and device connectivity
- Data/Voice traffic flows and service levels
- Traffic volume
- Traffic engineering
- Number of subscribers
- IP addressing
- Routing topology
- Types of technology
- Location of devices
- Data-link types
- Bandwidth requirements
- Protocols
- Wireless topology

The detailed topology is a functional design, not a physical design. The detailed topology is where client dreams become a reality. By this point the client should be fully aware of what they would like the network to offer, and your job is to make it happen. In addition to the documented results, you should have detailed drawings of the various topologies listed earlier. Once the detailed topology is complete, a detailed collocation design can be created.

# Creating a Detailed Service Collocation Design

As with the detailed topology, the detailed service collocation design builds on the collocation architecture. This step will provide the details necessary to install equipment in collocation facilities. Include the following information with the design:

- Network Equipment Building Standards (NEBS) compliance
- Facilities
- Cabling

Once the detailed service collocation design is complete and accepted by the client, it can be presented to the collocation vendor for approval. Once the vendor approves the design, the implementation phase for collocation services can begin.

# Creating the Detailed Services

This step will define and document the specific services that the client will offer to its customers. The services offered are a continuation of the services list identified in the high-level services design step. When creating the design, be sure to include information such as timeline for offering. This information will most likely be of interest to the client's marketing department. You can easily understand that in a service provider environment, the customers and the resulting revenue justify the network. Some of the information to provide with each service includes:

- Service definition
    - Service name
    - Description
    - Features and benefits
    - SLAs
- Service management
- Functionality

- Configuration parameters
- Access options
- Third-party equipment requirements
- Service provisioning
- Network engineering
- Customer engineering
- Service options

Not only do you need to provide information regarding when these services will be available, but you should include how they will be offered and how they will interface with the network. Once the detailed services have been created, they can be put to the implementation process.

## Creating a Detailed Physical Design

The detailed physical design builds on the high-level physical design. It specifies most of the physical details for the network including:

- Equipment model
- Cabling details
- Rack details
- Environment requirements
- Physical location of devices
- Detailed RF design

The detailed physical design builds on information identified in the following documents:

- High-level physical design
- Detailed topology
- Detailed service collocation
- Product evaluation
- Site survey details

The detailed physical design is a compilation of these items as well as finalized equipment configuration details including IP addressing, naming, RF details, and physical configuration. When you finish this step you should have a detailed physical drawing of the network as well as descriptions of each of the devices.

## Creating a Detailed Operations Design

The *detailed operations design* builds on the high-level operations design. The purpose of this step is to specify the detailed design of the support systems that will be implemented to support the network. Some of the results of this step include determining vendor products, identifying technical and support requirements, and determining costs. Major steps in this phase include:

- Develop systems management design
- Develop services design
- Develop functional architecture
- Develop operations physical architecture analysis and design
- Develop data architecture
- Develop OSS network architecture
- Develop computer platform and physical facilities design

The detailed operations design is complete when it is documented and reviewed. After it is complete, the detailed operating model can be designed. Due to the fact that the operations network can be very small (or nonexistent), or that it could be an entirely separate network with its own dedicated staff, the specific details for this step in the design process has been summarized. In large network projects, the operations design can be a completely separate project, consisting of the full NLM process.

## Creating a Detailed Operating Model Design

This step is intended to describe the operating model that will optimize the management of the network. The detailed design builds on the high-level operating model. When creating the detailed design you should answer as many of the following questions as possible:

- Which organizations will support what products and services, and how?

- Who is responsible for specific tasks?

- How will the organization be staffed?

- How do the different organizations interact?

- How long will a support person work with an issue before escalating it?

- How will an escalation take place?

- Which procedures will be automated?

- What tools are available to which organization?

- What security changes are required?

Depending on the size of the network, the management network may be integrated in the main network, or it could be its own network. Additionally, the management network might run on the single network administrator's PC (for a very small network), or it could be run in a large Network Operations Center (NOC) staffed 24 hours a day, or anywhere in between. Because of the variations in size and requirements to network management, only a brief description is provided on what needs to be done. On larger networks, often the management design is an entirely separate design project deserving its own NLM attention.

## Creating a Training Plan

Depending on the size of the new network and the existing skill set of the staff, the *training plan* can vary greatly. Interviewing existing staff, creating a skills matrix, and comparing the skills matrix to the skills needed to operate the network can help determine training needs. If the client wants to perform the implementation on his or her own, that needs to be considered when reviewing the matrix. Once the training needs have been determined, create a roadmap for each individual, keeping future technologies in mind. Once the roadmaps have been created and the client accepts them, this step is finished.

## Developing a Maintenance Plan

This step in the design phase is intended to plan and identify how maintenance and operations will take place once the network is operational. The *maintenance plan* should cover all pieces of the network including operations and management. Also, the plan needs to take the skill set and training needs into consideration. Once a maintenance plan is developed and the client agrees to it, the implementation plan can be developed.

## Developing an Implementation Plan

The *high-level implementation plan* should be an overview of the major steps required to implement the design. It should be comprehensive and it should highlight all steps from the design. Things to include in this step should be timelines, impact on existing network, and cost. The implementation plan and the detailed design documents will be the basis for the next phase: implementing the network design.

## Creating the Detailed Design Documents

The *detailed design documents* should be a summarized section of all of the documents from the entire design phase, as well as the architecture and plan deliverables. As with the architecture deliverable, we recommend that you present this information in several forms, including (but not limited to) CD-ROM, a single design document, or a dedicated Web site. Once this step is complete, the design phase of the project is finished. The next step is to move on to the implementation phase and install the new network. The details for the implementation phase are specific to each design.

   Now that you have been through a detailed examination of the how and why of network design, let's look at some design principles specific to wireless networking.

# Understanding Wireless Network Attributes from a Design Perspective

In traditional short-haul microwave transmission (that is, line-of-sight microwave transmissions operating in the 18 GHz and 23 GHz radio bands), RF design engineers typically are concerned with signal aspects such as fade margins, signal reflections, multipath signals, and so forth. Like an accountant seeking to balance a financial spreadsheet, an RF design engineer normally creates an RF budget table, expressed in decibels (dB), in order to establish a wireless design. Aspects like transmit power and antenna gain are registered in the assets (or plus) column, and free space attenuation, antenna alignment, and atmospheric losses are noted in the liabilities (or minus) column. The goal is to achieve a positive net signal strength adequate to support the wireless path(s) called for in the design.

As we continue to build a holistic view of the design process, it is important to take into account those signal characteristics unique to wireless technologies from several design perspectives. We will explore both sides of the spectrum, so to speak, examining characteristics that are unique and beneficial to implementation—as well as those that make this medium cumbersome and awkward to manage. Equally important is the ability to leverage these attributes and apply them to meet your specific needs. Ultimately, it is from this combined viewpoint of understanding RF signal characteristics as well as exploiting those wireless qualities that we approach this next section.

For the sake of clarity, however, it is worth reiterating that the wireless characteristics described in the following sections are not focused on traditional short-haul licensed microwave technologies. Furthermore, it is not our intent to delve deeply into radio frequency theory or the historical applications of line-of-sight Point-to-Point Microwave. Rather, the purpose at this juncture is to entice you into exploring the possibilities of unlicensed wireless technologies by examining their characteristics from several design perspectives.

# Application Support

Interest in wireless LAN technologies has skyrocketed dramatically over the last few years. Whether the increase in popularity stems from the promise of mobility or the inherent ability to enable a network with minimal intrusion, interest in wireless LAN technologies remains high. However, these aspects by themselves do not validate the need to embrace a wireless network—or any other network for that matter. To understand the real cause for adopting a network, wireless or otherwise, we must look to the intrinsic value of the network itself. What is the purpose of the network? How will the network enhance my current processes? Does the overall benefit of the network outweigh all operational, administrative, and maintenance (OAM) costs associated with deploying it?

In our search to find that intersection between cost and benefit, we ultimately come to the realization that it is the applications and services that are supported over the network that bring value to most end users. Except for those truly interested in learning how to install, configure, or support wireless or wireline networks, most users find the value of a given network to be in the applications or services derived from what is on the network. So then, how do unlicensed wireless technologies enhance user applications, and what are some of the associated dependencies that should be considered to support these applications or services?

It is undisputed that one of the key aspects of wireless technology is the inherent capability to enable mobility. Although wireless applications are still largely under development, services that accommodate demands for remote access are emerging rapidly. From *web clipping*, where distilled information requested on behalf of a common user base is posted for individual consumption upon request, to e-mail access and retrieval from remote locations within the network footprint, wireless personal information services are finding their place in our mobile society.

At this point, it should be realized that one wireless application dependency is found in the supporting form factor or device. Speculation is rampant as to what the ultimate "gadget" will look like. Some believe that the ultimate form factor will incorporate data and voice capabilities, all within a single handheld device. There is movement in the marketplace that suggests corporations and service providers are embracing a single device solution. We only need to look at their own cellular phones or newly released products like the Kyocera QCP 6035 that integrate PDA functionality with cellular voice to see this trend taking hold.

On the other hand, technologies like Bluetooth point to, perhaps, a model whereby applications and services are more easily supported by a two-form factor approach. Although still in the early development stage, with a Bluetooth enabled wireless headset communicating to a supporting handheld device or wristwatch, both voice and data communications may be supported without compromising session privacy or ergonomic function. As a result, from an applications perspective, knowing what physical platform will be used to derive or deliver your application or service is an important design consideration.

Power consumption and operating system efficiency are two more attributes that should be considered when planning applications and services over wireless LAN technologies. Many of us are aware of the importance of battery life, whether that battery is housed in a cellular telephone, laptop, or even the TV remote control. However, it should not go without mention that these two factors play a significant role in designing applications and services for wireless networking.

Unlike normal desktop operations, whereby the PC and supporting peripherals have ready access to nearby wall outlets to supply their power budget, developers that seek to exploit the mobile characteristics of wireless LAN are not afforded the same luxury. As a result, power consumption, heat dissipation, and operating system efficiencies are precious commodities within the mobile device that require preservation whenever the opportunity exists. Companies like Transmeta Corporation understand these relationships and their value to the mobile industry, and have been working diligently to exploit the operating system efficiencies of Linux in order to work beyond these constraints. Nevertheless, applications and service developers should take into account these characteristics in order to maintain or preserve service sessions.

Beyond these immediate considerations, the design developer may be limited in terms of what types of services, including supporting operating systems and plug-ins, are readily available. Synchronous- or isochronous-dependent services may prove difficult to support, based on the wireless transport selected. Therefore, take caution as you design your wireless service or application.

# Subscriber Relationships

Unlike wired LAN topologies, where physical attachment to the network is evidenced merely by tracing cables to each respective client, physical connectivity in a wireless network is often expressed in decibels (dB) or decibel milliwatts (dBm). Simply put, these are units of measure that indicate signal strength expressed in terms of the signal levels and noise levels of a given radio channel, relative to 1 watt or 1 milliwatt, respectively. This ratio is known as a signal-to-noise (S/N) ratio, or SNR. As a point of reference, for the Orinoco RG1000 gateway, the SNR level expressed as a subjective measure is shown in Figure 5.1.

**Figure 5.1** SNR Levels for the Orinoco RG1000

From a wireless design perspective, subscriber relationships are formed, not only on the basis of user authentication and IP addressing, as is common within a wired network, but also on the signal strength of a client and its location, a secure network ID, and corresponding wireless channel characteristics. Taking into account, as an example, the wireless channel plan defined in the 802.11b specification, remember that Lucent Technologies AP1000 access point affords the user with a total of 11 useable channels to transport data. It is imperative that the network design engineer understands the subscriber relationships to be supported and develops a channel plan accordingly. Let's take a closer look.

Like traditional short-haul microwave technologies, 802.11 direct sequence spread spectrum (DSSS) wireless technology requires frequency diversity between different radios. Simply stated, user groups on separate access points within a wireless LAN must be supported on separate and distinct channels within that wireless topology. Similarly, adjacent channel spacing and active channel separation play an important role when planning and deploying a wireless network. These aspects refer to the amount of space between contiguous or active channels used in the wireless network. From a design perspective, the integrity and reliability of the network is best preserved when the channels assigned to access points in the same wireless network are selected from opposite ends of the wireless spectrum whenever possible. Failure to plan in accordance with these attributes most likely will lead to cochannel interference, an RF condition in which channels within the wireless spectrum interfere with one another. In turn, this may cause your service session to lock up, or it may cause severe network failure or total network collapse. Other attributes that depend on subscriber relationships involve network security (we reserve discussion on this characteristic separately in order to consider this wireless attribute more carefully; see the Network Security section later in this chapter).

## Physical Landscape

Even if adequate channel spacing, sound channel management, and RF design principles are adhered to, other wireless attributes associated with the given environment must be taken into account. As mentioned at the onset of this section, antennas are constructed with certain gain characteristics in order to transmit and receive information. This attribute of the antenna serves to harness wireless information for transmission or reception; through the use of modulation and demodulation techniques, the transmitted signal ultimately is converted into useable information. However, the propensity of antennas to transmit and receive a signal is regulated largely by the obstructions, or lack thereof, between the transmit antenna and the receive antenna.

Make no mistake, although radio-based spread spectrum technologies do not require line-of-sight between the transmitter and corresponding receiver, signal strength is still determined by the angle in which information is received. The following diagnostic screens in Figures 5.2 (Screen A) and 5.3 (Screen B) show impacts to data when the angle of reception from the emitted signal is changed by less than five degrees.

**Figure 5.2** Diagnostic Screen A

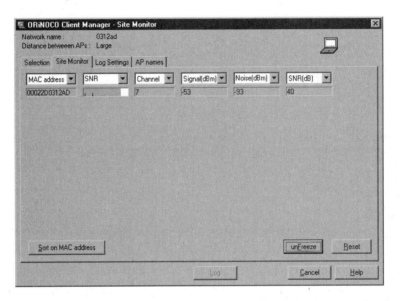

From a physical landscape perspective, we can easily see how physical obstructions may affect signal quality and overall throughput. As such, placement of antennas, angles of reception, antenna gain and distance to the radio should be considered carefully from a design perspective.

Obviously, with each type of antenna, there is an associated cost that is based on the transport characteristics of the wireless network being used. Generally speaking, wireless radios and corresponding antennas that require support for more physical layer interfaces will tend to cost more, due to the additional chipset integration within the system. However, it might also be that the benefit of increased range may outweigh the added expense of integrating more radios to your design.

**Figure 5.3** Diagnostic Screen B

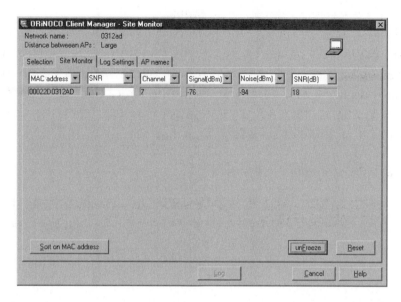

Beyond the physical environment itself, keep in mind that spectral capacity, or available bits per second (bps), of any given wireless LAN is not unlimited. Couple this thought of the aggregate bandwidth of a wireless transport with the density of the users in a given area, and the attribute of *spatial density* is formed. This particular attribute, spatial density, undoubtedly will be a key wireless attribute to focus on and will grow in importance proportionate to the increase in activity within the wireless industry. The reason for this is very clear. The wireless industry is already experiencing congestion in the 2.4 GHz frequency range. This has resulted in a "flight to quality" in the less congested 5 GHz unlicensed spectrum. Although this frequency range will be able to support more channel capacity and total aggregate bandwidth, designers should be aware that, as demand increases, so too will congestion and bandwidth contention in that spectrum. Because of the spectral and spatial attributes of a wireless LAN, we recommend that no more than 30 users be configured on a supporting radio with a 10BaseT LAN interface. However, up to 50 users may be supported comfortably by a single radio with a 100BaseT LAN connection.

# Network Topology

Although *mobility* is one of the key attributes associated with wireless technologies, a second and commonly overlooked attribute of wireless transport is the *ease of access*. Let's take a moment to clarify. Mobility implies the ability of a client on a particular network to maintain a user session while roaming between different environments or different networks. The aspect of roaming obviously lends itself to a multitude of services and applications, many yet to be developed. Is mobility the only valuable attribute of wireless technology?

Consider that market researchers predict that functional use of appliances within the home will change dramatically over the next few years. With the emergence of the World Wide Web, many companies are seizing opportunities to enhance their products and product features using the Internet. Commonly referred to as IP appliances, consumers are already beginning to see glimmers of this movement. From IP-enabled microwave ovens to Internet refrigerators, manufacturers and consumers alike are witnessing this changing paradigm. But how do I connect with my refrigerator? Does the manufacturer expect there to be a phone jack or data outlet behind each appliance? As we delve into the details of the wiring infrastructure of a home network, it becomes apparent that the value of wireless technology enables more than just mobility. It also provides the ease of access to devices without disrupting the physical structure of the home.

Whether these wireless attributes are intended for residential use via HomeRF, or are slated for deployment in a commercial environment using 802.11b, mobility and ease of access are important considerations from a design perspective and have a direct impact on the wireless network topology. From a network aspect, the wireless designer is faced with how the wireless network, in and of itself, should function. As stated earlier in this book, wireless LANs typically operate in either an ad-hoc mode or an infrastructure mode. In an ad-hoc configuration, clients on the network communicate in a peer-to-peer mode without necessarily using an access point via the Distributed Coordination Function (DCF) as defined in the 802.11b specification. Alternatively, users may prescribe to the network in a client/server relationship via a supporting access point through the Point Coordination Function (PCF) detailed in the 802.11b specification. It should be determined early in the design process how each client should interact with the network. However, beyond a client's immediate environment, additional requirements for roaming or connectivity to a disparate subnetwork in another location may be imposed. It is precisely for these reasons that mobility and wireless access must be factored in from the design perspective early in the design process and mapped against the network topology.

Finally, wireless access should also be viewed more holistically from the physical point of entry where the wireless network integrates with the existing wired infrastructure. As part of your planned network topology, once again, the impacts to the overall network capacity—as well as the physical means of integrating with the existing network—should be considered. The introduction of wireless clients, whether in whole or in part, most likely will impact the existing network infrastructure.

## Network Security

It is frequently said that an individual's greatest strengths are often their greatest weaknesses. The same can be said when examining the attributes of a wireless network. Both mobility and ease of access are touted as some of the greatest characteristics available when using a wireless LAN. Unfortunately, these same attributes give cause for the greatest concerns when deploying a wireless network.

Undoubtedly, it is in the best interest of all users on any given network, wired or wireless, to protect the integrity of the network. As a result, corporate network administrators that utilize both wired and wireless networks for corporate traffic normally employ high-level security measures like password authentication and secure login IDs in order to maintain network integrity. Lower level security measures, like installing corporate firewalls, are also commonly deployed in order to discourage or prevent undesirables from entering into both networks. It is at this point (that is, Layer 3 or the network layer of the OSI model) that security practices between a wired network and a wireless network typically traverse down different paths.

In a typical wired network, where Layers 1 and 2 (the physical and data-link layers) are regulated by supplying cable runs and network interfaces to known clients on the network, whereas wireless network emissions are distributed freely across numbers of users, in some cases unbeknownst to others in the same environment. However, because of the general availability of signals to users within the wireless footprint, wireless network providers counter the lack of physical control with additional security measures, namely encryption.

Within the Lucent product set, for example, where 802.11b is utilized, 64-bit key encryption, optional 128-bit key encryption schemes, and a secure network ID serve to counter unauthorized network entry. HomeRF standards leverage the inherent capabilities of FHSS, standard 128-bit encryption, and a user-specified secure ID to counterbalance unauthorized network intrusion. In both cases, encryption mechanisms are deployed over their wired network counterparts.

Many will argue the security merits of one wireless technology over another wireless technology. These arguments stem over ease of symbol rate conversion and unauthorized encrypted packet insertion. Still others may argue the merits of nonencrypted data over wired networks versus encrypted data communicated over a wireless network. Many US government agencies mandate TEMPEST-ready conditions, in which wired emissions are regulated to avoid intrusion. In either case, from a network design perspective, it is vital that the wireless network designer takes appropriate measures to ensure the security and stability of the wireless network. At a minimum, ensure that the logical placement of your wireless access points, if required, are placed appropriately in front of your network firewall. Finally, take into account the value of the information being transmitted and secure it accordingly.

# Summary

Designing a wireless network is not an easy task. Many wireless attributes should be considered throughout the design process. In the preliminary stages of your design, it is important to query users in order to accommodate their needs from a design perspective. Keep in mind that with wireless networks, attributes such as mobility and ease of access can impact your network in terms of cost and function.

The methodology used in this chapter incorporates elements of Lucent's Network Engagement Methodology (NEM). The design methodology is broken down into several parts, one being *execution and control*. This part has been categorized to include many of the most common types of projects; the category presented here is based on the service-provider methodologies. The execution and control part is broken down in this chapter into planning, architecture, and design.

The planning phase contains several steps responsible for gathering all information and documenting initial ideas regarding the design. The plan consists mostly of documenting and conducting research about the needs of the client. At the conclusion of the planning phase, documents that provide information such as competitive practices, gap analysis, and risk analysis can be presented to the client.

The architecture phase is responsible for taking the results of the planning phase and marrying them with the business objectives or client goals. The architecture is a high-level conceptual design. At the conclusion of the architecture phase, the client will have documents that provide information such as a high-level topology, a high-level physical design, a high-level operating model, and a collocation architecture.

The design phase takes the architecture and makes it reality. It identifies specific details necessary to implement the new design and is intended to provide all information necessary to create the new network. At the conclusion of the design phase, the design documents provided to the client will include a detailed topology, detailed physical design, detailed operations design, and maintenance plan.

# Solutions Fast Track

## Exploring the Design Process

☑ The design process consists of six major phases: preliminary investigation, analysis, preliminary design, detailed design, implementation, and documentation.

☑ In the early phases of the design process, the goal is to determine the cause or impetus for change. As a result, you'll want to understand the existing network as well as the applications and processes that the network is supporting.

☑ Because access to your wireless network takes place "over the air" between the client PC and the wireless access point, the point of entry for a wireless network segment is critical in order to maintain the integrity of the overall network.

☑ PC mobility should be factored into your design as well as your network costs. Unlike a wired network, users may require network access from multiple locations or continuous presence on the network between locations.

## Identifying the Design Methodology

☑ Lucent Worldwide Services has created a network lifecycle methodology, called the Network Engagement Methodology (NEM), for its consultants to use when working on network design projects. The design methodology contains the best-of-the-best samples, templates, procedures, tools, and practices from their most successful projects.

☑ The NEM is broken down into several categories and stages; the category presented in this chapter is based on the execution and control category, for a service provider methodology. The execution and control category is broken down into planning, architecture, design, implementation, and operations.

☑ The planning phase contains several steps that are responsible for gathering all information and documenting initial ideas regarding the design. The plan consists mostly of documenting and conducting research about the needs of the client, which produces documents outlining competitive practices, gap analysis, and risk analysis.

☑ The architecture phase is responsible for taking the results of the planning phase and marrying them with the business objectives or client goals. The architecture is a high-level conceptual design. At the conclusion of the architecture phase, a high-level topology, a high-level physical design, a high-level operating model, and a collocation architecture will be documented for the client.

☑ The design phase takes the architecture and makes it reality. It identifies specific details necessary to implement the new design and is intended to provide all information necessary to create the new network, in the form of a detailed topology, detailed physical design, detailed operations design, and maintenance plan.

## Understanding Wireless Network Attributes from a Design Perspective

☑ It is important to take into account signal characteristics unique to wireless technologies from several design perspectives. For example, power consumption and operating system efficiency are two attributes that should be considered when planning applications and services over wireless LAN technologies.

☑ Spatial density is a key wireless attribute to focus on when planning your network due to network congestion and bandwidth contention.

# Frequently Asked Questions

The following Frequently Asked Questions, answered by the authors of this book, are designed to both measure your understanding of the concepts presented in this chapter and to assist you with real-life implementation of these concepts. To have your questions about this chapter answered by the author, browse to **www.syngress.com/solutions** and click on the **"Ask the Author"** form.

**Q:** Several customers want me to give them up-front costs for designing and installing a network. When is the most appropriate time to commit to a set price for the job?

**A:** Try to negotiate service charges based on deliverables associated with each phase of the design process. In doing so, you allow the customer to assess the cost prior to entering into the next phase of the design.

**Q:** I'm very confused by all the different home network standards. Is there any way that I can track several of the different home networking standards from a single unbiased source?

**A:** Yes. There are several means of tracking various home network standards and initiatives. For comprehensive reports in the home network industry, I would suggest contacting Parks Associates at www.parksassociates.com. The Continental Automated Buildings Association (CABA) at www.caba.org is another good source for learning about home network technologies from a broad and unbiased perspective.

**Q:** I am trying to create a design of a wireless campus network and I keep finding out new information, causing me to change all of my work. How can I prevent this?

**A:** If you have done a thorough job in the planning phase you should already have identified all of the requirements for the project. Once you identify all of the requirements, you need to meet with the client and make sure that nothing was overlooked.

**Q:** How can I learn more about the Network Engagement Methodology (NEM)?

**A:** Lucent has a considerable amount of information available on NEM and all of their professional services on their Web site, www.network-care.com/consulting. From there you can learn more about the various services offered by Lucent ESS, see a live demo of NEM, and read about some of the successful engagements that Lucent has recently completed.

# Chapter 6

# Designing a Wireless Enterprise Network: Hospital Case Study

## Solutions in this chapter:

- **Introducing the Enterprise Case Study**

- **Evaluating Network Requirements**

- **Designing a Wireless Solution**

- **Implementing and Testing the Wireless Solution**

- **Lessons Learned**

☑ **Summary**

☑ **Solutions Fast Track**

☑ **Frequently Asked Questions**

# Introduction

An *enterprise network*, sometimes called a *campus network*, is a network that spans across multiple buildings. The case study we'll explore in this chapter follows the process of planning, designing, and implementing a wireless network in a hospital and associated medical buildings on the hospital campus. We will also review the advantages and cost savings associated with the implementation of this type of wireless networking versus leased lines.

We will walk through the steps you must complete first, gathering the network requirements and analyzing the current network. At that time, you will perform a site survey to determine the building infrastructure and see first-hand whether there are any line-of-sight issues. Based on the analysis of the current network and the site survey, you then develop a high-level design, and based upon the results, select the wireless equipment and develop the detailed design. Implementation of the network goes forward according to the high-level design. After the equipment is installed and configured, you make sure to perform acceptance testing to verify that the wireless links are working correctly.

Since these buildings are medical in nature, you must take special care when deploying wireless communications. Medical equipment in particular may be sensitive to wireless devices and channels. You must pay special attention to limiting radio frequencies in and around the emergency room area to avoid any interference. When you are writing the design, make sure that you speak to the Information Systems (IS) department to determine any concerns you need to be aware of while operating wireless equipment in the 2.4 GHz range.

# Applying Wireless in an Enterprise Network

Today, the IEEE 802.11b standard makes wireless networks possible. This standard enables you to implement frequencies around 2.4 GHz in North America without having to go through licensing paperwork. Wireless local area network (LAN) equipment using the 802.11b protocol provides for wireless capabilities with up to 11 Mbps of bandwidth. The wireless devices can be used to provide bridge extensions to existing wired Ethernet LANs. Other wireless devices act as access points (APs) and serve as a bridge to computers with wireless network interface cards into the network. Every computer accessing the same access point shares the bandwidth with all other computers using the same access point. This is the same technology used in wired Ethernet networks where all stations share the same 10 Mbps of bandwidth. Switched Ethernet networks do not share the same bandwidth.

Wireless devices help the campus networks evolve by providing users flexibility and mobility within the campus. Users are not limited to the locations or the number of available data ports in an office or conference room. They may now take their laptop computer and connect to the LAN virtually anywhere, even in hallways, within the access point range.

# Introducing the Enterprise Case Study

Our case study puts us in partnership with Jones Hospital & Associates. The IS manager from Jones Hospital has hired us as consultants to provide a wireless LAN solution for their hospital network. The hospital employs just over 800 employees, working in a complex composed of seven buildings in an urban area. All of the buildings are close enough in proximity that employees frequently walk between buildings.

The management staff wants to deploy wireless technology in their enterprise network. They have heard that this type of network will save them money as opposed to the current leased line network. They believe that the added mobility will also dramatically increase productivity. Since the staff moves from building to building, it seems to be the right idea to provide them with computer equipment and data that will roam with them.

## Assessing the Opportunity

Jones Hospital & Associates is composed of a group of affiliated primary care doctors and specialists. The hospital operates six leased satellite office buildings surrounding an eight-story central hospital tower. The IS department handles all LAN requirements. In preparation for this initiative, the IS department has gathered requirements with representatives from each medical area, including Administration, Pediatrics, Surgery, the Cancer Center, Heart Center, Pharmacy, Radiology, and Emergency departments. As consultants, we have been brought in to help the IS department assess the situation, gather requirements, and determine a wireless solution.

At this point we are in the planning phase of a wireless project. The first step in the planning phase is to gather the technical network requirements and current network architecture. To determine network requirements and current architecture, we will need to ask the following questions:

- What problems are you experiencing in the current network? Look for areas where wireless technology can help ease the IS burden as well as the departmental issues. By making the network easy to update, you've eliminated some issues.

- What is the architecture of the current network? Evaluate the current network to see how to integrate the wireless technology with the current network.

- What are the bandwidth limiting areas of your network? Obviously, you must limit the bandwidth in and around the surgery areas. Are there any other areas in which wireless technology could interfere with other medical equipment?

- Are there any applications that are limited by the current network? Or is there additional functionality required that the current network is not capable of? You may be able to increase productivity by overcoming any current obstacles.

- What is the building floor plan or layout? This information can help you plan where the wireless hardware equipment can be installed.

- Is there any equipment that might be susceptible to wireless frequencies? This should tell you whether the network transmission could possibly interfere with medical equipment. This is one area where research is very important.

- Are there any existing monthly costs that can be replaced with wireless link? The hospital administration staff wants to review the costs of the wireless network versus the current leased line system. The hospital Board of Directors is very cost-conscious.

- Are there any constraints in placing wireless equipment and antennas in computer rooms, communication closets, walls, roofs, offices, or conference rooms? If you can identify constraints at this time, you can save a lot of time during the implementation phase.

- What are the hospital plans for adding or deleting any office buildings? How accurate are the plans? Changes to the physical structure should be identified early to save time and effort.

These questions are important in understanding the current environment. They also help you design for constraints or limitations.

## Evaluating Network Requirements

After meeting with the hospital IS team, you determine the following requirements and constraints. It is important to define all requirements and constraints to ensure that your wireless solution falls within the expectations of your customer.

In the current physical network, all the satellite buildings use internal Category 5 Unshielded Twisted Pair (UTP) wiring. The Administration department expressed the need for LAN access in conference rooms in the main building. Since all employees are receiving laptop computers, all departments will require the ability to access the network from anywhere in the satellite buildings and in the conference room in the main hospital building. All users want the ability to use their laptops anywhere in any of the buildings. This will improve productivity because the medical staff often travels between the main hospital and the satellite buildings. The IS manager will provide building floor plans but foresees no physical limitations for placing wireless devices in the satellite buildings.

The satellite buildings are not owned by the hospital, they are leased. The satellite buildings connect to the main hospital via leased T-1 links. These leased links have become a recurring cost that the IS manager would like to reduce or eliminate. These links are highly utilized and the IS staff has received complaints from the different medical groups. There are no fiber lines to the satellite buildings and the cost to install fiber is not within the current budget. The IS staff wants to implement wireless technology to provide links from the main hospital to the satellite build-ings. The wireless network must provide security and encryption. The IS staff requires some level of redundancy for the site links.

Hospital officers mention that there are immediate plans to increase the hospital employee population. However, they want the developed solution to be scalable to support additional buildings in the future. They also express concerns about using radio frequencies in main hospital building, so they want to limit the wireless devices to conference rooms and site links within the hospital building.

## Assessing the Satellite Buildings' Physical Landscape

The IS manager has provided the floor plans. All of the satellite buildings were designed around the same floor plan, shown in Figure 6.1. Notice that there are communications and mechanical rooms in the center of the floor plan area; these rooms may generate noise and affect the wire-less design. The rest of the floor plan is open-area space with offices and a conference room. You will perform a walkthrough in each of the buildings to visually assess the environment.

## Evaluating the Outside Physical Landscape

The hospital campus area topography is shown in Figure 6.2. The main hospital is eight stories high and is separated from all other buildings with roads located in an urban zone. There is a park with high trees at the south of the main hospital building. Each satellite building is four stories high. There is a clear line-of-sight from the hospital to each

**Figure 6.1** Satellite Building Floor Plan

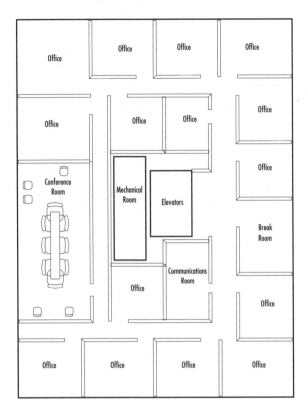

satellite building, and between the satellite buildings, except from Building 301 to Building 201. We must take this information into consideration to ascertain the redundancy requirements.

**Figure 6.2** The Topology of the Jones Hospital Buildings

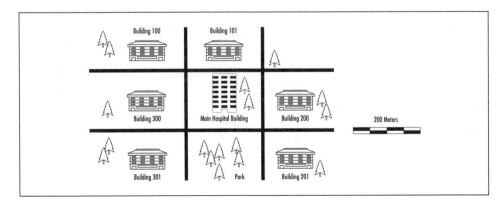

# Evaluating the Current Network

The current campus network has a router located in the computer center of the main hospital building with six serial interfaces. Each serial interface is used to connect to each of the satellite buildings via T-1 lines. Since the outside infrastructure is not privately owned, the T-1 lines are leased via the local exchange carrier. There is no fiber infrastructure between the buildings.

Each building has category 5 UTP wired infrastructure terminating into closet patch panels. Each LAN drop is terminated into a LAN switch. Fiber cables connect the LAN switches to the building router. As shown in Figure 6.3, the floor LAN switches connect to the building router, which has the T-1 line to the main building. This architecture does not provide for any redundancy, and the hospital wants to overcome this problem in the current architecture.

**Figure 6.3** Current Network Topology

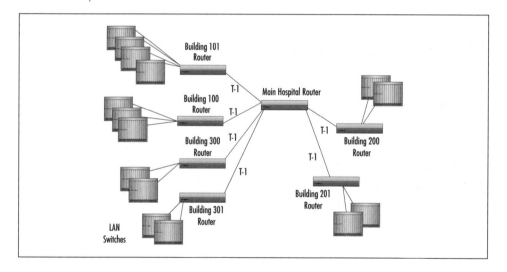

# Evaluating the Hospital Conference Room Networking Landscape

An assessment of the conference rooms in the hospital building shows four existing LAN drops in each room. The conference room layout is shown in Figure 6.4. Because the network connection already exists, and there is easy access to the drop, one of these drops can be used to place the access point bridge. As an additional benefit, the building infrastructure permits wireless LAN access from nearby offices.

**Figure 6.4** Conference Room Layout

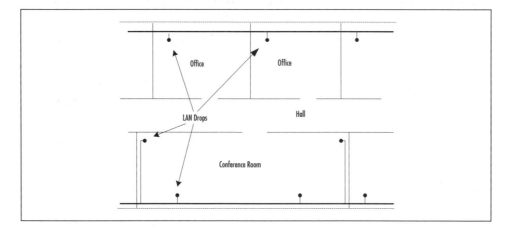

# Designing a Wireless Solution

Once we define the requirements and baseline the current network, we can move from the planning phase to the design phase. For convenience, we'll divide this wireless design project into three smaller projects, compartmentalizing the large project into smaller ones to make it easier to provide a solution for each project on a smaller scale. The first project provides *wireless access in the satellite buildings*. The second project simply adds *wireless LAN connectivity to the conference room* in the main hospital building. This enables the employees with wireless connectivity through the wireless interface cards in their laptops. The third project adds the *wireless links from the satellite buildings to the main hospital* and then adds the redundant links between each pair of satellite buildings. Let's review the design requirements:

- Provide wireless access for laptops in all satellite buildings.
- Provide wireless connectivity in conference rooms in the main hospital building.

- Provide a replacement to the leased T-1s that connect the satellite buildings to the main hospital building.

- Provide increased bandwidth to the satellite buildings.

- Provide redundancy to the satellite buildings.

- Maintain a level of security and encryption for the links.

# Project 1: Providing Satellite Building Access

When designing a wireless network in an enterprise building, you must determine the placement of antennas and access points for best coverage. In this example, the mechanical room, elevators, and communications room are sources of frequency interference that you need to consider. A single omnidirectional antenna might be capable of covering the office area in a satellite building (over 100 feet). However, with the interference items to consider, it would be better to place omnidirectional antennas (and access points) in each hallway, as shown in the Figure 6.5, to get better coverage. Also, each access point can provide redundancy. If one access point fails, the other provides access to all computers on the floor.

## Designing & Planning…

### Other Antenna and Access Point Bridge Placements

There are several methods of placing antennas to have full coverage in a floor. Directional antennas could be placed in each of the four corners of the floor aiming at a 45-degree angle toward the center of the building. To verify antenna placement, place an access point bridge at each location and test its range with a laptop with a wireless card. It is helpful to perform this test using a roll cart, so you can roll around the hallways, offices, and conference rooms to verify coverage.

**Figure 6.5** Project 1: Placement of Access Point Antennas in Satellite Buildings

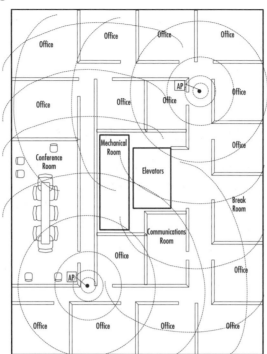

The access point wireless bridges will be placed on shelves near the antennas. The Ethernet ports of the access point bridges will be connected to the LAN switches that serve the floor. The LAN switch must be configured to permit multiple media access control (MAC) addresses on the data port.

# Project 2: Providing Wireless Technology to the Conference Rooms

For the conference room project, plan to install one access point wireless bridge. Users requiring wireless LAN connectivity will need to install wireless LAN network interface cards into their laptop computers. The access point will be configured as a bridge with the Ethernet port connecting to the LAN jack. An antenna will be installed in the conference room. This solution meets the requirement for access to the LAN from the hospital conference room.

As shown in Figure 6.6, the access point is placed on a shelf on the corner of the conference room. A directional antenna is also placed on the corner providing access to the conference rooms and nearby offices. The LAN switch that serves the conference room drop must be configured to permit more that one MAC address on the LAN port. This same solution is applied to each conference room in each satellite building.

**Figure 6.6** Project 2: Conference Room Solution

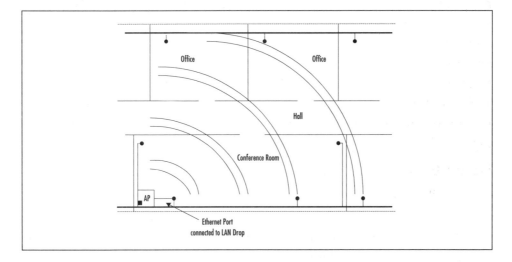

# Project 3: Providing Building-to-Building Connectivity

There are many different ways to provide a wireless solution for Jones Hospital's network. A single wireless link could be implemented between the hospital building and each satellite building, but this solution would not provide redundancy. A full mesh could also be implemented, but it might be an overkill solution.

The solution presented here is one design approach that meets the requirements. Let's review the design requirements for this connectivity:

- Provide a replacement to the leased T-1s that connect the satellite buildings to the main hospital building.

- Provide increased bandwidth to the satellite buildings.

- Provide redundancy to the satellite buildings.

- Maintain a level of security and encryption for the links.

Based on the requirements, the existing lease lines will need to be replaced with wireless links from the main hospital building to each satellite building. Data encryption will be enabled to provide link security. The wireless links will provide increased bandwidth from 1.5 Mbps to 11 Mbps. To provide redundancy, we could link every building in a loop, but this would add additional cost to the solution. The redundancy goal can be accomplished by just adding wireless links between building pairs; for example, adding a wireless link between Buildings 100 and 101, Buildings 200 and 201, and Buildings 300 and 301. A high-level illustration of the proposed solution for Jones Hospital is shown in Figure 6.7.

**Figure 6.7** Project 3: Proposed Building Wireless Connectivity

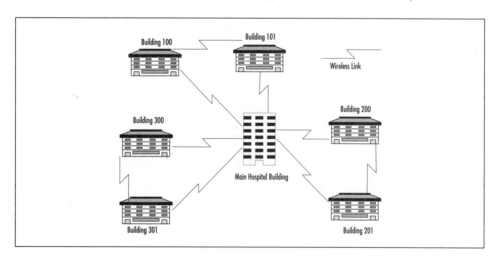

# Describing the Detailed Design of the Building Links

As previously described, we want to create point-to-point wireless links between buildings. Some vendors have wireless devices called *outdoor routers* that can provide a solution for Jones Hospital. We will create an architecture using the existing routers in each building. The access-point outdoor routers will connect via Ethernet to the hospital router. We'll use each outdoor router to create point-to-point links to each satellite building. As Figure 6.8 shows, Building 100 will use two wireless outdoor routers to link with the main hospital router and to Building 101 for redundancy. Data will be encrypted using 64-bit Wired Equivalent Privacy (WEP) or 128-bit RC4.

**Figure 6.8** Router to Router Wireless Connectivity

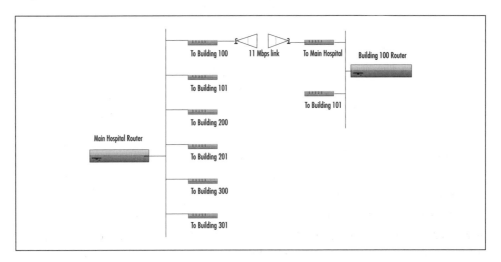

This solution provides for 11 Mbps of bandwidth between the buildings and the main hospital building, a significant increase from the 1.5 Mbps of bandwidth provided by the leased T-1 lines. Also, the hospital IS team will reduce costs by eliminating the monthly recurring costs for the leased lines.

Let's now look at how to add redundant links to provide backup connectivity in case of link or device failure. As shown in Figure 6.9, the main hospital router connects via Ethernet to the access-point outdoor routers. Each satellite building has two access-point outdoor routers to connect to the hospital and to the other building. If the link between Building 100 and the main hospital fails, the Building 100 router will still have access to the hospital via its link to Building 101. The same loop would be created for linking Buildings 200 and 201 to the main hospital route and for Buildings 300 and 301.

**Figure 6.9** Redundant Links: Hospital to Building 100 and Building 101

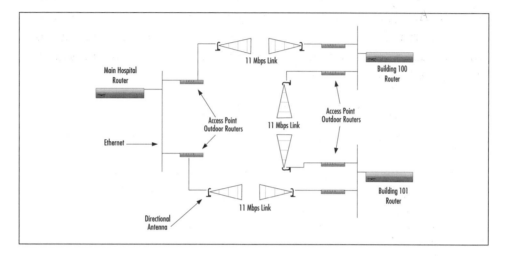

These designs will provide redundant connectivity for all satellite buildings. If there is a problem with any link or access point device, all traffic takes the redundant path to the main hospital router. These designs provide increased bandwidth to 11 Mbps. Also, users with wireless cards in their laptops will be able to meet in the conference room and access the local area network. Since the leased T-1 lines are not required, recurring costs also are eliminated.

Part of planning and design will be to reserve network closet and computer room space for the placement of the access point devices. We will need to estimate the distance of the antenna cables. Also, we need to determine the necessary equipment and obtain the building owner's permission to place the antennas on the building roof.

# Implementing and Testing the Wireless Solution

When the design phase is complete and all the equipment has been acquired, we can begin the implementation phase. The following sections describe the steps to follow when installing, configuring, and testing the wireless devices.

## Project 1: Implementing the Satellite Building LAN Access

Install the access point devices and antennas in the building floors as described in the design:

1. Mount the antennas in the hallways, and connect cables to the access point devices in the nearby offices.

2. Connect the access points to the floor LAN switch.

3. Configure the access point frequencies, keeping configuration information available for laptop configuration.

4. Configure the access point for bridging, and enable multiple MAC addresses on the LAN switch.

At this point we are ready to test wireless access throughout the floor plan. We begin by verifying access from each office and the conference room. The hospital laptops can be equipped with the wireless PC Memory Card International Association (PCMCIA) cards and configured to connect to the LAN via the access points.

## Project 2: Implementing the Hospital Conference Room

Implementation for the hospital conference room includes the same steps used in Project 1. For the conference rooms, install the access point and antenna at the corner of the room as described in the design diagram.

Place the directional antenna so that the antenna energy covers the conference room completely. The access point is configured for bridging (no routing). Connect the Ethernet port of the access point to a LAN drop. Configure the building switch that serves the used LAN drop to permit multiple MAC addresses on that port. The following steps provide a review of this implementation:

1. Mount the access point and directional antenna in the conference room.

2. Connect the access points to the floor LAN switch.

3. Configure the access point frequencies, keeping configuration information available for laptop configuration.

4. Configure the access point for bridging, and enable multiple MAC addresses on the LAN switch.

Use a laptop to verify access to the LAN in the conference room and nearby offices. Make sure that the connection is reliable.

# Project 3: Implementing the Building-to-Building Connectivity

The implementation of the wireless links between buildings is made in parallel to the current T-1 connectivity. No serial interfaces are used on the existing routers. In the server room of the main hospital, you connect the main router to six access-point outdoor routers. These routers reside in the server room, not outside. Install the directional antennas on the roof of the hospital, each pointing toward the direction of its respective satellite building. Install and configure the primary links between each satellite building and the hospital before installing the redundant lines. Figure 6.10 shows, at a high-level, the primary links. For implementation of the primary wireless links, follow these steps:

1. Install and configure the access-point outdoor routers.

2. Install the outdoor antennas and connect them to the outdoor routers.

3. Verify that the frequencies are configured and test the wireless link.

4. Verify that the received connection is strong enough to be a reliable connection.

**Figure 6.10** Primary Wireless Links

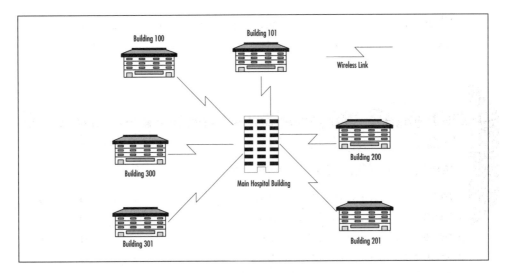

At this point we connect the outdoor routers to the existing building routers. Use the following steps to make these connections:

1. Connect the routers via their Ethernet ports.

2. Enable the encryption protocols for data security.

3. Configure the existing routers to forward packets via the wireless link.

4. Since the wireless link provides greater bandwidth, verify that the packets are getting forwarded via the wireless link over the leased T-1 lines.

When all six wireless links are installed and are passing traffic, install and configure the redundant links as shown in the steps for the primary wireless links listed at the beginning of this section. The next task is to test and verify the links:

1. Test the routing failover of wireless links by deactivating a primary link interface or an outdoor router.

2. Verify that the building still has access to the main hospital router.

3. Reenable the primary link or an outdoor router.

When all of the wireless devices and links are tested, the IS Manager can place cancellation orders for the leased T-1 links.

## Configuring & Implementing…

### Verify the Wireless Service

When installing the wireless antennas, use the testing capabilities of the access point devices to make sure that the wireless connection is reliable. If you encounter problems with the connection, try moving the antenna in one or the other direction to correct the problem. Verify that interference is not caused by trees or reflection from nearby buildings.

# Reviewing the Hospital's Objectives

Hold a follow-up meeting with the IS Department and hospital teams to demonstrate the functionality of the new wireless network and to determine the successes or failures of the wireless project. This meeting will help you determine whether you need to expand the wireless access points further in the satellite buildings. In the meeting held with Jones Hospital, we hear that the feedback received from the hospital groups is good. They are satisfied with their new ability to access the LAN from the satellite buildings and the conference room in the main hospital building. The medical staff is very happy with their new mobility.

The IS Manager is very pleased with the savings of leased line costs and the increased bandwidth to the satellite buildings. Since installing wireless devices is much faster than requesting that fiber cabling be installed, they are very pleased that the project was completed in a short time span.

# Lessons Learned

From this case study we learned how to deploy wireless technologies to extend wired Ethernet LANs for office and conference room areas. We also learned how to use wireless outdoor routers to provide campus links to an enterprise hospital network.

We learned to follow the process of planning, designing, implementing, and testing a wireless network. Following this approach makes wireless projects easier to manage. We learned to consider interference when designing for antenna placement for best coverage of the floor area, and decided on placing two access points in the satellite building floors because of interference in the mechanical, elevator, and communications rooms. In addition, having two access points increases the range and redundancy of the wireless network.

We decided to pair up satellite buildings to provide redundancy for the building links. This solution was not as costly as compared to creating a full mesh of wireless links. We enabled encryption to provide data security to the wireless links. We also learned that verification testing is very important. When the wireless network is implemented, testing access and routing will help validate the solution.

# Summary

In this case study chapter, we reviewed an enterprise network example involving a hospital. Wireless local area network (LAN) devices in this scenario were to help information services (IS) managers provide additional functionality and services. By installing wireless LAN access points, hospital personnel could access the LAN in the conference rooms and nearby offices. By installing IEEE 802.11b outdoor routers, the hospital was able to save leased line cost and increase bandwidth to 11 Mbps. Redundancy and security issues were also addressed in this case study.

We followed a wireless project approach of planning the project by gathering the requirements and baselining the current network before designing the wireless network. Implementation of the network was followed by testing and verification.

For Jones Hospital we gathered requirements for three projects broken out of the main challenge of providing a wireless solution: wireless access for laptops in satellite buildings, wireless access in the hospital building, and links between buildings. The requirements can be summarized as follows:

- Provide wireless access for laptops in all satellite buildings.

- Provide wireless connectivity in conference room in the main hospital building.

- Provide a replacement to the leased T-1 lines that connect the satellite buildings to the main hospital building.

- Provide increased bandwidth to the satellite buildings.

- Provide redundancy to the satellite buildings.

We designed a wireless access solution for the satellite buildings using two access points with omnidirectional antennas per floor in each satellite building. The design consisted of a wireless solution that contained an access point with a directional antenna in the hospital conference room. We designed a wireless solution for replacing the existing leased

T-1 lines with wireless links from the hospital to the satellite buildings. Data encryption provided security for the wireless links.

We outlined procedures to follow when implementing these projects. We discussed testing methods to verify that the wireless access devices and links are working and that the range of wireless access includes all locations within the building. At the conclusion of the project, a follow-up meeting was held to gather the client's feedback on the project.

# Solutions Fast Track

## Introducing the Enterprise Case Study

- ☑ Hospital requires wireless access for laptops in satellite buildings.
- ☑ Hospital requires wireless access in conference room.
- ☑ Hospital requires building-to-building wireless links.

## Examining Network Requirements

- ☑ The area in the satellite buildings has rooms that will cause interference to the wireless buildings.
- ☑ The area in the conference room is small.
- ☑ There is clear line-of-sight from the main hospital buildings to provide a wireless solution.
- ☑ The distance between buildings permits wireless links.

## Designing a Wireless Solution

- ☑ Use two access point bridges per floor in the satellite buildings with omnidirectional antennas.

- ☑ Add an access point bridge in the conference of the main hospital building.

- ☑ Use access-point outdoor routers with directional antennas for hospital to satellite building wireless connectivity.

- ☑ Add wireless links between building pairs for redundancy.

- ☑ Use encryption for security.

# Implementing and Testing the Wireless Solution

- ☑ Install, configure, and test the access points and antennas in the satellite buildings. Test that laptops can access the LAN from all locations in the floor.

- ☑ Install, configure, and test the access point in the hospital conference room.

- ☑ Install, configure, and test the outdoor routers and wireless links. Then install the redundant wireless links.

# Lessons Learned

- ☑ Using multiple access point devices on a floor will provide additional access range and redundancy.

- ☑ Using an access point with a directional antenna in the conference room will provide wireless access for those attending meetings.

- ☑ Using encryption will provide data security for the wireless network.

- ☑ Using IEEE 802.11b outdoor routers with wireless directional antennas provides increased bandwidth to 11 Mbps between buildings.

# Frequently Asked Questions

The following Frequently Asked Questions, answered by the authors of this book, are designed to both measure your understanding of the concepts presented in this chapter and to assist you with real-life implementation of these concepts. To have your questions about this chapter answered by the author, browse to **www.syngress.com/solutions** and click on the **"Ask the Author"** form.

**Q:** We have concerns about the security of our data—how is our data protected?

**A:** Wireless products come with varying levels of encryption methods to protect data. Some of the data encryption methods used are DES, 64- bit WEP, and 128-bit RC4. Also, MAC address-based access control table schemes are used.

**Q:** What are the ranges of wireless devices outdoors?

**A:** Directional antennas can provide a range of up to 16 miles.

**Q:** What routing or bridging functionality is available on access point devices?

**A:** Access point wireless devices can act as bridges or routers. They can be configured with static routers or with simple Routing Information Protocol (RIP). They can also be configured to filter based on a MAC address when acting as a bridge.

**Q:** How will wireless laptops acquire an IP address and other IP-related information?

**A:** When using wireless bridges, you still use your existing Dynamic Host Configuration Protocol (DHCP) servers on the network to acquire an IP address, subnet masks, default gateways, Domain Name System (DNS) server, and other IP information regularly configured via DHCP. No special changes are required to access the DHCP server.

# Chapter 7

# Designing a Wireless Industrial Network: Retail Case Study

## Solutions in this chapter:

- **Introducing the Industrial Case Study**
- **Designing and Implementing the Wireless Network**
- **Planning the Equipment Placement**
- **Lessons Learned**

- ☑ **Summary**
- ☑ **Solutions Fast Track**
- ☑ **Frequently Asked Questions**

# Introduction

Experts in the industrial environment acknowledge the growing need for wireless technology. The emerging wireless handheld devices dramatically expand mobility when applied to standard industrial activities like inventory and stock management. The increased productivity and cost savings far outweigh the cost of investing in new wireless technology. This chapter describes how to implement a wireless network in an industrial environment. Although there are various types of industrial applications, we will focus on applying wireless technology to a retail store environment. Retail stores implement wireless technology for a number of purposes, including helping their employees to track inventory using a mobile system, and allowing customers to self-scan purchases and check the price of items.

Although it may be easier to think of applying wireless technology to large superstores, the mobility that wireless provides offers a big advantage for smaller stores. Smaller stores cannot support the number of employees or merchandise that large superstores do, so if they implement wireless technology they are able to streamline the staff dramatically. By adding mobile devices, a store owner can provide customers with the ability to answer their own questions about pricing and inventory. Customers who are more self-reliant do not require as much help from staff. Similarly, employees with self-reliant customers do not require the same amount of support from their management.

Through the case study presented in this chapter, you will learn how a consulting company can apply the design principles described in previous chapters. The flow through the discovery and planning phases show typical real-world issues and events. The planning phase contains the details you must be aware of when implementing a similar type of wireless network. The implementation section of this chapter walks you through the process of integrating the existing wired network with the proposed wireless network.

# Applying Wireless Technology in an Industrial Network

In the past two years, companies like 3Com Corporation have designed wireless cellular digital packet data (CDPD) networks for consumer applications on popular personal digital assistants (PDAs). More recently, by coupling wireless 802.11b technology with their IPAQ PDA, the Compaq Computer Company is successfully implementing wireless technology in the industrial setting. With data rates that support up to 11 Mbps, companies are finding useful applications for everything from network troubleshooting for corporate LANs to inventory control directly from these mobile devices. Transmeta's TM3200 chipset provides more effective processing power. As this power is incorporated with the operating system efficiency of Linux in handheld technologies, an explosion of new and enhanced applications will find their way to these powerful devices.

Although size is an issue with mobile units, companies like Symbol Technologies are finding unique ways to shrink wireless devices to allow customers and employees to perform simple retail functions while roaming through a store. Beyond these immediate examples, several key benefits are inherent when wireless technology is incorporated into business processes.

The retail side of this industry is rapidly warming up to wireless technology. Recently, large department chains like Sears, Roebuck and Co. and Wal-Mart implemented handheld devices for employees. These devices enable the employee to check inventory quickly, make price changes, enable merchandise pickup, and maintain adequate stock. Customers benefit when companies like these use handheld devices to prescan items prior to checkout.

# Introducing the Industrial Case Study

In this case study, Bob Tucker, the owner of a large retail sporting goods store called Pro Sports, is interested in applying wireless technology to make his network more efficient and to increase customer service. His current sales figures are looking solid, but in his market environment, competitors could soon be moving in down the street. Future competition will drive prices, but it will more clearly drive service. Bob has kept up with wireless trends in the retail market, including the wireless checkout bays used in a few superstores in his area. It appears to him that customers are eager to use new technology.

He also knows that he needs to increase employee productivity and customer response. After analyzing current growth and predicting future sales trends, Bob believes he must either increase his full-time sales staff by three employees or implement technology that will likewise expand sales efficiency and customer response. This choice makes the incorporation of wireless technology a value proposition to weigh against future plans. One of the main reasons to implement wireless technology is to provide better customer service.

## Assessing the Opportunity

Bob Tucker evaluates Pro Sports' needs and develops a list of the benefits he wants to add for employees and customers. For the employees, he seeks to automate in-store inventory. Currently, employees manually track the inventory during off-hours. During regular hours, office personnel enter the inventory lists using the PCs in the company office. He figures that he can save money when employees take inventory via handheld devices. This eliminates the reentry performed in the office, and the employees can take the inventory during normal working hours.

Bob wants his shipping clerk to place items in inventory as they are unloaded in the docking bay. He projects that the handheld devices will enable the shipping/receiving clerk to add to the inventory real-time as merchandise comes off the truck. This activity will eliminate the extra effort it takes to provide the paperwork to the office for manual entry. This automation will also enable other employees to check stock accurately and quickly for items that just arrived. Another advantage to adding this capability to the shipping/receiving area is that wireless technology will enable the shipping/receiving clerk to access the current wired network. The PC used in the shipping/receiving department currently is not connected to the office PCs. It is a stand-alone PC with a separate software package that is not tied to the company accounting system.

Handheld devices will enable the employees to respond to customer pages. These devices will make it easy to assess the customers who need assistance and respond to them quickly. When a customer requests specific information, the sales associates with that particular expertise can respond. Since employee incentives are based on commission and customer satisfaction, handheld devices will become sales associates' pagers. What better chance of earning a commission can Pro Sports offer to the employee than answering a customer's page?

Bob figures that the customers will benefit from the wireless technology by enabling them to check for stock and prices. For example, as the sports seasons change, the shoe department is often one of the busiest departments. By giving customers handheld devices and allowing them to scan the bar codes of the display shoes, the customers can check to see if the inventory contains shoes of that type in their size. Although Bob's office team works hard to print price tags for incoming items, human errors occur and sometimes items show up without price tags. The handheld device enables the customer to scan an item's bar code for pricing if a price tag is not available. This device will also provide a map to help the customer locate items within the store.

Handheld devices can eliminate the customer's wait in long lines. Customers can scan their items and present the device to the cashier at the register. The cashier downloads the information from the handheld device. This step is particularly useful on weekends and holidays when the store is very busy. Bob figures that this feature may eliminate his need to hire extra holiday seasonal help.

After careful consideration, Pro Sports contacts your wireless networking firm to create a design to see if these goals can be met by implementing wireless technology in the store. The results of the wireless implementation in this store might open up additional opportunities throughout the chain. The opportunity for future sales and support makes it clear that your planning must be thorough, your design must be efficient, and your hardware selections must be cost-effective.

# Defining the Scope of the Case Study

This is the first implementation of wireless technology in the individually owned Pro Sports chain, so the current intention for this network is limited to the single store and does not include network access to other stores at this time. However, the results could lead to adding wireless networks to other stores within the chain. The existing computer network is in place and running fine. There is no need to modify the existing computer network other than to integrate the wireless system with the existing network.

Pro Sports is located in a spacious two-story building. Both floors contain merchandise that is organized to attract customers and lead them through the store. The attached warehouse acts as a receiving dock for merchandise. Employees use the warehouse for inventory overflow and office activities, like general company accounting (accounts payable, accounts receivable, and payroll). For convenience, the company offices are located in the warehouse.

The existing wired network consists of an Ethernet local area network (LAN) that connects the registers to the computer system in the company offices. The company offices consist of several desktop computers, three network servers, an Ethernet switch, and a router for wide area network (WAN) and Internet access. The wireless technology that will be implemented includes handheld scanning devices and a wireless card for an existing PC.

We will not address data security in this case study. No confidential data will be transmitted using the handheld devices. The handheld devices have the capability to swipe credit cards for payment, but Bob Tucker has stated that he does not want any credit card transactions transmitted over the wireless network, not wanting to risk the possible interception of personal customer data.

# Reviewing the Current Situation

To make sure that your team understands the situation, Bob outlines his need to add wireless technology to Pro Sports. To recap, he needs to tie the shipping/receiving PC into the existing network and enable instant stocking by the shipping/receiving clerk through the use of a handheld device. The system must provide customers more autonomy by enabling price checks, inventory checks, a virtual shopping cart, an online store directory, and customer assistance paging. These features must be implemented on handheld devices. The intended benefit is to save time and money by making the employees mobile and more responsive.

# Designing and Implementing the Wireless Network

The approach is straightforward—you must determine how to address the customer's needs and make sure they are well defined; the owner and his management team must verify information about the employees and the customers for you. After the approach is determined, you'll begin the planning by defining the network elements and their placement, and gathering details about the physical space and the intended use.

After ample design time, your team will purchase the hardware elements, then implement the design by installing and configuring the hardware elements and making the necessary software changes. During implementation, you'll have to test every aspect of the system, including the range of the handheld devices and the ability to check bar codes on the loading dock. At the end of the implementation phase, you should be able to verify that the results fulfill the needs of Pro Sports.

## Creating the High-Level Design

Your team considers setting three subdomains to make it easier to divide the work and find where to place the access points. They will also make it easier for you to categorize and track progress as you set up the network. These subdomains include the first floor, the warehouse, and the second floor. Two of the subdomains are divided because of the physical boundaries between floors; it is easier to plan the integration of the wireless elements and the existing network elements by floor. The functional boundary of the warehouse naturally makes it a separate subdomain. The warehouse does not need to address any customers; only a few employees work in or around the warehouse.

It is determined that handheld devices will be used in each of the subdomains. Employees and customers will use handheld devices in the first floor and the second floor. Only a few of the employees will use handheld devices in the warehouse. These employees perform specialized tasks, like shipping/receiving or accounting. The team identifies the additional need for a wireless-enabled PC in the shipping/receiving area of the warehouse.

At this point, the owner wants to make an investment of 100 hand-held devices. He feels that the majority of these devices should be available for the customer. He does not want so many that they end up hanging on the wall, but he does not want the customers to have to wait for the use of a handheld device. As a result, Bob chose a number that he felt would be balanced between the two situations. You will have to determine with his help the total number of employees that will use handheld devices and the division of the work force per floor. His responses will help in determining where the access points will be located later on in the design.

# Creating a Detailed Design

Your consulting company invests some time into the planning and design of the wireless network for Pro Sports, addressing the following tasks:

- Obtain a physical map to chart all aspects of the building, including electrical outlets, Ethernet cabling, and existing network elements. Since the new wireless network will have to interface with the existing one, knowing the details of the current network will help you make decisions.

- Talk to the owner about expected user density. How many customers does he expect to have on either of the floors at one time? How does he assign employee activities? What is the maximum number of employees scheduled to work on each floor? The answers to these questions help determine the number of access points required for efficient transmission, as well as where to put the access points.

- Identify any constraints that may limit the design of the wireless network. When you identify constraints early, you have more time to work around the issues. Constraints can be physical, such as no access to electrical outlets. The consumer can also mandate constraints.

- Conduct a walk-through to verify information on the physical map. This helps you account for any deviance from the physical map to the existing structure. A deviance can occur when store improvements are not added to existing documentation. Walk-throughs also provide you with additional information. For example, if there was no access to an electrical outlet but a light fixture was located nearby, you could assume that an electrical connection can be established close to the light fixture.

- Identify any potential radio frequency (RF) interface sources. Any electrical appliances using the 2.4 GHz range can affect the reliability of the wireless network, such as microwaves and 2.4 GHz cordless phones.

- Determine the size of the store and the radius of RF transmission. Apply the facts regarding the size of the store and the expected user density to determine the required range of RF transmission. While planning this radius, make sure you record any overflow coverage.

- Plan the access point locations to take advantage of transmission coverage. Make sure one or two radios are added to the access point as needed for transmission. Extend the radio antennas as needed for coverage.

- Determine Internet Protocol (IP) addresses. You can identify network elements (wired and wireless) by IP addresses. The IP addresses must be unique within the network. The Dynamic Host Configuration Protocol (DHCP) server enables you to set the IP range and monitor use of the addresses.

■ Define the process to integrate the new wireless infrastructure into the existing computer network. Certain capabilities, like IP addressing and tracking are available in the existing network. The new wireless system can rely on the same DHCP server that controls the existing IP range.

All of these points must be addressed as you progress through the network development phases of planning and design.

## Obtaining a Physical Map

The physical map contains information about the placement of the different areas of the store, information about the current wired network, and other physical characteristics, like access to electricity. These particulars provide the physical details used when combining the wireless elements to the wired elements. For example, if there is no access to electricity, a network element cannot be plugged in. An additional physical requirement is that access points must connect to the Ethernet cable of the existing network.

The ten-year old steel-framed Pro Sports building projects a spacious feeling with 20-foot high ceilings. The 18,000 square foot retail store is composed of a 10,000 square foot first story, a 4000 square foot warehouse expansion at the back of the first story, and an 8000 square foot second story. The load-bearing first floor contains four columns that dissect the room. The second floor does not contain any columns. The drop ceilings for each floor allow for four feet between the second-story floor and the first-story ceiling, and the roof and the second-story ceiling. The drop ceilings can provide enough room to accommodate the weight and the space requirements of the access points.

Figure 7.1 illustrates the layout of the departments on the first floor of Pro Sports. The first floor contains various clothing departments, a shoe department, a baseball/soccer department, a golf department, a seasonal department, and a sunglasses department. Generally, the most active of all the first-floor departments is the shoe department, which contains tennis shoes, cleats, boots, and specialty sports shoes for everyone in the family—note that the merchandise planners placed the most active department in the back of the store. The planners implemented this store design to influence customers to buy other items as they walk through the store.

**Figure 7.1** Layout of the First Floor

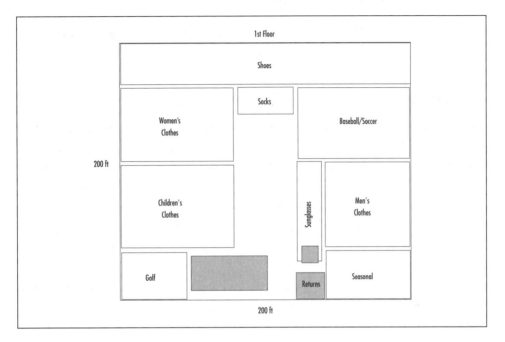

The owner has placed ten checkout registers near the outside doors on the first floor. During the weekdays, up to seven of the ten are available for checkout. On weekends and during holidays, all ten checkout registers are open for business. As a rule, Bob Tucker does not like to see more than two people waiting per checkout line. There is one register at the return counter to enable the employee to process customer requests for exchanges and returns, and to return items to inventory. One register is available in the sunglasses department. All sunglass purchases must be made using this register; this is a physical security implementation due to the ever-increasing prices in the sunglasses department and the portability of the merchandise.

The first floor spans 200 feet by 200 feet. The main entrance to Pro Sports is on the north side of the building. The entrance implements glass panes to let natural light filter into the store. An escalator, which enables customers to move to the second story, divides the store horizontally and vertically. An additional escalator on the reverse side enables customers to go to the first floor to check out at the register. The 40,000 square foot measurement does not include the warehouse on the south side of the first floor; it will be addressed as a separate subdomain.

The warehouse contains a shipping/receiving area for processing items coming into the store and items being shipped from the store. Trucks haul merchandise to the loading dock. The shipping/receiving clerk verifies the receipt of the items and stores them in the warehouse until an employee can stock the merchandise. The warehouse also contains the company office, where the administrators run the store's accounting software and track employee database information. As Figure 7.2 shows, the warehouse also contains the computer closet, which holds most of the existing network equipment.

**Figure 7.2** Layout of the Warehouse

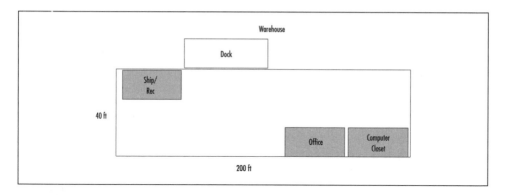

The warehouse extends 40 feet in length parallel to the south side of the first floor. Loading docks extend beyond the warehouse for merchandise that is trucked to the store. Trucks arrive at various times of the day and the shipping/receiving clerk tends to each shipment. Because the warehouse stores merchandise until an employee has time to stock it, much of the warehouse appears to be pallets that are stacked high with boxes.

The second floor contains the largest items sold by the store. Pro Sports sells merchandise for water and snow sports, camping, fishing, and hunting (the department layout is shown in Figure 7.3). The store design includes many demonstration displays on the second floor, from assembled tents to hanging kayaks. Employees carry large purchases downstairs using a freight elevator on the northeast corner of the first and second floors. Many of these departments require salespeople who are very knowledgeable about the subject to be constantly available to customers to answer questions.

**Figure 7.3** Layout of the Second Floor

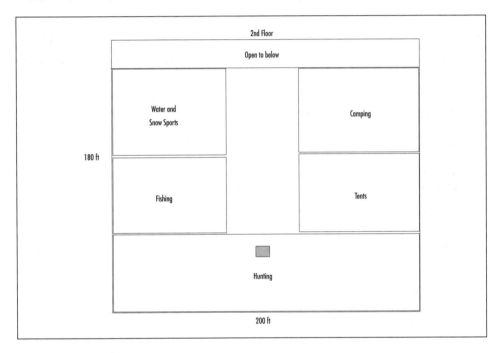

The 180 by 200 square foot second floor is open so that customers can view the last 20 feet of the first story. Future plans include the placement of a children's play area in the first-floor area that can be viewed from the second floor. A floor-to-ceiling fence surrounds this overlook. Electrical outlets exist every 20 feet across the east and west walls. Droplights hang from the ceiling at 20-foot intervals. A single register is available on the south side of the second floor in the hunting department. This register is used to license firearms, process security clearances, and purchase firearms.

Figure 7.4 shows the current wired network for the first floor and the warehouse. This network contains a server farm for the existing LAN. The server farm is located in the computer closet. There is also a router in the closet. As mentioned earlier, the router provides connectivity to the Internet as well as other Pro Sports stores. The computer closet is a basic wiring closet with a DHCP server to handle IP addressing for the store PCs and registers. Other servers in the server farm address the database and processing needs of the existing network. An Ethernet switch, located in the middle of the false ceiling in the first floor, connects the cash registers in the front of the store to the server farm.

**Figure 7.4** Existing Network for the First Floor and Warehouse

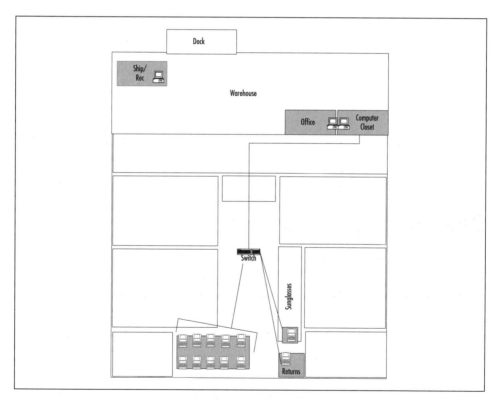

The Ethernet switch is located in the middle of the first-floor false ceiling for a single purpose. It can reach the only register found on the second story. The Ethernet switch registers connections shown in Figure 7.5. The Ethernet switch is connected to the current network via Ethernet. You decide that an access point should be placed in the proximity of the Ethernet switch so that the access point can be connected to the existing network.

**Figure 7.5** Existing Network for the Second Floor

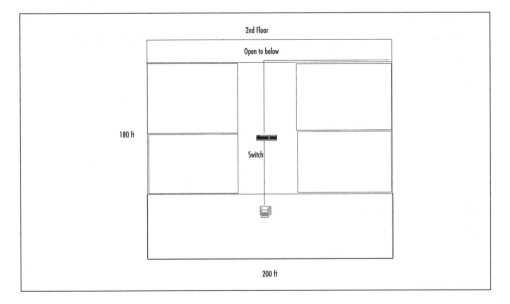

# Determining User Density

Next you need to talk to Bob Tucker about user density; that is, the maximum number of customers and employees that could co-exist on the first floor, second floor, and warehouse subdomain of the store. Bob reviews current employee placement records, takes averages, and applies a slight increase (+ or − 15%) to answer questions about the number of people per subdomain. The user density helps your team determine the number of users that need to be addressed via access points.

Bob explains that he expects to provide one handheld device to every employee in the store. During store hours, management assigns employees to cover static positions in a particular department or dynamic positions within the departments of a floor for employees to roam between departments for additional coverage. These employee positions are shown in Table 7.1.

**Table 7.1** Employee User Density

| Floor | Department | Number |
|-------|-----------|--------|
| First floor | Shoes | 2 |
| | Seasonal | 1 |
| | Men's Outdoor Clothing | 1 |
| | Ladies Apparel | 1 |
| | Children's Apparel | 1 |
| | Sunglasses | 1 |
| | Roaming throughout floor | 3 |
| Warehouse | Shipping | 1 |
| | Office | 1 |
| Second floor | Camping | 1 |
| | Hunting | 1 |
| | Roaming throughout floor | 3 |
| Roaming Management | Store Manager | 1 |
| | Floor Managers | 2 |

Two handheld devices will exist within the warehouse. The shipping/receiving clerk needs a handheld device to check stock into inventory. The office needs a handheld device to track employee time. In addition to employee positions, three managers walk the floors to ensure quality customer service. These managers are not assigned to stay on a particular floor, but may all be on the first floor, the second floor, or dispersed throughout the floors.

# Identifying Constraints

All constraints must be identified to make sure that the plan can be as foolproof as possible. When you identify constraints early in the planning stage, you have more time to work around your findings; also, constraints identified during implementation clearly add to the schedule and scope of the project.

The only physical constraints are that the owner of Pro Sports does not want the access points viewable by his customers. It's a matter of aesthetics, Bob explains. He wants customers to concentrate on merchandise, not network equipment. One of the benefits to wireless technology is that the hardware is low profile and easy to conceal. Knowing this constraint, you propose that the access must be concealed in the false ceiling if at all possible.

## Conducting the Walk-Through

After gathering building facts such as square feet per floor from the physical map, you conduct a walk-through to identify construction materials between ceiling and walls. Walk-throughs identify elements that do not exist on the physical map, such as improvements beyond the original design. They also help to locate additional resources, such as AC availability through light fixtures and other wired elements. This walk-through identifies no issues, as you find the steel construction with wood floorboards and drop ceilings.

## Identifying RF Interface Sources

Your team identifies potential RF interface sources. They check for these sources because certain electrical appliances can provide interference to wireless transmissions in the form of static on the receiver side. They look for cordless 2.4 GHz phones and microwaves. Pro Sports does not use cordless phones, but the break room in the warehouse contains a microwave that runs at 2.4 GHz. You can identify the microwave as a potential risk but you will not know the impact of the interference until the wireless network is tested during implementation.

## Plan the RF Pattern for the Network

After executing the walkthrough, your team plans the RF pattern for the network. You determine the size of the store and radius of antenna transmission. Since the handheld devices will be roaming throughout the three subdomains, you overlap the RF patterns to create accessibility to more radios. Overlapping the RF patterns makes the signal stronger and transition between access points less noticeable.

The proposed design covers a dense population of handheld users in a small area where there are few planes for interference sources. The RF pattern is designed so that any spot in the store is covered by at least three radios, with some areas being covered by five radios. This extra coverage ensures that every user is provided coverage that is transparent as the user roams throughout the building.

You note that with an 802.11b extender antenna with a 100 foot by 100 foot footprint, distance is not an issue, but density may be an issue if employees and customers use the 100 handheld devices at the same time. It is assumed that if the 100 handheld devices are used at once, they will be divided within the floors. So, you design the first floor for a density of 13 employees and 80 shoppers. The density for the second floor can be set at eight employees and 50 shoppers. You count the density for the warehouse to be five employees and managers.

Your team follows the general application rules. Current equipment guidelines state no more than 30 users per radio. You apply the density to the amount of users that one radio can handle. From the outset, with the projected densities per floor, it appears that there will be four access points throughout Pro Sports.

# Planning the Equipment Placement

Before you can determine the placement of the equipment, your team checks for Ethernet connections, electricity availability, and physical access. The access points must connect to the existing network using a RJ-45 wire. An electrical outlet must be available for the access point. Physical access can be an issue if wires cannot be concealed or wire length exceeds CAT5 limitations.

Ethernet connections are available in the center of the drop ceiling for the second floor. This is the location of the existing wired switch. Ethernet connections are also available when strung to the computer closet in the warehouse. The amount of wire needed does not appear to be an extraordinary amount.

Electrical outlets exist on the east and west sides of the building on both floors. Lights hang from the false ceiling on the first floor and the ceiling on the second floor. You arrange to have an electrician install an electrical outlet six feet away from the light in the center of the false ceiling.

The building is steel construction and there are no columns on the second floor. Measurement of the length comes to 20 feet of slack in the computer closet, 20 feet up the wall to the ceiling, and 20 feet up to the second floor. A diagonal to the center of the second-floor ceiling requires 70 feet. This makes a total of 130 feet of cable (this amount of cable is reasonable because it is under the CAT5 cable length limitation of 100 meters).

# Determining Where to Place the Access Points

Handheld devices search for and use the access point with the strongest signal. Therefore it is important that the access points be placed where the signal will optimally cover the area. Since the handheld devices will be roaming throughout the three subdomains, you overlap the access point ranges to create a stronger signal. Overlapping makes the transition between access points invisible to the mobile consumer or employee carrying the handheld device.

Your team decides on the best location for the access points. They take into consideration that the location must be close to the Ethernet switch in the center of the first-floor ceiling. They place the access points in a centralized location because the dimensions of the store are small enough that they do not have to worry about coverage within the building. They will install the equipment in fairly close proximity at the center of the building, to make it easier and more convenient to service the equipment.

To address the second-floor density of 58, one access point will be placed in the center of the ceiling. The access point contains two radios. To span the width of the floor, the antennas for each radio are extended six feet to the east and west of the access point, as shown in Figure 7.6.

The access point diagrams shown in Figures 7.6, 7.7, and 7.8 represent the access point as a diamond, the radios as ovals, and a small antenna tower as an extended radio antenna. The RF patterns for the second-floor overlap, as shown in Figure 7.6. This overlap provides double coverage on the second floor.

**Figure 7.6** Access Points on the Second Floor

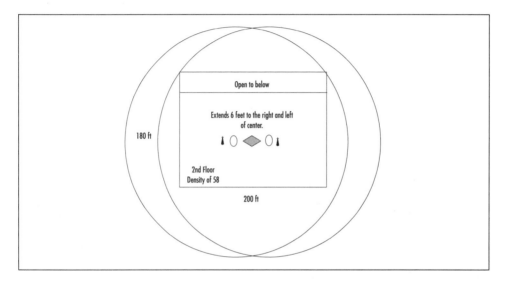

To address the first-floor density of 93, two access points are used. One access point is located three feet west of the center of the false ceiling on the first floor. This access point contains one radio. The second access point is located ten feet diagonally to the northwest (front) corner of the building. This access point contains two radios. To make sure that connection is made evenly throughout the store, the antenna on one of the radios is extended toward the middle of the store. The warehouse needs a single access point located near the computer closet. This access point contains one radio, as shown in Figure 7.7. This access point provides an overflow into the southwest corner of the store.

Note how the RF patterns overlap on the first floor and the warehouse. The overlap ensures that the large amount of handheld users will have adequate coverage. The RF pattern for the warehouse extends outside of the physical building. This pattern allows for coverage at the dock so the shipping/receiving clerk can check merchandise into inventory. It also gives the clerk space so that he can actually go in the trucks while he checks the merchandise.

**Figure 7.7** Access Points on the First Floor and Warehouse

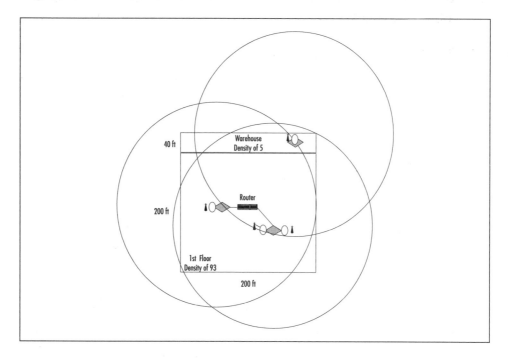

The access points provide plenty of coverage for the predicted user density. Remember that these figures represent only a two-dimensional representation of the pattern—the RF pattern actually covers a three-dimensional range. Coverage for both floors is represented more accurately in Figure 7.8. This figure shows the RF pattern for the first floor overlaid with the RF pattern of the second floor. The RF pattern shows that almost all areas of the store are covered by at least three RF patterns. In fact, most areas in the store are covered by five RF patterns. This extra coverage ensures coverage for the estimated user density.

You have determined a total of four access points and six radios. To recap, you plan one access point and two radios on the second floor, one access point and one radio in the warehouse, and two access points and three radios on the first floor. This plan allows for the future expansion of two radios.

**Figure 7.8** The RF Pattern Overlay for Both Floors

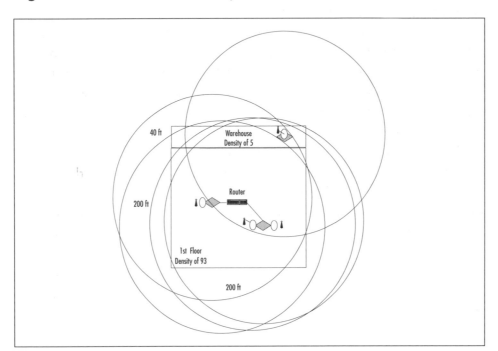

# Determining the RF Channel Optimization

Since the radios in the access points will be very close in proximity to each other, it is very important that they all operate on different 802.11b frequency channels. The 802.11b specification provides 11 different frequency channels. It is also important that the channels that are chosen be as separate as possible from each other. In other words, you cannot set one radio to channel 1 and the next one to channel 2. Most access point vendors recommend a three-channel spacing between useable channels; however in certain cases it is possible to push that limit to a two-channel spacing. A three-channel spacing will allow for three usable channels. Since you have split the RF spaces into three separate subdomains, you will not have a problem with channel overlap.

There are a total of two access points and three radios on the first floor. The access point with a single radio will be configured to operate on channel 3. The other access point will have one radio on channel 7 and the other on channel 11. When your team has determined the operational frequency channels for the first subdomain, they will reuse the same settings for the other subdomains. For the second floor, they will set one radio to channel 3 and the other to channel 7. In the warehouse, they will set the access point to channel 11. If Bob Tucker decides to add additional capacity in the future, the RF channel pattern will most likely need to be modified. Configuring and modifying channel patterns is a simple software change.

With this configuration, a shopper will connect to the radio with the strongest signal. Since the flooring between the first floor and the second floor, as well as the wall between the store and the warehouse, is made of concrete, the radios operating on the same channel will not be a problem (the concrete will absorb most of the RF energy from one subdomain to another, and the stronger access point will always be in the subdomain of the user). If all of the radios were set to operate on the same channel there could very possibly be any number of unexplainable RF problems. It is always a good idea to ensure that access point radios that overlap RF patterns be set to different channels.

## Identifying IP Addresses

The existing wired network has a DHCP server in the server room of the warehouse. Pro Sports currently is using typical Class C IP addresses in a range from 192.168.1.0 to 192.168.1.255. Of these 256 addresses, they currently are using 20. That leaves 236 available to use in the same range.

You plan to use the same address range for the handheld units through DHCP, reserving addresses from 192.168.1.100 to 192.168.1.225 for the full 100 handheld devices. This schema leaves 25 additional IP addresses for future growth.

## Implementing the Wireless Network

The design is in place and your team begins to implement the design. Begin by identifying the hardware required for the installation. In this case, hardware must be provided for the access points, the handheld units, and the wireless card required in the shipping/receiving PC. After the hardware is selected, begin installing the wireless network.

## Selecting the Hardware

As stated, the wireless hardware elements required to connect the wireless aspects of the network to the existing network include access points, handheld devices, and a wireless PC card. You review the hardware elements used in previous commitments against new wireless network element technology, also taking into account pricing and availability.

The first element you select is the access point. You select this element first because the other wireless components must be compatible to it. The access point acts as a wireless hub, receiving and transmitting information over a radio frequency of 2.4 GHz. Requirements for the access point include 802.11b compliance and a throughput of up to 11 Mbps. After weighing many of the available access points, you select the Agere Orinoco AP-1000 access point, because it is expandable. The AP-1000 provides two radio slots. Multiple radio slots enable you to load balance access points when they are heavily used. Each of the radios can operate on a different frequency channel. Also, if only one radio is used, the network becomes scalable. This access point is easy to configure using Windows-compatible software and provides an integrated Ethernet interface. The AP-1000 can perform many functions, serving as a router, bridge, or DHCP server.

The compatible Agere Orinoco PC Memory Card International Association (PCMCIA) cards serve as the radios in the AP-1000 access point. Besides the six radios that are chosen for the access points, you purchase one hundred more to go in the handheld devices.

An Orinoco Range Extender antenna is purchased for each radio attached to an access point. The Range Extender is compatible with the AP-1000 and the Peripheral Component Interconnect (PCI) cards, and is a 5-dBi indoor omnidirectional antenna. These antennas can boost coverage up to 50 percent, based on the physical environment.

The manufacturer recommends that at least one of the two PC cards should be equipped with a range extender to create a distance of at least one meter between the antennas of the two PC cards. You decide that all of the radios should have the Range Extender. Orinoco also recommends that you set each of the two PC cards to a different frequency channel and to optimize capacity and minimize channel crossover, and suggests that you separate the two channels as far as possible. The shipping/receiving PC requires an Orinoco PCI/MCA (microchannel architecture) card to interface with the wireless and existing networks. These cards are designed to interface with the AP-1000. The card fits in the PC casing and boasts sufficient range and stability, and will transmit data over a radio frequency of 2.4 GHz.

Since the shipping/receiving PC runs stand-alone applications, the application must be integrated with the standard networked PCs used in the office. You evaluate the changes (and your software consultants join the process) and revamp the networked software with the shipping/receiving application.

Price checks and inventory control require a means for efficient scanning. You review a number of handheld devices that have 802.11b LAN access with scanning capabilities. It is important to note that these are two very different functions. 802.11b allows access to the existing LAN and is the Institute of Electrical and Electronics Engineers (IEEE) standard for wireless. These scanning devices must interface with existing peripherals, including the registers. Because employees must carry a handheld device throughout their shift, the device must be lightweight. It must also have a large viewing screen for ease of use by the customer and employee. Bob Tucker has also asked that the cost of the handheld devices be within an estimated cost range. Handheld devices that did not meet these needs were not considered.

The SPT1700 model from Symbol Technologies met all the requirements, including the scanning capability and 802.11b; it is lightweight and easy to use. The devices implement a Web browser interface for accessing the in-store network. A great feature of the SPT 1700 is that the IP address is stored in the handheld device. Perhaps the most important aspect, however, is the cost—it fits the projected budget supplied in the consultant's equipment proposal.

When the owner of Pro Sports is presented with the pricing scheme for this model, he asks about security of the handheld devices. You assure him that tags are embedded into the devices and that the outside doors scan for these tags just like the ink tags placed on large ticket inventory items within the store.

# Installing the Wireless Components

At this point in the process, you and your team must install the wireless network elements that were chosen. The installation includes adding the PC card and testing its functionality, setting up the access points, configuring the access points, setting up the IP address range, and testing the handheld devices. Testing, performed after each step of the implementation, ensures proper communication with the existing network.

Create an installation checklist and verify the steps on the list. The checklist contains the following high-level actions, which are described in detail in the following sections.

- Set up the IP information
- Install the access points
- Install the AP Manager software
- Test the wireless network
- Review the client's objectives

## Setting Up IP Information

As the first step in the implementation, set up the IP addresses by adding the media access control (MAC) addresses of the access points to the IP configuration table in the existing DHCP server, which is located in the server closet on the first floor. Reserve the IP address range of 192.168.1.100 to 192.168.1.225 for the 100 handheld devices.

## Installing the Access Points

After the IP information is provided, mount the access points as shown previously in Figure 7.6 (second floor) and Figure 7.7 (first floor and warehouse). The following list summarizes the placement of the access points and the placement of radios (PC cards):

- **Warehouse** This subdomain contains one access point located in the ceiling above the computer closet. Mount this access point four feet from the southwest corner of the warehouse. Insert one PC card into this access point.

- **First Floor** This subdomain contains two access points. Mount the first access point in the drop ceiling four feet west of the center of the room. Insert one PC card in this access point. Mount the second access point in the drop ceiling, ten feet from the center of the room diagonally across to the southeast corner. Insert two PC cards and extend the antenna three feet towards the center of the ceiling.

- **Second Floor** This subdomain contains one access point, mounted in the center of the drop ceiling. Insert two PC cards and extend antennas from both cards six feet east and west to the outer walls.

Your team performs the following steps for each of these access points:

1. Mount the power supply in the desired location.

2. Mount the processor module.

3. Connect the network interfaces by inserting the PC cards into the processor module.

4. Connect the Ethernet cable to the 10/100 Base-T Ethernet interface on the access point.

5. Mount the cover plate.

6. Power up the unit.

7. Verify that the LCD lights show the availability of the unit.

# Install the AP Manager Software

After the access points are installed, install the AP Manager software on a Windows NT server in the server closet. This server has a 486 processor with 32 MB of RAM and two gigabytes of hard disk space. The consultants compare the specifications of this PC with the required specifications to make sure that they can run the AP Manager software on the PC.

This software establishes the connection of the AP-1000s. Since there are multiple AP-1000s, the consultants configure the other AP-1000s to match the values for the first access point. Make the following setting changes for each access point:

1. Set the PC card settings to "Access Point."

2. Set the network name to the name of the existing network.

3. Verify the IP addresses the consultants provided to the DHCP server that were automatically assigned.

4. Continue steps 1 through 3 to configure each access point.

# Installing the PC Card in Shipping/Receiving

Add a Lucent PCI-to-PCMCIA card to the shipping/receiving PC to enable communication to the network. To test this card, you deploy a handheld device. When the hardware is deployed you make minor changes to the shipping/receiving software so that the scan directly feeds to the wired accounting system. Test this functionality and make adjustments as needed.

# Testing the Wireless Network

After the configuration is performed, test the links to make sure they are active on the network. At this point the links test correctly. However, in the middle of the testing process, your team learns that Bob Tucker just received funding for an extension to the warehouse. Bob provides you with the physical layout of the extension and it appears as if the wireless design will cover the extension without a problem.

Just before you install the access point in the warehouse, you talk to the heating and air conditioning contractor who will work on the warehouse extension. When your team had performed the walk-through, you made sure there were no potential interference or physical placement issues with the ventilation system. However, the contractor explains that the ventilation duct close to the hub will now need to be split to flow properly into the extension. Rather than install the access point now and move it in a few months, you move the warehouse access point ten feet to the west.

During the RF pattern discovery, another microwave was found. After the network is installed, you run the microwave at various power levels while using handheld devices. The test proves that the microwave does not interfere with network communications.

You and your team thoroughly test the handheld devices using the wireless access points to ensure connectivity. You test the devices in major area of the store as well as areas with less regular traffic. The devices prove to be functional and responsive in testing. Access is also addressed, and you restrict access accordingly based on IP addresses.

## Reviewing the Client's Objectives

After thoroughly testing the wireless portion of the network and testing the interaction between the wired and wireless aspects of the network, you can take the owner of the store on a tour. You show Bob Tucker how the shipping/receiving clerk can enter inventory at the dock. As you do this, a truck rolls up to the dock. You follow the clerk into the truck and watch as the clerk records the merchandise. At the shipping/receiving desk, the merchandise information is downloaded to the wireless PC, which in turn adds the information to the store database and accounting system.

On the first floor, you show Bob how to use the employee handheld devices to scan items for pricing and inventory. He takes a consumer handheld device, goes to the shoe department, and looks up the price and inventory for several types of shoes. He takes both handheld devices to the second floor and performs price checks; he successfully pages an employee for the hunting department; the store map also works. He takes the employee's handset and scans items for a customer. When that information is successfully downloaded to a register, Bob is satisfied that all his objectives were met.

# Lessons Learned

After the job is finished, your team meets to perform a *post mortem* of the installation. In this meeting, you can identify major lessons to apply to future jobs. The most important lesson is to adequately evaluate software development. The accounting software was proprietary software. It required changes from the software vendor, the Accounting/Informational Technology expert, and your team of software developers. It was obvious that you should have included the software team much sooner in the design process.

The warehouse extension was not planned at the outset of the wireless network planning stage. The owner did not get funding until the wireless network was in the implementation stage, but you had not known the changes were even imminent, so the possible ductwork changes had not been factored in when you had evaluated impacts in the ceiling. Fortunately, you found out about the changes in time to move the access point in the warehouse before the work on the ventilation ducts began.

# Summary

To summarize, combining wireless technology with an existing wired network empowers industry owners, managers, employees, and customers with scalability, flexibility, and mobility. In this case study, the owner of a retail store called Pro Sports defines the updates he wants to provide his employees and customers. He is able to tie his shipping/receiving PC into the existing network and enables instant stocking. The system gives customers the ability to check prices, inventory, stock a virtual shopping cart, and find items using the online store directory. The same mobility is provided for customers as it is for the employees. By checking prices, inventory, and store maps, customers can be more self-reliant and more efficient.

The owner successfully assessed the opportunities that wireless technology could provide to his store. By taking time to develop his goals, he was able to present you, the consultant, with a vivid picture of the expected results. This eliminated what is sometimes the hardest part of a project—getting the client to provide a set of goals. Although it is tough getting this information, it's the only way to measure whether the job is completed satisfactorily.

Your team walks through the planning stages quite efficiently, obtaining the background information, including the physical map, talking to the client about the expected user density, and recording any constraints. They perform a thorough walk-through of the building to look at building materials, access in the ceiling, and the current network elements. Potential radio frequency (RF) interface sources are found to be negligible. The team determines the location of the access points and tracks the RF patterns to make sure that adequate coverage is provided. IP ranges are established.

When the planning stage is complete, implementation begins with a selection of hardware. Most of the equipment is manufactured by the same company (in this case, Orinoco) to ensure compatibility. After the hardware is purchased, it is installed and configured, and you test the component functionality and review all new features and functionality with the client.

The resulting network proved to meet all of the client's requirements. It has added extensibility. When there is a need for more handheld devices for customers or employees, the owner can purchase more of the SPT1700 devices and PCI cards. When the serial numbers for the new hardware are configured in the access point software, the devices are ready to use.

# Solutions Fast Track

## Introducing the Industrial Case Study

☑ Wireless technology addresses the emerging mobility needs in the industrial setting. Recent coupling of 802.11b technology with handheld devices promotes widespread uses, from mobile inventory to network administration, to increase employee productivity and customer service.

☑ In the case study, the store owner wants to make his existing wired network more efficient and address customer needs. Handheld devices must be implemented to provide mobility.

☑ By streamlining the network, the store owner provides employees and customers easy access to store data, such as pricing and inventory.

## Designing and Implementing the Wireless Network

☑ The network consultants approach the design by categorizing the physical store into three subdomains: the first floor, the warehouse, and the second floor.

☑ The consultants obtained a physical map and reviewed the existing network.

☑ The store owner provided estimates of the maximum number of customers and employees on each subdomain.

☑ The store owner also provided the constraint that all network elements must be hidden for aesthetics.

☑ Planning for the RF patterns took place. The consultants planned the placement of the network elements. IP addresses were established.

## Planning the Equipment Placement

☑ The following hardware was selected: the Orinoco AP-1000 access point, the Orinoco PCI card, the Orinoco Range Extender, the Orinoco PCI/MCA card, and the SPT1700 handheld device.

☑ The consultants set up the IP addresses, installed the access points, and installed the related software. They installed the radios in the access points and handheld devices and installed the PCI/MCA card in the shipping/receiving PC. All of the hardware and software underwent testing to ensure functionality.

## Lessons Learned

☑ You learned how a consulting company can apply the design principles described in previous chapters.

☑ The planning phase contains the details you must be aware of when implementing a similar type of wireless network.

☑ The implementation section of this chapter walks you through the process of integrating the existing wired network with the proposed wireless network.

☑ The most important lesson is to adequately evaluate software development.

# Frequently Asked Questions

The following Frequently Asked Questions, answered by the authors of this book, are designed to both measure your understanding of the concepts presented in this chapter and to assist you with real-life implementation of these concepts. To have your questions about this chapter answered by the author, browse to **www.syngress.com/solutions** and click on the **"Ask the Author"** form.

**Q:** What are my choices in alternative handheld devices for a retail application?

**A:** There are many handheld devices on the market. Any industrial handheld device that is capable of scanning and is 802.11b compatible would work—the greater decision is in the pricing of the device.

**Q:** How can I make sure that the handheld devices do not leave the store?

**A:** There are various ways to add security to the physical device itself. One method is to implant a chip inside the device. Alternatively, you could add a magnetic bar code on the bottom of the cover. Either of these methods requires you to add the code information to a sensing mechanism at the exit, which will activate an alarm when the handheld device nears the door. Similar security is often used in retail stores that attach sensor tags to merchandise.

**Q:** Can wireless technology actually save you money?

**A:** The flexibility of a wireless network can save you money. This flexibility enables you to quickly add networked devices and peripherals, temporary networks, or make changes within the company. When your needs change, modification costs are low. You save a tremendous amount of money by not paying utility companies for leased lines, construction workers for trenches and holes, or linesman to string cable. With wireless, you do not have to worry if a cable is cut or goes bad. Wireless technology is so flexible that you can quickly and easily network hard-to-reach areas like a connection between buildings.

You can count other savings in personnel. The network is efficient, extensible, and static. There is less need for senior IT personnel. The software (in the case study, the AP Manager tool) often runs on Windows 98, Windows 2000, or Windows NT. As compared to network administration in fixed network elements, wireless software is explanatory and user-friendly. For example, you do not need an IT manager to set up the security for accounts. Security management is more manageable because of the application of per-user, per-session keys. These keys make it easy to create and maintain security.

**Q:** How can the Pro Sports store in the case study increase the number of supported units?

**A:** The design has made the wireless network extensible. Using the current access points, you can add an additional radio to the warehouse access point. You can add another radio to one of the first-floor access points. These additions will add two more overlays of RF patterns. Since each radio can cover 50 units, you could add up to 100 more handheld devices or wireless PCs. These points assume that you are not going to buy additional hardware. You can also connect additional AP-1000 access points to the network to extend it further.

**Q:** What additional wireless technologies and improvements could be applied to the retail market?

**A:** Traditionally static products like printers, weight scales, and time clocks can be integrated with new technology. Symbol Technologies is a leader in this industry. Specialty products like IP video cameras also adapt well to wireless implementation. Other improvements benefit retail management. For example, consider that a store manager can access sales reports, current transactions, inventory, and employee scheduling from anywhere in the store. This effort brings new meaning to the management style "management by walking around."

# Chapter 8

# Designing a Wireless Campus Network: University Case Study

## Solutions in this chapter:

- Introducing the Campus Case Study

- Designing the Wireless Campus Network

- Implementing the Wireless Campus Network

- Lessons Learned

☑ Summary

☑ Solutions Fast Track

☑ Frequently Asked Questions

269

# Introduction

This chapter will take you through the detailed steps in designing a wireless *campus network*. The steps in this chapter are paramount to the success of any wireless design and implementation project. This chapter will describe the basic characteristics of a campus network, and what we use to define a campus architecture. After reading this chapter, you should have enough information to determine if the project you are working on fits into the campus model. We will also uncover the potential pitfalls in designing and implementing a wireless network and the capabilities available to overcome those issues. In general, our use of the term *campus* refers to a university, hospital, or company that resides in an area such that all the buildings in that area belong to the organization; the hospital case study in Chapter 6 focused on the particular needs of a medical facility in avoiding problems with interference. A typical requirement of campus networks is the increased mobility or an "always connected" capability for the individuals present at that campus. Note also that although we use the term campus in the subsections, these principles pertain to all wireless network designs in varying degrees.

## Applying Wireless Technology in a Campus Network

There are numerous benefits to using a wireless campus network over a traditional wireline network in this type of environment. Benefits include cost savings: no labor cost for digging trenches and limited time stringing cable. With wireless technology, you can rapidly deploy a new architecture. From a maintenance standpoint, a wireless network enables you to create a more dynamic and cost efficient architecture to support the rapid changes and flexible management demanded of a campus. Wireless technologies are evolving at a much higher rate than traditional wireline technologies. With new technology at your fingertips, you have the ability to upgrade a wireless architecture quickly to meet the organization's growing demands as they occur.

# Introducing the Campus Case Study

This case study of a fictional university shows the detailed process of a design project. It will provide a taste of the requirements development process to empower you with the skills necessary to conduct a similar undertaking, and presents a structured approach to implement the design methodologies laid out in earlier chapters.

# Assessing the Opportunity

Faber University has recently been experiencing a decreasing level of enrollment. Faber was built in the early 1900s, and until ten years ago, was known as one of the finest centers for higher education on the eastern seaboard. In the last ten years, however, enrollment seemed to plateau and then slowly decline. Faber's Chancellor Jennings has hired a polling agency and also formed an action committee composed of faculty, students, and administration to determine the causes of the university's decline in enrollment.

The polling agency surveys the graduating seniors and reports that the emerging needs of students are not being met. The new generation of student that the university wants to attract is the technically elite who are known as early technology acceptors. Faber's rich history and, consequently, its old network architecture and lack of technical infrastructure, are its downfall in this new, technological environment.

The action committee finds that various departments in the university lack advanced technological capability. The internal committee also links this lack to the decline in the student's perception of the quality of education provided to the student body. The internal committee decides that they must undergo a massive funding exercise to upgrade Faber's technological capabilities as well as reconstruct the university's technological image. Since this image is a major attractant to new enrollments, the decision is to go after funding as soon as possible.

Once the funding is secured, the university must develop a strategy to allocate the newly found wealth to bolster their technology. Chancellor Jennings creates a committee called the Concerned

Emergent Network Technology Staff, known as CENTS. The CENTS committee is composed of prominent members of the university's departments: the Administration department, the Athletic department, the Engineering department, the Biological Sciences department, the Liberal Arts department, and the Student Union. This committee is formed to develop a list of functional requirements for each organization and the university as a whole. The university will save expensive consulting fees by utilizing their own Engineering department—the Engineering department will refine the requirements into detailed design requirements, create subsequent implementation plans, and implement new network architecture to facilitate the university's needs. The following sections in this case study describe the gathering of these network requirements.

As previously stated, the functional requirements will be formulated by the functional elements of the university. A working group within the Engineering department will derive a set of general assumptions and general constraints and combine those with the functional requirements to develop a set of detailed design requirements. Once all the requirements are developed, reviewed, and approved, the Engineering department work group (known as the *Tiger Team*) will develop an implementation plan. The implementation plan will consist of both physical and logical deployment plans.

After the new architecture has been successfully deployed, the Tiger Team will develop a set of "Lessons Learned" results, based on experiences documented throughout the whole process. The results of the Lessons Learned will be integrated into the design methodologies used by the Engineering department.

# Defining the Scope of the Case Study

This case study addresses the administrative, athletic, and academic areas of the campus. At this time, only three academic areas are addressed. The planned network must be easy to adapt as these areas of study increase or change. For example, the Math and Computer Sciences department may break from the Engineering department to become its own department.

The network structure must be flexible to assist the changing priorities of the university.

# Designing the Wireless Campus Network

As you read in Chapter 5, there are many steps to the design process. This case study shows the university groups determining the functional requirements as the first design step. After these needs and desires are recorded, the design team identifies the constraints and assumptions. Then, they begin the detailed design by planning the equipment placement for each department and user group. After the detailed design is finished, the design team implements the physical and logical aspects of the wireless network.

## The Design Approach

The Tiger Team's approach to revising the existing design is first to work with the CENTS committee to determine what they want out of the new network architecture. The final determination from this committee will become the functional requirements. The Tiger Team will sift and refine these requirements by conducting a walk-through, obtaining a physical map, determining user density, identifying constraints, identifying radio frequency (RF) interface sources, and then creating a detailed design plan. After the design is created and traced to make sure the design addressed all of the objectives of the CENTS committee, the Tiger Team will become the Program Managers and Lead Designers for the implementation crew.

## Determining the Functional Design Requirements

The CENTS committee brainstorms and formulates lists of what each organization requires of this new architecture. The functional requirements that each organization presents must support existing capabilities as well as new desired capabilities. A common practice in determining the existing capabilities required is first to identify the different functional groups within each organization. For example, the academic organizations have functional groupings of staff and students. The Athletic department may have functional groups of coaches, players, and the press. The Administrative department may designate a Financial functional group, as well as Student Records and Management functional groups.

Once the subgroups within the organizations are identified, the current requirements can be determined by going through a "day in the life" scenario with each subgroup. In a nutshell, this means that you will step through the day-to-day job requirements that the subgroup performs to determine what it is that they do and the support they need. The desired requirements can be determined by individual interviews or surveys within each of these subgroups. These surveys must convey the university's desire to improve their environment both from a job satisfaction standpoint as well as an efficiency standpoint.

Each respective group presents its functional requirements based on this methodology. The functional requirements are listed categorically and numerically later, to exemplify the formal process of developing and presenting these requirements in a clear and universally complete format. This also provides a way to trace requested requirements to the engineer's design.

## Tracking the Administration Needs

The Administration department serves three very distinct purposes: accounting, enrollment, and marketing. In the accounting area, clerks perform the day-to-day income and expense record keeping and budgeting. Student records are maintained in the enrollment area. The marketing area, responsible for recruiting, sees great opportunity in the new network architecture. They plan on creating a Web site advertising the new technologies to inform and entice new students. All in all, the Administration department requires the following capabilities:

- High-speed network availability on every floor of the administration building to support the high data rate requirements of administration's existing staff

- High-speed connectivity *between* floors to support the current exchange of information between functional elements within Administration

- High-speed connectivity between the floors and the *database* and *servers* to support current access to these assets

- Broadband access to the Internet for online enrollment to provide a desirable and enticing marketing tool to promote the new image and capabilities that Faber University desires

## Tracking the Athletic Needs

The business-related activities of the Athletic department take place in the Field House. These activities include purchasing gear, tracking statistics, and evaluating possible recruits. Using the new network architecture, the Head Coach plans to create an Intranet Web site where his employees can interactively track statistics and game plans. During practices and game time, the coaches need the ability to communicate with each other and with the athletic teams. To accomplish these goals, the Athletic department requires the following capabilities:

- Connectivity to the Internet at the stadium and field house to track players' statistics on the Athletic department Web pages and to provide access to recruiting information for the coaches.

- Wireless mobile connectivity at the stadium and field house for press connectivity to the Internet for online filing of articles. This will provide a desired capability to the press and hopefully will attract more coverage of Faber athletic events.

- Wireless mobile data communications at the stadium for data communications between staff on the field and the coaching staff in the scouting booth. This capability will replace existing wireline technologies and will be used to showcase Faber's advancement as a leading edge technological institution.

- The administrative staff, located in the stadium, requires high-speed connectivity to the University Administration building for transfer of financial data. This requirement addresses the transfer of information relating to items such as ticket sales and expenses resulting from athletic events.

# Tracking the Academic Department Needs

The Engineering, Biological Sciences, and Liberal Arts departments have very similar needs. The instructors need the ability to access every classroom and office within their department. A myriad of research opportunities would be available to them if they had broadband access to the Internet. Each department needs to be able to connect to the administration building to update student records with grades. These departments require the following capabilities:

- High-speed mobile connectivity on all floors of the department building for virtual access of instructors in every classroom and office. This is a desired capability that will provide the engineering staff with mobility throughout each department in an "always connected" environment.

- Broadband access to the Internet for educational collaboration with other universities and research projects. This requirement supports access to research material throughout the academic community.

- Separate administrative connectivity to administration building for records and enrollment purposes. This requirement supports the transfer of student records information such as grades and course completion.

In addition, the Engineering department will provide the connectivity for the Liberal Arts and Biological Sciences buildings. This capability puts the Engineering department at the core of the academic connectivity within Faber. This action places the responsibility for these connections with the Engineering department and provides a working environment to teach the technologies to the engineering students.

## Tracking Student Union Needs

The Student Union wants to provide network capability to employees and students within the building. The Student Union requires separate high-speed mobile connectivity on all floors for staff offices. This is a current capability that will support the transfer of data between functional groups within the Student Union.

## Tracking Student Needs

The students want to be online and remain online as they travel within their dorms, at the Student Union, and within the floors of the academic departments. The students require the following capabilities:

- Broadband access to Internet and student access from the dorms for research and e-commerce

- Separate high-speed mobile connectivity on all floors of all academic departments for students

- High-speed mobile connectivity on all floors of the dorms

- High-speed connectivity between dorms and Union building

# Constraints and Assumptions

All network architecture designs begin with a set of assumptions. It is important to document these assumptions so that others involved with the project can see the logic that was used when the design was developed. Some assumptions may seem obvious to you at the time, but less experienced or new engineers assigned to the project may not understand the driving influences or the technologies available to you at the time of the development.

Assumptions can also provide shortcuts in the design. For example, if there is an assumption that multiple functional organizations want the same requirement, you can provide a homogeneous design that can be applied to those organizations. If this type of assumption is not made, you must provide a detailed design for each of those functional organizations.

Assumptions also clarify the meaning of commonly used terms so that all parties have a clear understanding of what those terms actually refer to. An example of this would be the term *broadband* or *wireless*. A good procedure to use in developing your assumptions is first to list the common terms that require specific understanding and define the assumptions associated with them. Next, list the common sense assumptions such as privacy requirements on student records, if they were not specifically listed under functional requirements.

To ensure the success of any design, the design team must perform a level of due diligence in determining any "showstoppers" that may occur during implementation. These are listed as constraints and should be properly documented for an accountability tool to justify the technologies selected. In other words, this list of constraints gives a historical reference as to why a certain technology was selected. Constraints fall into two categories, *functional* and *physical*. Functional constraints include logical items such as limited IP addressing space, or lack of licenses for spectrum use. Physical constraints include building conditions and materials, distance between buildings, obstructions, and interference sources. You can identify physical constraints during walk-throughs, spectrum testing, and inspection of site and building maps. A good starting point for determining constraints is to list the possible technologies being considered and then list the operating requirements of those technologies. You should have the list of requirements with you during your inspections and identify any specific showstoppers for a particular technology. For example, large obstructions between buildings will constrain the use of line-of-sight technologies to create links between those buildings. Sheer distance between buildings may constrain certain technologies as well.

The Tiger Team, tasked with building the new communications infrastructure, runs across several hurdles or technology eliminators during the discovery phase of the project. They will have to make some assumptions to proceed in certain areas of the detailed design. The next section provides both general constraints and general assumptions that were encountered and formulated during the discovery phase.

## Identifying the Assumptions

The Tiger Team begins documenting their assumptions. At the top of this assumption document is a list of how they define terms used in their design. These definitions, shown in Table 8.1, help focus the requirements set by the CENTS committee.

**Table 8.1** Terminology and Definitions

| Terminology | Assumption |
|---|---|
| High speed | With respect to individual local area network (LAN) connectivity, this refers to speeds exceeding 10Mbps. With respect to LAN-to-LAN or Floor-to-Floor connectivity, this refers to speeds of at least 100 Mbps. |
| Broadband access | This refers to access speeds of at least 1.5 Mbps or more. |

The Tiger Team further assesses the situation by reviewing the physical aspects of the communication area, using physical maps and wiring maps. Wiring maps help them assess the current physical capabilities (power and air conditioning). They assess usage and security, and define domains and equipment. As a result of this assessment, they document a list of general assumptions. In an effort to ensure the satisfaction of the committee with the proposed design, the following general assumptions are reviewed and approved by the CENTS committee before the Tiger Team proceeds through the design phase:

- **Current Use** Determining current usage patterns are not required for design since all current network capacity will be upgraded with current technology.
- **Physical Framework** Required power and cooling is available in each building's wiring closets due to a recent upgrade in those areas.

- **Timeframe** All departments of the university require this upgrade to be performed in the Summer Session to limit disruption. This translates to an accelerated implementation schedule and will direct the design towards technologies that can be deployed quickly.

- **Security** Higher security levels are required on staff, administration, and e-commerce networks, and these networks will remain separated from public networks such as the student and press networks.

- **IP** The network will use the Internet Protocol (IP). Allocation of IP addressing will be dynamic based on the location of the addressable device and a login/authentication procedure. After a detailed analysis, the Tiger Team determines that not more than 250 students would be present at any one time in any of the academic buildings. Therefore, it is assumed that a standard Class C IP subnet supporting 256 addresses (254 usable) per building is sufficient for the student network.

- **Equipment** Students are to be issued and sold necessary equipment (laptops and wireless access cards) through enrollment and the Student Union. The Engineering department sees this effort as an opportunity to expose engineering students to new technologies.

- **Stability** Any leading-edge technologies selected with higher risk of data loss will be used only on noncritical networks.

- **Domains** Each individual floor of the buildings serves a functional purpose for that organization. Therefore, each individual floor will be treated as a separate logical domain or subnetwork for IP addressing purposes. This is true only for administrative and staff networks. Student connectivity will be treated as a single domain or subnetwork for each building. In other words, floors with student access will be bridged (not routed) together to create one logical network domain for that building.

- **Network Type** Wireless technologies will be used for horizontal applications (LANs on floors and links between buildings) and wireline technologies will be used for vertical applications (connections between floors).

## Identifying the Constraints

The Tiger Team documents the general constraints they encounter while analyzing the technologies and the physical environment of Faber University. These constraints are listed next, categorized under cabling, cost, interference, physical interference, and Internet access. These constraints must be reviewed and acknowledged by the CENTS committee before the Tiger Team may develop the detailed designs.

- **Cabling Issues** Existing cabling systems cannot be used with the new technologies and bandwidth requirements, since the existing cables are based on the old coaxial Ethernet technologies. Trenching new cables between buildings is not practical because of cost and regulatory issues with city streets and the local telephone company. Due to the historic nature of Faber's buildings (asbestos health issues), the Tiger Team will run all interfloor cables through existing elevator shafts. Existing wiring closets located next to these elevator shafts will be used to house equipment such as routers, switches, and access points.

- **Cost Issues** The licensing of spectrum for point-to-point links is prohibitive in both time and cost.

- **Interference Issues** The interference in the 2.4 GHz spectrum is unacceptable due to a large number of cordless phones in the area. (802.11b and Bluetooth are not acceptable technologies in this environment). However, the 5 GHz spectrum is clean in this area, allowing the use of 802.11a technology.

- **Internet Access** There are two demarcation points for Internet access at Faber. One demarcation point is in the Student Union and the other is in the Administration building. Each point has 45 Mbps (DS3) access. The Student Union access is meant for e-commerce and student access to the Internet. The Administration access is meant for educational collaboration and online enrollment.

- **Physical Interference Issues** Since Faber is an older university, it has a large amount of tall foliage and most buildings consist of three floors or less. The height of the buildings presents a problem with absorption since many trees are located in the fresnel zone of any rooftop point-to-point link with line-of-sight requirements. Additionally, adjacent Faber Lake might create multipath problems for any line-of-sight technology links in its vicinity.

Figure 8.1 shows a map of the Faber campus. The Tiger Team used this map to determine the physical restraints. Topographical information, such as the location of trees and lakes, supports the constraints just noted. Maps provided later in this case study do not show this level of physical detail; instead, they are designed to allow more clarity in the depiction of the proposed infrastructure.

**Figure 8.1** Faber Campus Map

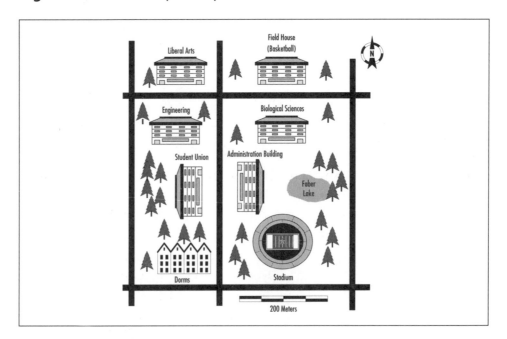

# Planning the Equipment Placement: Detailed Design Requirements

The Tiger Team meets with the CENTS committee and clears up any questions with the original functional requirements. In addition, the Tiger Team presents and receives approval on all the assumptions and constraints previously identified from the committee's review board. They are granted authority by Chancellor Jennings to proceed with the detailed design of the architecture and can now begin the process of defining the detailed design requirements to implement the approved functional requirements.

The Tiger Team is addressing the functional requirements sequentially from the bottom up for both the physical and logical components of the design. Basically, they design the wireless networks at the building's floor-level LAN first. Once all of those have been defined, they can determine the relative bandwidth requirements between floors and apply the appropriate technologies to those connections accordingly. Once the individual building networks are defined, the Tiger Team can determine the relative bandwidth and reliability requirements for links between buildings and create a design using technologies that support those requirements. At each level, the number of IP addresses required and allocation methods are defined. This process creates a logical evolution of the design and reduces the amount of reworks of the architecture. The detailed design requirements developed in this section provide the guidelines for the implementation plan.

## Providing Detailed Administration Requirements

The Administration department requires high-speed network availability on every floor of the administration building. In response to this functional requirement, 802.11a wireless technology will be used to provide LAN connectivity to each individual floor of the Administration building. This will provide a mobile communication environment for administrative staff on their respective floors. This method does not affect the movement of employees between offices on that floor because of the individual's network settings.

Wireless LANs will connect to the building's backbone via Fast Ethernet (100 Base T) to routers located in central wiring closets on that floor. The size and functionality of each group within the Administration building warrants the use of a separate IP subnet for each group. Routers will provide the necessary service between the various groups that are delineated by the floor on which they are located. Fast Ethernet provides the additional bandwidth required to connect the various floors and does it in a cost-efficient manner. A wireline technology is selected to reduce the complexity of channel allocation between domains of the wireless LANs on the individual floors.

Since the Administration department also requires high-speed connectivity *between* floors, Fast Ethernet will be provided as the transport technology between floors. This defines the physical technology that will be used for this connectivity. Access between floors will be *daisy-chained* or hopped from floor to floor. This defines the logical topology used to connect the floors. By daisy-chaining the access, the Tiger Team will sequentially connect routers on each floor. This means that a data packet that needs to get from the subnet on the third floor to the subnet on the first floor actually passes through the router on the third floor, through the router on the second floor, and finally to the router on the first floor.

The Administration department additionally requires high-speed connectivity between the floors, the database, and the servers. Access from each floor to the router on the database and server floor will be provided with a dedicated Fast Ethernet line from each floor. Since the bandwidth requirements to these servers are higher due to large file transfers, dedicated wire line connections are provided from the individual routers to the router servicing the database and servers. Access from the database and servers to the router will be via Gigabit Ethernet. The combination of the 100 Mbps Fast Ethernet lines on each floor create a requirement to provide a connection between the router and the servers that would support the aggregated bandwidth of those connections. Gigabit Ethernet will provide the necessary bandwidth required to support that requirement.

Finally, the Administration requires broadband access to the Internet for online enrollment. The administration networks will have access to the Internet via the DS3 (45 Mbps) connection provided at the ground floor demarcation point in the building. This requirement provides the connectivity to the existing Administrative connection. Administrative access to the Internet will be provided under the protection of a proper firewall located between the Internet access point and the Administrative LANs. See Figure 8.2 for the detailed Administrative building network design.

**Figure 8.2** Detailed Administrative Building Network Design

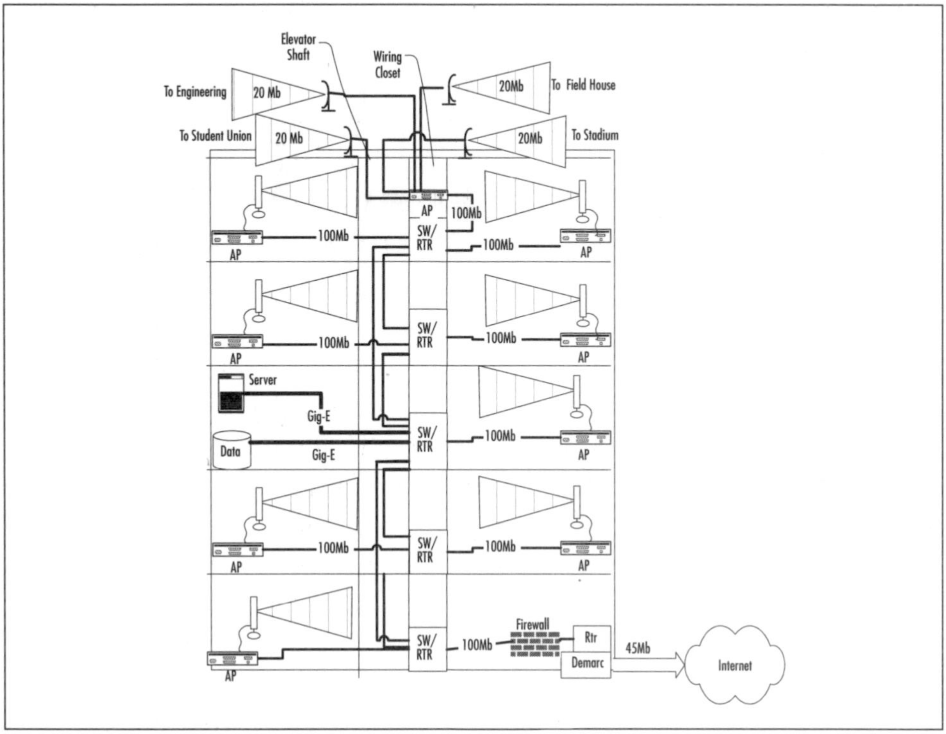

# Providing Detailed Athletic Department Requirements

The Athletic department requires connectivity to the Internet at the stadium and field house. The stadium access to the Internet will be provided via an 802.11a link to the Administration building. This requirement defines the physical connection between the stadium and the Administration building. The Tiger Team chooses the 802.11a technology due to the close proximity of the two buildings, the bandwidth requirements, and the obstructions provided by the trees between the two structures. Field house access to the Internet will also be provided via an 802.11a link to the Administration building, chosen for the same reasons. Yagi antennas will be used to focus the 802.11a signals for peak performance.

The Athletic department requires wireless mobile connectivity at the stadium and field house for press connectivity to the Internet for online filing of articles. See Figure 8.3 for a depiction of the press connectivity. Wireless public coverage will be provided in the stadium press box and the field house press tables via 802.11a. This provides dynamic access for members of the press by enabling Internet communication between members of the press and their employers. They will be able to access the Internet via public accounts administered by the Athletic department's staff. Members of the press will be allocated a wireless card along

**Figure 8.3** Stadium Press Internet Connectivity

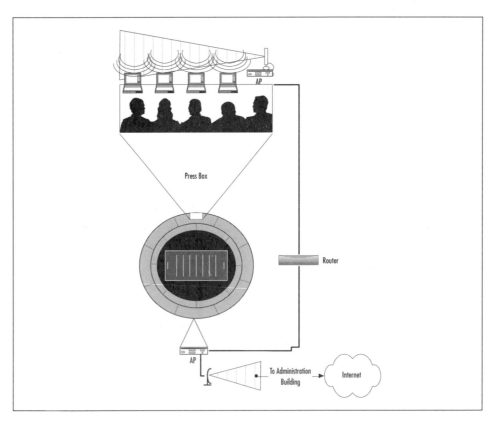

with their press passes and will be given the necessary connectivity information to access the network. The press box hospitality staff will collect the wireless cards upon the departure of the individual. Members of the press will have access to the Faber University Athletics Web page for useful statistics and information as well as information on the Internet. They will be able to submit their articles or reports online via guest e-mail accounts.

Connectivity from the public wireless network to the stadium and field house backbones will be via Fast Ethernet, with continued connectivity to the Internet through the Administration building link. Fast Ethernet provides the required bandwidth in a cost efficient manner, while reducing the complexity of channel allocation for the wireless networks in proximity to the stadium and field house.

The Athletic department also requires wireless mobile data communications at the stadium for data communications between staff on the field and the coaching staff in the scouting booth. See Figure 8.4 for a depiction of the coaches' connectivity. Wireless mobile connectivity will be provided to both teams via 802.11a. This will replace the existing wireline technologies of the coaches' headsets and provide a mobile data interface between the coaches on the field and the coaches in the box. The coaches in the box will be able to send digital pictures of opposing team formations with instructions to the coaches on the field. Faber will showcase this capability to raise national perception of Faber's technological position. Omnidirectional antennas will be used to focus the coverage zones on the stadium field.

Each team will be given a separate domain. This will protect the privacy of each team's communications. Visiting teams will be given instructions on how to configure security features such as encryption and password allocation to ensure the concept of fair play and remain within NCAA rules and guidelines. Both teams must have equal capabilities to meet NCAA rules. Visiting coaching staffs will be given laptop computers with the required wireless cards to enable the capability by the stadium hospitality staff. The Faber coaching staff's laptops will be configured initially by the Engineering department staff. Faber's staff will be able to use this capability both during games and during practice sessions to evaluate the team's performance.

**Figure 8.4** Coaches' Connectivity at the Stadium

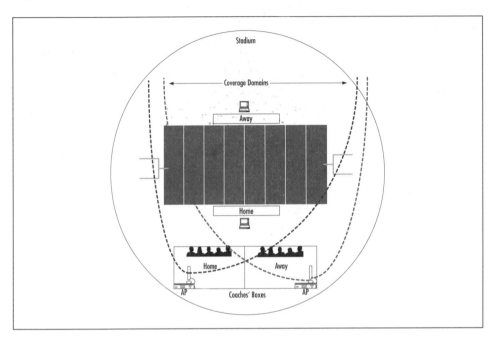

The Athletic department's administrative staff, located in the stadium, requires high-speed connectivity to the university's Administration building for transfer of financial data. High-speed connectivity is provided between the stadium and the Administration building via an 802.11a link. This requirement is satisfied with the previously described link design.

# Providing Detailed Academic Department Requirements

Each academic department requires high-speed mobile connectivity on all floors of each building for virtual access of instructors in every classroom and office. A wireless LAN using 802.11a technology will be installed on every floor of each academic building. These LANs are totally exclusive to the teaching staff. The staff network is maintained as a separate network from the student network to help maintain data privacy such as student grades and the content of course-related tests.

Each floor of each of the buildings will be bridged together to form one logical staff network via Fast Ethernet switches. By bridging the floors together, the staff will be able to move from floor to floor without having to reset their TCP sessions and rerequest a new IP address. The Fast Ethernet switches have this capability built in, and the IT department will make the necessary changes to them.

Each department requires broadband access to the Internet for educational collaboration with other universities and research projects. Access to the Internet is provided via a direct link to the Administration building using 802.11a technology. The 802.11a technology is chosen due to the close proximity of the two buildings, the bandwidth requirements, and the obstructions provided by the trees between the two structures.

Each department also requires separate high-speed mobile connectivity on all floors for *students*. A student wireless LAN using 802.11a technology will be installed on every floor of each building that is to be used by both students and staff. The reasons for choosing 802.11a for the student network are the same as for the staff network. The staff is being provided with access to the student network as an additional courtesy and to ensure that if there are labs or other types of network related courses, the instructor can connect to the student network to remain consistent with the students' configuration. The administrative policies that will provide students with access to Faber University networks will also be provided to staff so that they may access wireless networks in areas dedicated to student use, such as the Student Union.

Each floor of each of the buildings will be bridged together to form one logical student network via Fast Ethernet switches. The reasoning for this design is the same as for the staff network.

Each department requires a separate administrative connectivity to the Administration building for records and enrollment purposes. Access to the administrative network is provided via a direct link to the Administration building via 802.11a.

In addition, the Engineering department will provide an optical link to the Liberal Arts building and to the Biological Sciences building for connectivity purposes. The Engineering department is using this opportunity to provide access between academic buildings to expose its staff and students to emerging technologies. An optical solution was selected since there are no obstructions or reflective objects between the Engineering building and the Liberal Arts building or the Engineering building and the Biological Sciences building. The optical link does not require licensing and can provide scalable levels of high-speed access between the two buildings. The Engineering connectivity design is shown in Figure 8.5.

**Figure 8.5** Engineering Connectivity

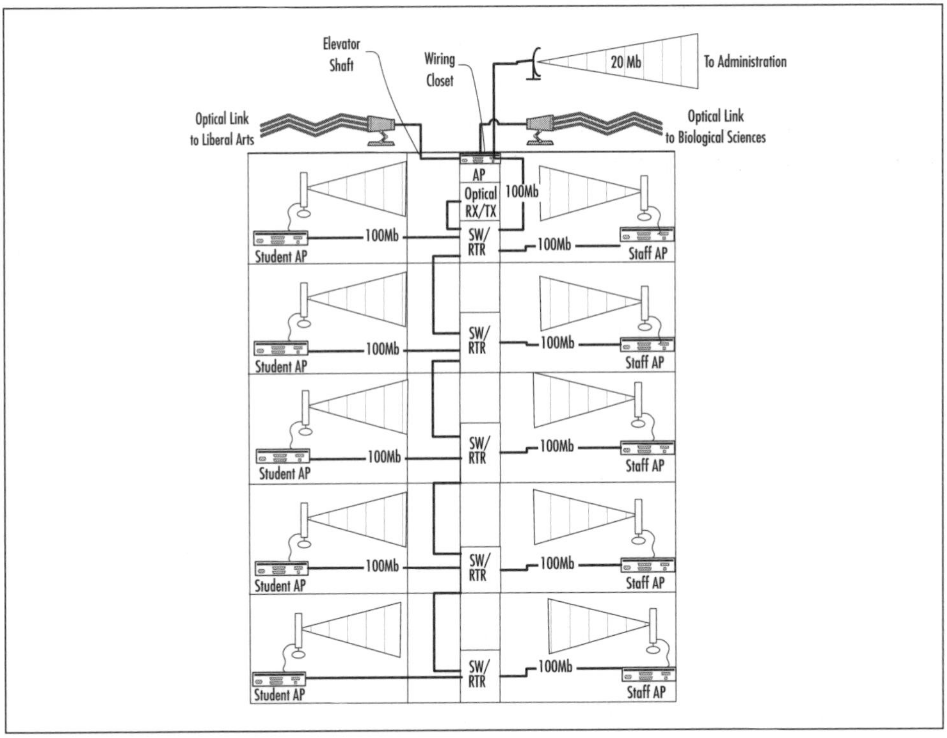

## Providing Detailed Student Union Department Requirements

The Student Union requires separate high-speed mobile connectivity on all floors for staff offices. A staff wireless LAN will be installed on every floor of the Student Union building, which is totally exclusive to the Student Union staff. 802.11a will be used. This requirement is similar to that of the academic staff and will utilize the same basic design as the academic networks. Each floor of the Student Union building will be bridged together to form one logical staff network via Fast Ethernet switches. As in the other bridged networks on campus, this design provides mobility to the Student Union staff by not requiring them to reestablish the IP session on different floors of the Student Union.

The Student Union requires broadband access to Internet for e-commerce and student access from the dorms. The Student Union networks will have access to the Internet via the DS3 (45 Mbps) connection provided at the ground floor demarcation point in the building. This requirement simply defines the connectivity to the existing Internet service provider's access point in the Student Union. Student Union access to the Internet will be provided under the protection of a proper firewall located between the Internet access point and the Administrative LANs. This requirement underlines the obvious security restriction on the Internet access point.

The Student Union also requires separate high-speed mobile connectivity on all floors for students, and will be provided by implementing an 802.11a network on all floors.

## Providing Detailed Student Requirements

Student access from the dorms to the Internet and other university networks is provided via an 802.11a link between the dorms and the Student Union. The Tiger Team chooses the 802.11a technology due to the close proximity of the student dorms to the Student Union, as well as the obstruction provided by the trees between the two structures. Individual student dorm rooms will be connected via wireless 802.11a domain networks in the dorms. The access points in the dorms will connect via Fast Ethernet backbone switches as one bridged network to support roaming within the dorms without making the student reestablish IP sessions. The student dorm bridged network will be routed to the Student Union to provide Internet access. IP addressing for student access will be addressed dynamically using the Dynamic Host Configuration Protocol (DHCP) and Login/Authentication via Radius and DHCP servers. This access method will remain consistent across all student networks so that the access method of the student is standardized and easy to implement and understand. See Figure 8.6 for a depiction of student access.

**Figure 8.6** Student Access

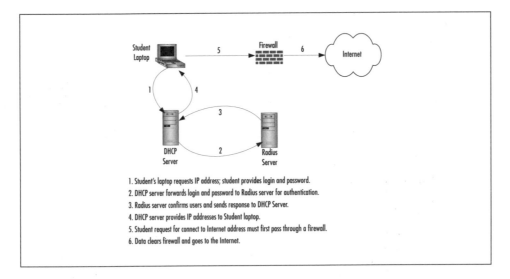

The students also require high-speed mobile connectivity on all floors of the dorms. Mobile student connectivity will be provided on all floors of the dorms using an 802.11a network on all floors. For students requiring high-speed connectivity between the dorms and Student Union building, connectivity will be provided via a high speed 802.11a link.

# Implementing the Wireless Campus Network

The Tiger Team finalizes the detailed design requirements and submits them to the CENTS committee for approval. They also want to make sure that no *scope changes* (the addition or subtraction of requirements for capabilities) will occur once the implementation is under way. Scope changes are one of the most damaging obstacles to completing projects on time and within budget. When scope changes occur, the Tiger Team must restart the previously defined design processes, to ensure proper integration of the requirements and to mitigate the risk of the new requirements overloading or impacting the previously designed links and LANs.

Once the detailed requirements are finalized, the Tiger Team must begin developing an implementation plan. Implementation plans include the identification of resources and skill sets required, as well as a projected project plan with timelines and dates for the completion of tasks (*task tracking*).

Since issues involving licensing, right-of-way permissions, and trenching under city streets have been avoided, the implementation phase for the Faber University technology upgrade consists mainly of deploying and tuning the RF and optical equipment. This project really falls into two categories. The first category is the physical layer that refers mainly to the deployment of the RF access points (APs) and the optical receiver/transmitters. The second category is the logical layer and involves IP address management, network security, and user administration. As with any implementation, the fundamental project management is critical to the success and speedy deployment of the design.

# Implementing the Physical Deployment

For the overall physical deployment, the implementation should start with the three main focal points of the network—in this case, the Administrative, Engineering, and Student Union buildings. The physical deployment consists of two main skill sets. The first is *internal access* and basically involves the construction of the wireless LANs (WLANs) within each of the University buildings. This skill set involves tuning and placement of the access point as well as frequency management of the various domains or coverage areas so that interference is reduced. The second skill set involves the *external installation* of the various building-to-building links prescribed in the design. This group requires both 802.11a knowledge as well as optical knowledge. As with the WLAN group, this group will also need to manage the frequencies used.

The distance links should be established before the WLAN groups begin, so that frequency use on these links can be determined and avoided by the WLANs. The 802.11a signal is amplified for the links so the chance of interference to other domains using the same frequency in the vicinity is increased. The optical links are line-of-sight technologies, so this team must address issues relating to obstruction in the line of sight. The primary links to and from the Administration, Engineering, and Student Union should be deployed first so that the WLAN teams can begin deployment in those building as soon as possible. Figure 8.7 shows the high-level inter-building connectivity.

**Figure 8.7** Inter-Building Connectivity

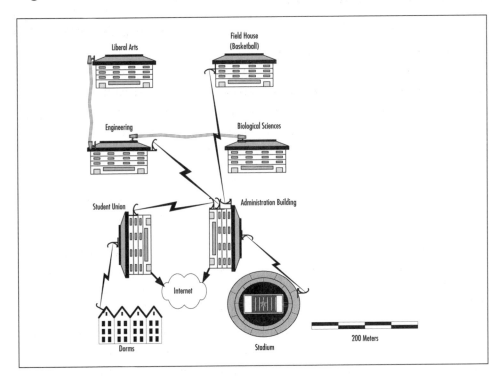

## Implementing the Logical Deployment

The logical deployment involves the configuration of the routers and switches to support the individual WLANs created throughout the campus. This requires the creation of subnets and/or virtual LANs (VLANS) that support the separation requirements between staff and student networks. The configuration of the DHCP servers and the fire-walls are also a part of this team's tasks. This team will also develop and distribute the methodology for the dissemination of the necessary software and account information so that the end users can access this wireless network. End users include staff, students, and the press. Accessibility instructions must be simple and easy to follow to minimize the amount of support required. This team must establish and implement policies on Internet use.

# Lessons Learned

The Tiger Team completes the technology upgrade just prior to the summer enrollment session at the university. Now it's time for the various groups involved with the discovery, design, and implementation to get back together to discuss the perceived successes and failures of the process. This falls under the conventional wisdom that states, "the definition of insanity is doing the same thing over and over and expecting different results." The Tiger Team documents their findings so that in their future methodologies and engineering practices the successes can be repeated and the failures avoided.

This process includes the evaluation of everything from technical issues to project management and administration. Sometimes simple logistics can delay projects more often than the difficult technical problems. This is often the case when engineers that are focused on the technical issues assume without verification that the administrative pieces will fall into place. In Faber's case, the implementation team ran out of access points just prior to the Fourth of July holiday. The wireless vendor was unreachable for four days, so the Tiger Team had to reshuffle tasks during that time to remain on schedule. Another lesson learned involved the discovery that wasps had built nests under the overhangs on the optical gear, thus blocking the link. The lessons learned process is paramount to the successful honing of an organization's engineering procedures and its ability to adapt to change.

# Summary

This case study provided a basic understanding of the detailed steps required in conceiving, designing, and implementing a wireless campus network as well as the high-level steps that apply to all wireless design projects. It outlined the path from the discovery phase to the design phase, and finally to the implementation phase while using the wireless campus model to illustrate the main points. The discovery phase entails physical inspections, technology research, user surveys, and brainstorming sessions to build the groundwork on which the design phase operates. Functional requirements, constraints, and assumptions were identified, documented, and approved before the design phase could begin.

Once the discovery phase was completed, the Engineering department work group showcased in the case study (the Tiger Team) matched the best technologies with the organization's desired capabilities. They were required to eliminate technologies that did not meet Faber's requirements or were not possible within the defined constraints. Once the detailed requirements were finalized, the Tiger Team revisited and represented the proposed detailed design to the overseeing university committee (CENTS). This helped to ensure their buy-in on the design and mitigated the risk of scope creep during the implementation phase.

After the Tiger Team received administrative approval on the design phase, they moved on to the implementation phase. Project plans were developed with task-tracking timelines. Resource requirements, both physical and human, were identified and administrative measures to fill them were put in place. Once a definitive plan was in place and approved, the work began and the Tiger Team became the program managers of the effort. They made sure that the individual tasks of the project remained on schedule and identified and rectified any issues that affected the interdependant tasks.

The methodology you execute in your own projects can be as important to the success of the project as the technology itself since it is the methodology that enables you to select the technology that best suits your organization's requirements. This process is a highly dependent interworking of the individual steps.

# Solutions Fast Track

## Introducing the Campus Case Study

☑ Faber University requires an upgrade of its technological capabilities and image. It has funding for the implementation.

☑ Faber consists of very old buildings that are not conducive to wire line technologies. The buildings are in close proximity, but constraints include the fact that the line of sight is mostly blocked by trees. Also, trenching and burying cables is not an option for building links.

☑ Students require mobile and Internet access in academic buildings, the Student Union, and dorms.

☑ The teaching staff requires separate access in academic buildings.

☑ The resident and visiting coaching staff and the press require cordless access in sporting facilities.

☑ The administrative staff needs mobile access on respective floors.

## Designing the Wireless Campus Network

☑ 802.11a is used for all the wireless LAN applications.

☑ Wireless is used horizontally on floors, and wireline Fast Ethernet is used for the vertical interconnection of floors.

☑ Two access point bridges using 802.11a are placed per floor in the academic buildings with omnidirectional antennas. One access point is for students and one access point is for faculty.

☑ 802.11a is used to provide mobile access and communications for coaching staff at the stadium and to provide mobile access to the press at the sports facilities.

☑ Free Space Optical links are used between academic buildings as a teaching element.

☑ DHCP is used for dynamic allocation of IP addressing.

☑ Authentication/Logon is used for user identification.

## Implementing the Wireless Campus Network

☑ Resource requirements are identified.

☑ Task tracking timelines are created.

☑ Implementation tasks are divided into physical and logical deployment schedules.

☑ Tasks are rescheduled to keep on schedule and within budget.

☑ Scope creep is mitigated with prior authorization processes.

## Lessons Learned

☑ The design methodology is paramount to the success of project.

☑ The design team must continually retool methodology to remain current with technology.

☑ The design team must protect the project from scope creep and delays.

☑ Administrative issues are just as important as technological issues.

# Frequently Asked Questions

The following Frequently Asked Questions, answered by the authors of this book, are designed to both measure your understanding of the concepts presented in this chapter and to assist you with real-life implementation of these concepts. To have your questions about this chapter answered by the author, browse to **www.syngress.com/solutions** and click on the **"Ask the Author"** form.

**Q:** What is the difference between a *functional* requirement and a *design* requirement?

**A:** A functional requirement defines "what" you want to do. A design requirement defines "how" you will do it.

**Q:** Who generally defines the requirements?

**A:** End-users generally define the functional requirements, and the network architects and designers define the design requirements.

**Q:** What is an access point (AP) and what is its main function?

**A:** An access point is a wireless bridge that provides access to a wireless station so that it can communicate with a wired LAN. An access point can also be a bridge used to communicate with other wireless stations.

**Q:** What are possible interference sources in an 802.11 network?

**A:** If it is an 802.11b network, common interference sources include 2.4 GHz mobile phones, Bluetooth, other 802.11b network wireless devices, and microwave ovens. If it is an 802.11a network, the main sources of interference are other 802.11a networks.

**Q:** What determines the range of an 802.11a link?

**A:** Signal power and antenna type are the two primary factors in the range of the signal. Noise levels can also affect it since longer distances may provide more interference sources and reduce throughput.

**Q:** What is the difference between *bandwidth* and *throughput*?

**A:** Bandwidth refers to the amount of raw data passed through a link or network and includes both overhead signaling data as well as user data. Throughput refers to the actual amount of user data passed through the link or network.

**Q:** What determines the coverage zone in an 802.11 wireless network?

**A:** The antenna type is the primary factor in the shape of the coverage zone.

# Chapter 9

# Designing a Wireless Home Network: Home Office Case Study

## Solutions in this chapter:

- Introducing the Wireless Home Network Case Study

- Designing the Wireless Home Network

- Implementing the Wireless Home Network

- Designing a Wireless Home Network for Data, Voice, and Beyond

- Lessons Learned

☑ Summary

☑ Solutions Fast Track

☑ Frequently Asked Questions

# Introduction

One of the most exciting applications for wireless technologies is the wireless home network. Home networks allow you to network PCs and other devices for peripheral and file sharing, online gaming, and shared Internet access. As new Internet-ready devices flood the marketplace and a whole new range of household, business, and entertainment services become available with expanded broadband access, a home network will become a must for many households. With a wireless home network, you will be free from the need to install wired connections where fixed Internet-ready devices are desired. You will also be able to control those devices as you move in and around your house.

The business-related advantages of a network are widely recognized, but most home PC users have not yet recognized the advantages a home network can provide. Online gamers have long been using networked PCs in the home to play multiplayer games. Small home office users, along with some other multi-PC families use home networks for peripheral, file, and Internet sharing. But for the most part, the possibilities of a home network, particularly a wireless home network, have yet to be tapped.

This chapter and its case study explore the possibilities of a wireless home network, both today and in the near future. It explains the potential benefits and the options available for the type of home network that will meet your needs and your budget.

# Advantages of a Home Network

Already, the popularity of online music services has begun to demonstrate the potentials and the pitfalls of electronically distributed entertainment. As broadband access has expanded, we've also begun to see video-on-demand services appear on Internet sites. What's more, a proliferation of Internet-ready entertainment devices is hitting the marketplace. Set top boxes are currently available for using Web services from your analog television. Network-ready MP3 players are available for your home music systems. Moreover, the market will soon be flooded with a range of telephony products (fixed and mobile) that support both voice and Internet services. With technologies and services available today, you can control and distribute entertainment services throughout your home.

In the area of household automation, appliance makers are building or considering network-ready appliances of nearly every kind. Home network and Internet services are envisioned for virtually every type of kitchen appliance, as well as heating, cooling, and lighting systems. Services range from remote control and maintenance of your stove, washing machine, furnace, or coffee pot, to enhanced services, such as automated grocery lists generated from your refrigerator, or home security systems that will alert you remotely when they are activated. Appliance manufacturers envision a $21^{st}$ century kitchen where many of today's routine household tasks can either be automated or remotely controlled, either in your home or out of it, from mobile wireless devices.

For the home office user, broadband services can now offer complete integration into corporate networks. Large business users can operate from the home with much the same security and access to network resources as those at work. Small business users are better able to host their own Web sites and will see a whole new array of small-business services.

Telecommunication and cable companies are integrating expanded home services into their broadband portfolios. Many complex services will require more than broadband Internet access, especially when voice and data integration are required or when access is required away from your home. Remote, mobile, and integrated access, whether to outside services when you are at home or to home devices when you are away, will be the next great achievement of the broadband industry.

## NOTE

As service logic is developed in our telecommunication networks, services such as enhanced home security systems and automated shopping will begin to emerge.

Enhanced security systems will allow you to monitor your home, whether you are in it or away. With cameras mounted in and around your house, your home security system could feed full-motion video of what is currently happening in your home to your mobile wireless device. When notified that the alarm has sounded, you would be able to alert your security service or notify them of a false alarm. With connections to the lighting and entertainment subsystems of your network, you could make your lights flash to alert your neighbors to a burglary, or control lights and entertainment devices as if you were home, to prevent one.

Appliance manufacturers and grocers envision a day in the very near future where you'll use scanners on your refrigerator, your cabinets, and possibly even your trashcan to generate grocery lists. Using the refrigerator's video screen, you'll be able to edit your grocery list if necessary and send it to the supermarket for home delivery. Alternatively, you could use the screen to browse the Internet for recipes or store them for later retrieval.

## Advantages of a Wireless Home Network

Although home networks can be created with wired technologies, wireless technologies offer far greater convenience and mobility than the wired options. Wireless networks are more convenient because they don't require the installation of new wires or new network access points where broadband services are desired. Even though new technologies for providing broadband data access over existing home wiring (telephone and even power lines) are becoming available, the convenience of wireless cannot be matched. Even if every power and telephone outlet in your home could become a potential broadband data port, wireless still offers the convenience of locating your Internet-ready devices in places where the physical outlets do not exist.

Even more advantageous, wireless networks allow you to use Internet-ready devices while mobile. Whether you want to move your laptop to your living-room couch, to your bed, or to your deck at the back of the house, a wireless network will let you move without the need to "plug in" to a new connection. Even better, you can stay connected while you are moving. This becomes particularly useful when using devices such as personal digital assistants (PDAs) or cell phones. With a wireless home network, you could have the power to control lighting, music, or other services while moving about your house, all from your hand-held control center.

# Introducing the Wireless Home Network Case Study

The following case study illustrates the design of a simple home network intended for a home-office user. The user is interested in high-speed data services only and needs to build the network with technology available today. She has no immediate plans for expanding the network beyond her current home-office needs. This section will describe the user's current situation, a statement of her problem, her proposed solution, and how she implements her solution. It will also describe the lessons she learned during the process.

## Assessing the Opportunity

Under doctor's orders for more bed rest, Jan received authorization from her employer to work from home during and immediately after her pregnancy. However, to do her job effectively, she routinely needs to retrieve large files from the corporate local area network (LAN), modify them, and return them to another location on the LAN. She also occasionally likes to print something for convenience or record keeping, and she needs convenient access to a telephone. Jan has received instructions from her company's Information Technology (IT) staff regarding how to connect to the corporate LAN.

Jan currently has broadband access to her home. However, the only access is to a PC in a family room in the home's finished basement. Jan's family uses this PC for Internet access, online gaming, and as a resource for school projects. The PC is connected to a color printer.

Jan wants to create a home office in an unused upstairs bedroom. During the later stages of her pregnancy, she wants the convenience of working from more comfortable locations, such as her couch or bed. She already has a cordless phone and is planning to purchase a laptop PC and perhaps a second printer. However, a quick call to her broadband provider has caused her to question the financial feasibility of running new wiring for broadband access in other locations of her home. Perplexed with her problem, Jan talks to some of her coworkers, and one of them mentions wireless. Jan does a little investigation of the wireless LAN products available and decides many of the products are within her budget.

## Defining the Scope of the Case Study

The scope of Jan's solution will be limited by the fact that she already has broadband access installed in her home. She also has instructions for connecting to the corporate LAN. However, she has not checked to see if the wireless home network will affect these instructions.

Jan's challenge is that she needs reliable high-speed access to the corporate LAN from the new home office and other convenient locations in the house. She wants to interfere as little as possible with use of the PC in the family room, and she needs her laptop to be inaccessible from the family PC. She would like to have printing capability in the home office. However, her solution must fit within a limited budget. Finally, all equipment that she uses for her solution must be immediately available.

# Designing the Wireless Home Network

This section explains how Jan determines the need for, plans, designs, and implements a wireless home network. As a part of these processes, Jan learns more about the strengths and weaknesses of wireless networks, and about the costs and advantages of different vendor solutions. The processes she follows are:

- Determining the requirements
- Analyzing the existing environment

- Creating a preliminary design
- Developing a detailed design
- Implementing the network

Using this design methodology, Jan decides to conduct her investigation as if she is designing a network for a business, making appropriate changes as the situation warrants. Jan begins her investigation by performing the following tasks:

- Determining the functional requirements of her manager and family
- Talking to her company's IT staff
- Drawing a physical map of her home

# Determining the Functional Requirements

The actual users of Jan's home network will be Jan, her husband, and their children. Since Jan's manager will be auditing her work, she also feels that her manager must give her advice regarding what is expected. Jan works with her manager and family to define their expectations of the home network.

## Determining the Needs of Management

At work, Jan discovers that her manager is concerned primarily about the security of the files she will be using. Will the security of the corporate LAN be compromised by the wireless connection? Can the home network be child-proofed? Based on this conversation, Jan decides that the connection between her laptop and the corporate LAN must be secure from the family computer and safe from Internet hackers. Another concern is risk mitigation—basically, what happens if Jan's laptop goes down? What backup procedure does Jan envision? Jan believes that she will copy her work to the company network on a daily basis. This practice should limit the amount of loss to a single day.

# Determining the Needs of the Family

Though intrigued by the possibilities of a wireless network, Jan's husband is concerned primarily about the impact on the family's budget, and the future value of the new equipment. Although the home network will benefit Jan's employer, the employer will not finance any of Jan's home networking needs. Since home networks, and wireless technology in particular, are considered "new technology," he reasons that the costs will be significantly higher now than they will be in the future.

Jan and her husband are so afraid that the cost will be phenomenal that she limits her desires to the basic necessities. Since Jan plans to buy a new laptop PC and another printer, they want to hold the cost of the network to a few hundred dollars. They consider running wires to her home office themselves if that would be a less expensive alternative. Her husband even suggests, somewhat jokingly, moving the printer to Jan's office during the day and back to the family room for schoolwork at night. Although moving the printer is not practical, Jan considers moving the printer permanently to the home office. The children debate this idea because they frequently need the printer to print papers and book reports for school. The children also are concerned about how a network will affect the bandwidth for their online gaming.

# Talking to the IT Department

Jan calls Diane, a network engineer in the company's IT department. Diane tells her that to secure her laptop from the family PC, she must purchase a wireless access point (AP) rather than network the PC and the laptop. Without the access point, the family PC would have to act as a server to the laptop, since the wired broadband connection is near that PC. However, with the wireless access point, Jan can make either PC the server, or even purchase an access point that would perform that function. She also needs the access point if she wants to connect any other devices wirelessly, such as the printer or another PC. Of course, in doing so, Jan needs to remember that each device requires a wireless network card.

Diane regards the security risks of the wireless LAN to be acceptable as long as Jan's browser uses standard encryption technology. Since the range of home wireless LANs on the market today is about 100 meters, she does recommend that Jan not make it well known outside of the office that she's using a wireless LAN for company business. Diane also recommends that Jan purchase a home firewall to protect her from Internet hackers over her broadband connection. However, she assures Jan that the wireless network will cause no serious configuration issues in connecting to the corporate LAN. The configuration steps will be the same.

Jan also discovers that one of her coworkers has a wireless network at home, so she talks to him about his experiences. He is largely happy with his home network. His brother connected it for him, so he can't say much about network design or the advantages of various vendor solutions. However, one problem he's had is that the network seems to cause a "popping and cracking" noise in his cordless phone. He has noticed that the noise is more serious when he is transferring data.

## Creating a Site Survey of the Home

In preparing to conduct her site survey, Jan decides she needs to consider the following factors:

- Whether any locations where she wants to use the laptop will be more than 100 meters (over 300 feet) away from the access point.

- Whether any potential sources of interference will cause any problems with the network. The attention Jan's coworker brought to this issue made her realize that she needs to learn more about interference issues. Her cordless telephone will be important for her work activities.

Since the access point must be located near the Broadband connection, Jan decides to measure her house and create a diagram showing all the relevant distances. She also decides to note any sources of interference. With a little investigation, she finds that many cordless telephones do in fact experience interference from the current generation of wireless LANs. Even more, she finds that radio frequency (RF) leakage from microwave ovens also can cause wireless LANs to experience a loss in the data rate.

## Assessing the Functional Requirements

Based on her preliminary investigation, Jan comes up with the following list of design considerations:

- She needs to purchase a wireless access point.

- She needs to purchase wireless network cards for any devices she may want to connect wirelessly.

- She should purchase a home firewall to protect from Internet hackers.

- The location of all wireless devices must remain within 100 meters of the access point for connectivity.

- She must consider sources of interference and their locations.

- The printer in the family room is used considerably.

- The wireless network will not cause any problems in configuring access to her corporate LAN.

Jan also completes a site map of her house showing the approximate location of the wireless accent point, all relevant dimensions of her house, and the types and locations of any interference sources. Her diagram is shown in Figure 9.1.

## Analyzing the Existing Environment

The next step in Jan's design methodology is to analyze her existing environment. Her analysis includes the following processes:

- Identifying current technology options and constraints

- Investigating the costs

- Weighing the costs and benefits

Jan decides that her current applications consist mostly of entertainment and school content. She and her husband also occasionally use the family PC and printer for work. The two children both use the PC and printer for homework. By observing the computer use, Jan has discovered

**Figure 9.1** Jan's Site Map

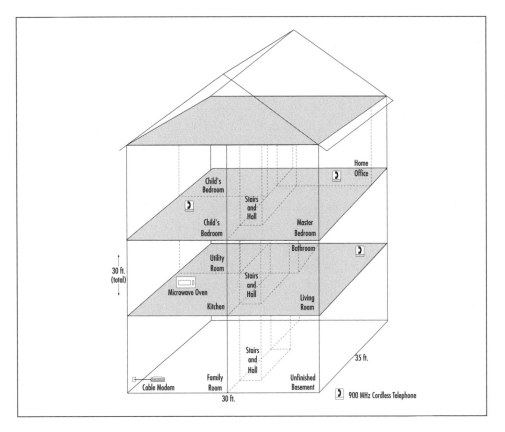

that the kids use the printer more than she had thought, so moving the printer from the family room is probably not a viable option. Both also use the Internet for various activities, including online games, so Jan is concerned about how that might affect her bandwidth while she is working.

Jan's existing network is simple. She has Broadband Internet access available in the family room only. The Broadband service is delivered into the house from a cable modem. From the cable modem, the service is wired to the family PC via a Category 5 Ethernet cable. The printer is a peripheral of the PC via the PC's serial port.

# Identifying Current Technology Options and Constraints

Although Jan has already done some preliminary investigation of the technology, that investigation has led her to realize that she needs to know more. By using key words such as *wireless LAN* and *home networking* on her Internet searches, Jan is able to learn a considerable amount about both the benefits and drawbacks of wireless home networks. She also discovers that she can consider using existing telephone wires in her home to wire her network. Although she doesn't have a telephone outlet in her home office, she decides to add existing telephone outlets throughout her house to her site map.

Jan learns that she has several options in configuring her wireless network. Some wireless access points can be configured as routers or Dynamic Host Configuration Protocol (DHCP) servers, whereas others simply bridge Internet traffic from the modem to a single device. She also learns that a home firewall can act as a server or router, making all other devices (including the wireless access point) clients of the firewall. Finally, she finds at least one vendor solution that serves as both firewall and wireless access point.

Jan also learns more about interference issues. She discovers that the current generation of home networks operates on the IEEE 802.11b specification. Thus, all current devices will suffer from interference from certain cordless phones. However, she discovers that the interference is limited to phones operating on the 2.4 GHz band. Phones using the 900 MHz band won't suffer from the same interference.

In addition to the interference from microwaves and 2.4 GHz phones, Jan learns that glass objects, particularly windows and mirrors, can reflect the wireless signal occasionally, causing some minor interference issues (from multiple reflections). She also discovers that dense material, such as concrete and metals, can block the signal.

In the area of security, Jan confirms Diane's risk assessment. Although the wireless signal can be intercepted anywhere within 100 meters of the wireless access point, encryption on her browser offers the same security as crossing the Internet.

# Investigating Costs

While investigating her technology options, Jan has been noting the costs of various components. She now makes a more thorough cost investigation by documenting the expense for purchasing and installing any components she thinks she might use in her design. The cost factors Jan considers for three different network types are:

- **Completely Wired Solution** Jan uses the installation costs quoted by her Broadband provider for extending wired access, which are relatively high. She also investigates the cost of having her husband run the wire instead. Although the costs of this are low, the level of effort required is very high.

- **Completely Wireless Solution** In a totally wireless solution, Jan will need not only a wireless access point and wireless network cards for every device, but she will need to buy two new printers, since her current printer won't support the wireless card. The cost of the network-compatible printers and network cards make this solution even more expensive than paying for wire installation.

- **Hybrid Wired/Wireless Solution** This solution seems to offer the most cost-effective approach. By maintaining her current wired connection to the family PC, Jan can achieve her primary requirements with the purchase of only two new components: a wireless access point and a wireless network card for the laptop PC. However, if she wants to connect her home-office printer wirelessly, the cost will be relatively high.

# Weighing Costs and Benefits

Given her investigation of costs, Jan is now prepared to weigh the costs and benefits of various designs for her network and review them with the only other decision maker: her husband. Although a wired solution would be inexpensive if they do the wiring themselves, they decide that it's probably beyond their expertise to install the wiring in an inconspicuous fashion. A wired solution would also offer Jan less convenience and no mobility.

A completely wireless solution, though offering the maximum in mobility and convenience, is far beyond their budget for the project, mostly due to the cost of the wireless printers. This solution also goes well beyond the family's network needs. There is not really any reason to make the family PC and printer wireless components. They serve their functions well where they are.

They agree that the best choice is probably a hybrid wired/wireless network. The wireless network can be purchased inexpensively, and it offers the convenience and mobility that Jan considers the most important of her requirements. Adding a wireless printer in the home office will probably be outside of their budget, but Jan decides convenient printing is a less important requirement. She figures she'll still have access to the printer in the family room, or she can buy a standard printer for the home office and connect it to the laptop when she needs it.

## Assessing the Existing Environment

Jan comes up with the following list of additional considerations and conclusions:

- She has determined her current applications and network design.

- She learned that she has some options for which device to use as her server.

- She has discovered that interference can also be caused by windows, mirrors, and dense metal or concrete objects.

- She has discovered that the wireless network's interference with cordless phones is limited to those operating in the 2.4 GHz band. There is no issue with phones that operate in the 900 MHz band.

- Through her cost/benefit analysis, she has decided that the most feasible design is probably a hybrid wired/wireless solution.

- She is still uncertain about exactly how she will solve her printing problem.

Jan also updates her site map to identify her existing network, the location on the network where particular applications are used, and additional sources for potential interference. Jan's updated site map is shown in Figure 9.2.

**Figure 9.2** Jan's Updated Site Map

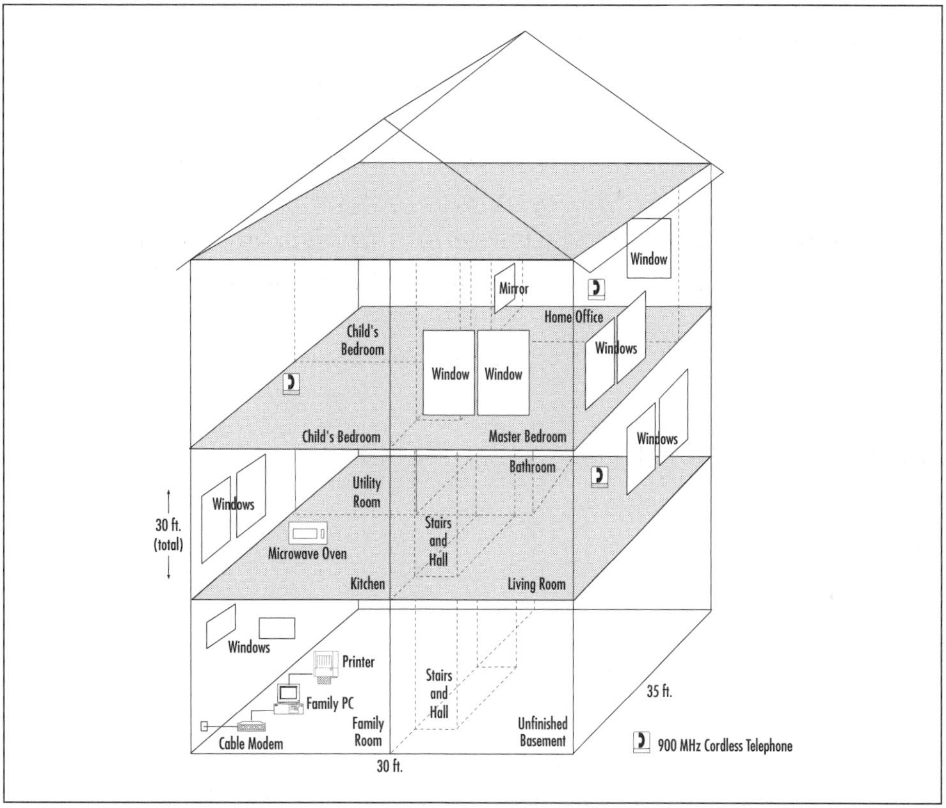

# Developing a Preliminary Design

In this section, Jan plans her preliminary design and chooses the vendor solutions. Jan begins designing her network by drawing it out on her site map. She assumes for now that she will buy a combined firewall and wireless access point. Her initial network design is shown in Figure 9.3. Even though her network is very simple, Jan quickly realizes the benefit of drawing it out. First, she sees that her wireless access point/firewall must serve as a DHCP server since multiple PCs will connect as clients to it. Secondly, the wireless access point/firewall must also have an Ethernet port for her family PC.

**Figure 9.3** Jan's Preliminary Design

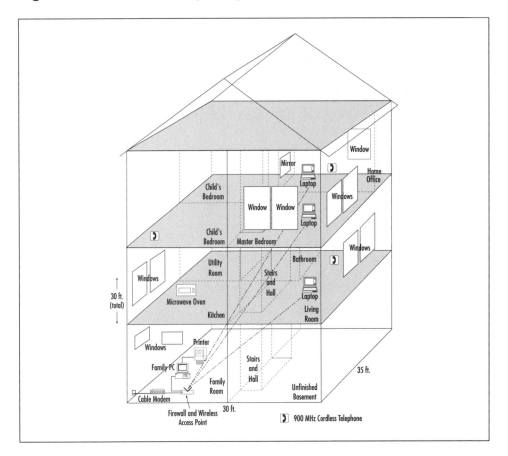

In reviewing her site map, Jan decides that the only serious interference source (the microwave oven) is far enough away from her access point and the places she will be using the laptop that it won't be a significant problem. However, the telephone connection near the family PC causes her to recollect that on one occasion in the past, her Broadband connection went down for several days. If this were to happen again, the only way she could work at all would be to dial up to the corporate LAN using a 56 K modem. She decides she should consider support for dial-up access as an additional backup requirement for her network.

# Choosing Vendor Solutions

Finally, Jan considers her options with various vendor solutions. Based on her previous investigation and analysis, her requirements for the wireless access point are as follows:

- Support for DHCP
- Support of both wireless and Ethernet
- Firewall protection
- v90 modem support

Based on product reviews, prices, and product features, Jan narrows her options to the following two solutions:

1. Linksys Wireless Access Point and Home Firewall. This product supports DHCP, provides firewall protection, and has multiple Ethernet ports. However, it does not provide a modem port.

2. Agere Systems Orinoco RG1000 Wireless Access Point. This product supports DHCP and does provide a modem port. It doesn't provide firewall protection for the wired computer and doesn't have any Ethernet ports. However, Jan can purchase a separate home firewall from Linksys, which will provide both the firewall function and the Ethernet port.

Although the first solution will be somewhat less expensive and will be contained in a single box, Jan decides that she is concerned enough about losing her Broadband connection that the analog modem support is worth paying a little more. She therefore chooses the second solution.

The RG1000 requires that the wireless network card for her laptop support 64-bit encryption. She is also concerned that with a new technology, she should use the same vendor as she does for the access point. She therefore decides to purchase her wireless network card from Agere Systems as well.

# Developing a Detailed Design

Jan purchases her products and makes her final considerations. She updates her site map to show the final components, and she considers her configuration options. For configuration, her primary consideration is which devices should implement DHCP.

Since the firewall will have multiple clients, she decides it should implement DHCP. The access point, on the other hand, can serve simply as a bridge between the laptop and the firewall. She decides to disable DHCP on it. Jan's detailed design is shown in Figure 9.4.

**Figure 9.4** Jan's Detailed Design

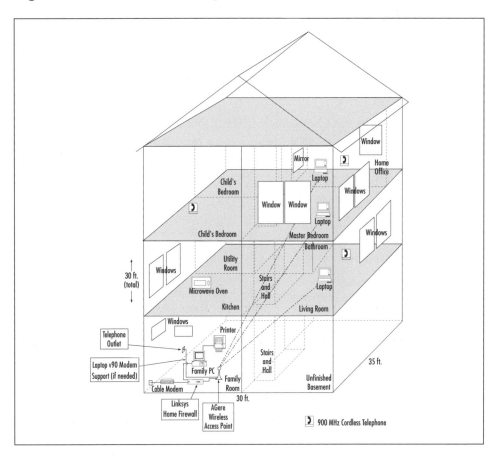

# Implementing the Wireless Home Network

This section describes, at a high level, how Jan builds her home network. Jan approaches the implementation by:

- Assembling the network components

- Determining Broadband configuration

- Installing the hardware

- Installing and configuring the software

- Testing the network

## Assembling the Network Components

Having planned and designed her network, Jan purchases the following components:

- One Agere Systems Orinoco RG1000 Wireless Gateway

- One Linksys BEFSR41 4-Port, 10/100Mbps Home Firewall

- One Agere Systems Orinoco Silver PCMCIA Wireless Network Card for her laptop PC

- One Dell laptop PC with open PCMCIA slot with Windows 2000 installed and an open parallel port

- Two short Category 5 Ethernet cables

The other components of Jan's network that she already owns are:

- One fully equipped Gateway PC with Ethernet network card and Windows 98 installed

- One Hewlett-Packard color printer with parallel port and cable

Jan assembles all of the components in her basement family room since all of her network installation and configuration can be done from there.

# Determining Broadband Configuration

Jan begins by reading the instructions for all the components of her network. She discovers that before installing her network, she needs to know whether her existing PC is given a static IP (Internet Protocol) address or whether her Broadband provider supplies her a dynamic address from their DHCP server. Whichever the case, Jan will need to set her firewall to the same setting. To determine her Broadband settings, Jan completes the following procedure:

1. From the Windows Start menu, she selects **Settings | Control Panels**.

2. In the Control Panel window, she selects the **Network** icon.

3. In the Network Properties window (**Configuration** tab), she selects **TCP/IP** and then the **Properties** button.

4. In the TCP/IP Properties window, shown in Figure 9.5, Jan sees that her IP address is dynamically assigned to her PC (**Obtain an IP address automatically** is checked). Thus, she knows to configure her firewall in the same fashion.

5. Jan closes the TCP/IP Properties window and all other windows without making any changes.

**Figure 9.5** TCP/IP Properties Window with Dynamic IP Address

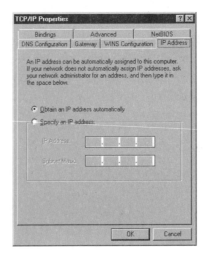

Had the other option (**Specify an IP address**) been selected, Jan would have needed to take note of her IP Address and Subnet Mask information from the IP Address tab of the TCP/IP Properties window. She would have also needed her Gateway and WINS Configuration information from the TCP/IP Properties window. However, most Broadband service providers set up services using a DHCP server, as Jan's did.

# Installing the Hardware

Jan decides to install the hardware. With the exception of the software for the wireless network card, she installs all of the network's hardware before doing any software installation or configuration. She uses the following procedure:

1. Jan powers on the laptop and inserts the wireless network card in the PCMCIA slot. Windows recognizes the hardware and offers to configure it for her. She declines and instead uses the software accompanying her network card. (At the time of this book's writing, the driver supplied with Windows 98, Windows 2000, and Windows Millennium is not the correct version for the Agere Systems wireless network card. It is important to note that you must manually install the driver provided by Agere for the Orinoco Silver card.)

2. She shuts down and disconnects electrical power from all other network components except the cable modem. Some cable and DSL service providers recommend that you do not disconnect the power supply from their network devices. They may be grounded against electrical storms through the power line.

3. She disconnects the family PC from the cable modem (at the cable modem), leaving the Ethernet cable attached to the PC.

4. Using one of the new Category 5 cables, she connects the cable modem to the **In** Ethernet port on the home firewall.

5. Using the other new Category 5 cable, she connects an **Out** Ethernet port on the firewall to the **In** port on the wireless access point.

6. She connects the Ethernet cable from the family PC to another **Out** port on the home firewall.

7. She connects (or reconnects) all wired network components to electrical power.

# Installing and Configuring the Software

Jan now begins to install software and configure her network. To install and configure the software for the firewall and wireless access point, she needs to use a computer that is directly attached to them. She therefore uses the family PC to configure the firewall and the laptop to configure the wireless access point. Jan follows the procedures outlined in the following section.

## Installing and Configuring the Software for the Home Firewall

The Linksys instructions indicate their software is configured directly to the firewall through a Web interface. Following the instructions, Jan performs the following steps (note that her installation and configuration are particular to her situation):

1. She turns on both the home firewall and the family PC.

2. She opens a Web browser and enters the default IP address into the browser of **http://192.168.1.1**.

3. She enters the default user and password (no user and admin).

4. Once she has logged into the firewall, she sees the setup page shown in Figure 9.6.

5. Jan follows the instructions provided by Linksys to set up features of her firewall. She accepts the defaults on most features,

such as whether to use Network Address Translation (NAT). Typically, the defaults are the most desirable configuration.

**Figure 9.6** Jan's Completed Setup Page

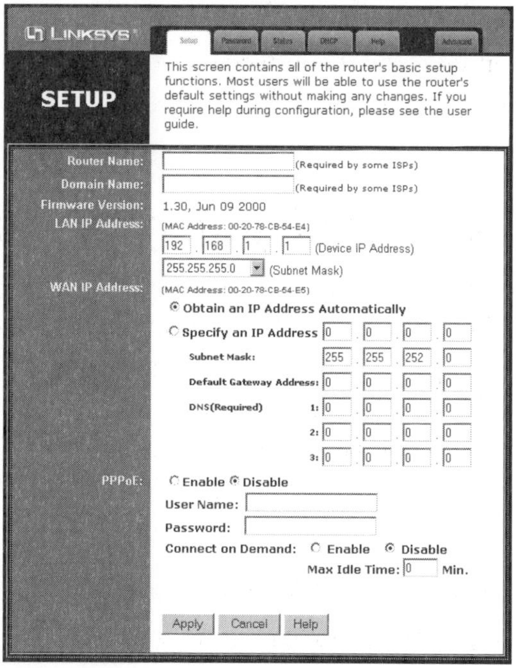

The most important configuration features for Jan to consider are how the firewall communicates with her Broadband provider and how her network devices communicate with her firewall. Since she checked the configuration information on her PC earlier, Jan knows her Broadband provider supplies a dynamic (DHCP) address rather than a static IP address. She therefore needs to instruct her firewall to **Obtain an IP address automatically**. Jan also knows she wants to set up her firewall as a DHCP server to the rest of her network. She therefore wants to **Enable** DHCP on the firewall. These are typically the default settings for these two features, since most users will want this configuration.

Jan's completed Setup page for the Linksys configuration software is shown in Figure 9.6. Note that she has selected **Obtain an IP Address Automatically**. She has also left the settings for the LAN IP address and Subnet Mask at the defaults supplied by the software. These two addresses are supplied by default because Jan "enabled" DHCP on an earlier page. They define how the firewall will communicate with its DHCP clients.

## Installing and Configuring the Software for the Wireless Access Point

As with the Linksys firewall, the Agere Orinoco instructions indicate their software must be installed on a PC to configure it. In this case, Jan installs the software for the wireless access point on the laptop since it has a connection (a wireless one) to the access point.

**NOTE**

Because Jan purchased her wireless network card from the same vendor as the wireless access point, her laptop was configured to communicate with the access point during the network card installation. Had she used a different vendor, she would have needed to set the Subnet Mask in the laptop's TCP/IP Properties to the correct Subnet Mask for the wireless access point.

Jan follows this procedure to configure the wireless access point:

1. She turns on both the wireless access point and the laptop PC.

2. When her Windows desktop has appeared on the PC, Jan inserts the Orinoco CD and installs the software.

3. She selects the Custom installation because she does not want to enable DHCP on her wireless access point. There is no reason to set up DHCP since she has only one wireless device. If she were creating a complex network, Jan might want to create a wireless subsystem (most likely for security reasons). In that case, she would enable DHCP.

The key window in the custom installation is Network Topology. The three tabs of this window define how the wireless access point communicates with the firewall and the laptop as follows:

- On the DHCP Server tab, Jan leaves the boxes unchecked because she does not want the access point to act as a server (see Figure 9.7).

**Figure 9.7** Network Topology DHCP Server Tab

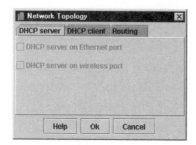

- On the DHCP Client tab, she identifies the access point as a DHCP client of the firewall attached to its Ethernet port (this performs the same function as selecting Obtain an Address Automatically in Windows and the Linksys software). This is shown in Figure 9.8.

**Figure 9.8** Network Topology DHCP Client Tab

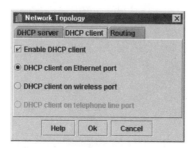

- On the Routing tab, she identifies the access point as a bridge, as shown in Figure 9.9. Notice she does not enable NAT because it was already enabled.

**Figure 9.9** Network Topology Routing Tab

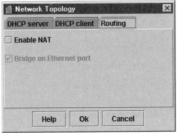

# Testing the Network

After completing her installation and configuration, Jan tests everything to make sure she has all the functionality she was expecting. She verifies that both her family PC and her laptop have Internet access. After configuring her corporate LAN access, she verifies that it is functional. Access from her laptop doesn't appear to be affected by where she is in the home, except she thinks it may be slower when she's in the kitchen with the microwave oven in operation.

Jan realizes at this point that she isn't able to access her family PC from the laptop. Thus, she can't reach the family printer either. When she is unable to understand why, she calls her IT contact Diane. Diane explains that for a peer-to-peer session on her LAN, she would need to configure the NetBEUI protocol in Windows (which creates the Network Neighborhood). However, Diane also explains that this would expose her laptop to the family PC. She could password-protect her laptop, but it would still be an unacceptable security risk for the company's information. Jan therefore decides to just buy a printer for the home office and connect it to the laptop when she needs it.

# Designing a Wireless Home Network for Data, Voice, and Beyond

Another colleague and friend of Jan's, called Dennis, is very excited by the convenience and mobility offered by Jan's wireless network. Dennis is an audio and video enthusiast and is interested in using a home net-work to create an audio/video server on his home PC. He begins reading about home networks in general, and wireless home networks in particular. He learns that he easily could build his audio/video server with an existing IEEE 802.11b-based home LAN, a network-ready MP3 player for his home sound system, and a network-ready set top box con-nected to his existing TV. However, Dennis also discovers that there may be good reason for him to wait just a little while.

# Current State of the Home Wireless Marketplace

First, Dennis learns that there are currently three wireless standards com-peting for the wireless home-network space: IEEE 802.11b, Bluetooth, and HomeRF. Unfortunately, the technologies are, for the most part, incompatible, and it is still unclear which will eventually emerge as the technology (or technologies) of choice. However, the capabilities of each are beginning to suggest some trends.

Products based on the IEEE 802.11b standard have been available for some time, particularly for business applications. The major drawbacks of 802.11b products are their interference with 2.4 GHz phones and the fact that they support data only (no native voice integration). New products based on the IEEE 802.11a standard will be emerging in the near future. These products will support an even higher bandwidth and will not interfere with the cordless phones. Major players in the industry, such as Intel and Microsoft, are currently moving toward adoption of the 802.11a standards. However, the lack of an integrated voice signal in these standards severely restricts their applications.

Bluetooth is another standard that is likely to find a place in the home network marketplace. Bluetooth provides for voice and data inte-gration. However, it currently operates on Class 2 devices, and will therefore be limited to bandwidths under 1 Mbps. Bluetooth devices will most likely be limited to voice and command-and-control services. However, its strength is in merging the home and public network spaces. Bluetooth devices are a likely solution for control of home devices when at work or in a public space such as an airport or retail establishment with a wireless public network.

Probably the most exciting of today's home wireless technologies are based on the HomeRF 2.0 standard. HomeRF 2.0 delivers up to 10 Mbps of bandwidth for data. But even better, it provides a fully integrated 2.4 GHz voice signal with up to 8 high-quality 2.4 GHz voice channels and all the Custom Local Area Signaling Service (CLASS) calling features like call waiting and caller ID. The HomeRF standard also uses a *frequency hopping* technology that avoids interference with existing 2.4 GHz devices. It will also likely provide greater security from someone intercepting your RF signal.

The key advantages of the HomeRF 2.0 standard are that it integrates the voice and data channels over the same wireless transport protocol, handles multimedia streams effectively, and supports synchronous full-duplex voice traffic. Because the voice and data signals are integrated, products using the HomeRF standard should find voice recognition and automation applications easier to develop and support.

Products based on the HomeRF 2.0 standard will likely be emerging in the second half of 2001. Siemens has been working closely with Proxim (the HomeRF 2.0 chipset manufacturer) to integrate HomeRF 2.0 and the Digital Enhanced Cordless Telephone (DECT) specification natively. It is expected that Siemens will leverage these integrated capabilities to support new and innovative products.

## Designing & Planning...

### Home Networking Technologies

Although wireless offers the greatest convenience and mobility for home networking products, it is certainly not the only solution for building a home network. Products using Home Phoneline Networking Alliance (HPNA) standards are currently on the market, which allow you to use existing Category 3 telephone lines in your home to deliver your existing voice signal and up to 10 Mbps of

**Continued**

data simultaneously. Similarly, power-line technologies are emerging that will carry even larger data bandwidths over your electrical power lines (simultaneously with the electrical power).

Most likely, all of these technologies eventually will be used in the home network. Fixed devices with ready access to an electrical plug-in may use power-line technology, whereas mobile devices or those you move frequently may use wireless. The access method you'll want to use for any given device will probably be determined by the network access points available in the locations where you expect the device to reside.

A key question in all of this is where the network hub will reside. Most likely, you will want to have control of many of your devices from a single mobile device such as a cell phone or PDA. However, for security reasons, you will also want to have network subsystems (requiring DHCP servers) for general categories of devices (for example, heating and cooling, lighting, kitchen appliances, and entertainment devices).

Two major players are emerging in the command and control arena: Microsoft's Universal Plug and Play (UPnP) and Sun Microsystems' Genie. Not surprisingly, Microsoft's approach is "PC-centric," meaning a PC will serve as the central hub and quite likely as the servers for the various subsystems. Sun's approach, on the other hand, is device-centric, meaning that a wide array of devices could serve these functions. Which solution will win the battle and which device will be the central hub remains to be seen, but the solution should certainly become apparent in just a few years.

# A Proposed Solution for the Future

Jan's colleague Dennis was initially planning to use a wireless home network just to build an audio/video server. However, after learning more about the home networking marketplace and its future, he decides he would rather choose a solution that will be expandable to meet his future home-networking needs. He therefore decides to apply Jan's design methodology to his own situation with an eye to the future.

Although the technology is not yet available for much of the home automation possibilities, Dennis decides to include these in his preliminary design to better decide which products he will eventually purchase.

Dennis completes the same investigation, analysis, and design process as Jan did. The preliminary design that Dennis develops is shown in Figure 9.10.

**Figure 9.10** Dennis's Preliminary Design

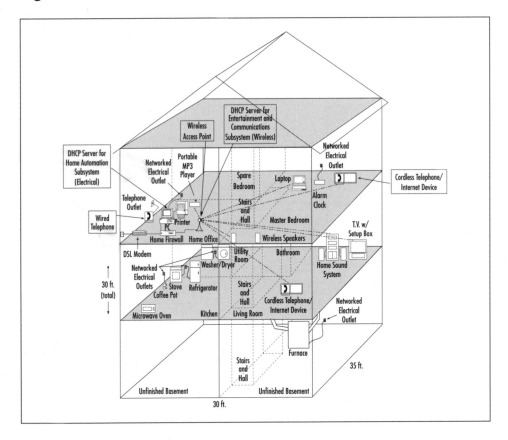

# Lessons Learned

Both Jan and Dennis have learned a number of lessons while planning, designing, and building their home networks. First, Jan has learned that no matter how much she investigates the technology and plans her network, there is always something new to learn and there will always be missteps. Even though a simple home network can be built without a lot of difficulty, there is always another technology to consider.

Jan has learned that the processes outlined in her methodology are not as neat and clean as they may first appear. As with any technology, there are drawbacks (such as interference and technology incompatibilities) that must be considered and a complex array of choices to be made.

Both Jan and Dennis have learned that there are considerable risks in purchasing any home wireless technology today, given that it is likely to become obsolete as new technologies, services, and applications become available. The key is to determine as much as possible your immediate and long-term needs, the costs you are willing to incur for various benefits, and the solutions that will address these issues most effectively. However, just as with other emerging technologies, the chances are that the products available today will have a very limited capacity to address the needs of future services and applications.

# Summary

Along with other home networking technologies, wireless home networking is seeing an explosion of activity. Home networking applications are foreseen for nearly every electronic device in your home. The advantages of wireless are that it offers you mobility and is available in locations where a wired outlet doesn't exist. The disadvantages include some minor interference problems and a quickly evolving and competitive group of standards.

Building a simple home network is a relatively easy and inexpensive task that can be completed with technology available today. However, as with any network, you should complete a thorough process of investigation, analysis, and design before purchasing any wireless networking solutions.

Preparing for the more complex wireless home networks of the future can be a more daunting task and will require a more thorough investigation of emerging technologies.

# Solutions Fast Track

## Introducing the Wireless Home Network Case Study

- ☑ New technologies and services include online music services, video-on-demand, and Internet-ready entertainment devices. Companies are also networking kitchen appliances, heating and cooling appliances, lighting, and security functions.

- ☑ This case study explores the user's opportunities in designing and implementing a home network with high-speed access to the company LAN and to a printer. The user in the case study has an existing PC with broadband access that is for family use only, and is located far from the home office.

**Chapter 6** Continued

# Designing a Wireless Solution

☑ Use two access point bridges per floor in the satellite buildings with omnidirectional antennas.

☑ Add an access point bridge in the conference of the main hospital building.

☑ Use access-point outdoor routers with directional antennas for hospital to satellite building wireless connectivity.

☑ Add wireless links between building pairs for redundancy.

☑ Use encryption for security.

# Implementing and Testing the Wireless Solution

☑ Install, configure, and test the access points and antennas in the satellite buildings. Test that laptops can access the LAN from all locations in the floor.

☑ Install, configure, and test the access point in the hospital conference room.

☑ Install, configure, and test the outdoor routers and wireless links. Then install the redundant wireless links.

# Lessons Learned

☑ Using multiple access point devices on a floor will provide additional access range and redundancy.

☑ Using an access point with a directional antenna in the conference room will provide wireless access for those attending meetings.

☑ Using encryption will provide data security for the wireless network.

**Chapter 6** Continued

☑ Using IEEE 802.11b outdoor routers with wireless directional antennas provides increased bandwidth to 11 Mbps between buildings.

# ❖ Chapter 7 Designing a Wireless Industrial Network: Retail Case Study

## Introducing the Industrial Case Study

☑ Wireless technology addresses the emerging mobility needs in the industrial setting. Recent coupling of 802.11b technology with handheld devices promotes widespread uses, from mobile inventory to network administration, to increase employee productivity and customer service.

☑ In the case study, the store owner wants to make his existing wired network more efficient and address customer needs. Handheld devices must be implemented to provide mobility.

☑ By streamlining the network, the store owner provides employees and customers easy access to store data, such as pricing and inventory.

## Designing and Implementing the Wireless Network

☑ The network consultants approach the design by categorizing the physical store into three subdomains: the first floor, the warehouse, and the second floor.

☑ The consultants obtained a physical map and reviewed the existing network.

☑ The store owner provided estimates of the maximum number of customers and employees on each subdomain.

**Chapter 7** Continued

☑   The store owner also provided the constraint that all network elements must be hidden for aesthetics.

☑   Planning for the RF patterns took place. The consultants planned the placement of the network elements. IP addresses were established.

# Planning the Equipment Placement

☑   The following hardware was selected: the Orinoco AP-1000 access point, the Orinoco PCI card, the Orinoco Range Extender, the Orinoco PCI/MCA card, and the SPT1700 handheld device.

☑   The consultants set up the IP addresses, installed the access points, and installed the related software. They installed the radios in the access points and handheld devices and installed the PCI/MCA card in the shipping/receiving PC. All of the hardware and software underwent testing to ensure functionality.

# Lessons Learned

☑   You learned how a consulting company can apply the design principles described in previous chapters.

☑   The planning phase contains the details you must be aware of when implementing a similar type of wireless network.

☑   The implementation section of this chapter walks you through the process of integrating the existing wired network with the proposed wireless network.

☑   The most important lesson is to adequately evaluate software development.

## ❖ Chapter 8 Designing a Wireless Campus Network: University Case Study

## Introducing the Campus Case Study

☑    Faber University requires an upgrade of its technological capabilities and image. It has funding for the implementation.

☑    Faber consists of very old buildings that are not conducive to wire line technologies. The buildings are in close proximity, but constraints include the fact that the line of sight is mostly blocked by trees. Also, trenching and burying cables is not an option for building links.

☑    Students require mobile and Internet access in academic buildings, the Student Union, and dorms.

☑    The teaching staff requires separate access in academic buildings.

☑    The resident and visiting coaching staff and the press require mobile access in sporting facilities.

☑    The administrative staff needs mobile access on respective floors.

## Designing the Wireless Campus Network

☑    802.11a is used for all the wireless LAN applications.

☑    Wireless is used horizontally on floors, and wireline Fast Ethernet is used for the vertical interconnection of floors.

☑    Two access point bridges using 802.11a are placed per floor in the academic buildings with omnidirectional antennas. One access point is for students and one access point is for faculty.

☑    802.11a is used to provide mobile access and communications for coaching staff at the stadium and to provide mobile access to the press at the sports facilities.

☑    Free Space Optical links are used between academic buildings as a teaching element.

**Chapter 8** Continued

☑  DHCP is used for dynamic allocation of IP addressing.

☑  Authentication/Logon is used for user identification.

## Implementing the Wireless Campus Network

☑  Resource requirements are identified.

☑  Task tracking timelines are created.

☑  Implementation tasks are divided into physical and logical deployment schedules.

☑  Tasks are rescheduled to keep on schedule and within budget.

☑  Scope creep is mitigated with prior authorization processes.

## Lessons Learned

☑  The design methodology is paramount to the success of project.

☑  The design team must continually retool methodology to remain current with technology.

☑  The design team must protect the project from scope creep and delays.

☑  Administrative issues are just as important as technological issues.

# ❖ Chapter 9 Designing a Wireless Home Network: Home Office Case Study

## Introducing the Wireless Home Network Case Study

☑  New technologies and services include online music services, video-on-demand, and Internet-ready entertainment devices.

**Chapter 9** Continued

Companies are also networking kitchen appliances, heating and cooling appliances, lighting, and security functions.

☑ This case study explores the user's opportunities in designing and implementing a home network with high-speed access to the company LAN and to a printer. The user in the case study has an existing PC with broadband access that is for family use only, and is located far from the home office.

## Designing the Wireless Home Network

☑ The functional requirements include the security of files passed to the company's LAN, the family budget, and the accessibility of the home office.

☑ The user identifies her options, investigates costs, and weighs the results.

☑ In the preliminary design, the user checks for interference, opts for a DHCP server, and reviews the access points within her budget.

## Implementing the Wireless Home Network

☑ In the detailed design, the user assembles the network components, determines the Broadband configuration, installs the hardware, installs and configures the software, and tests the resulting network.

## Designing a Robust Wireless Home Network for Data, Voice, and Beyond

☑ A user in a related case study is excited by the convenience and mobility of a wireless home network. He wants to create an audio/video server on his home PC.

## Chapter 9 Continued

☑ Currently there are three wireless standards competing for the wireless home-network space: IEEE 802.11b, Bluetooth, and HomeRF. The technologies are, for the most part, incompatible, and it is still unclear which will eventually emerge as the technology (or technologies) of choice.

☑ The major drawbacks of 802.11b products are their interference with 2.4 GHz phones and the fact that they support data only (no native voice integration). New products based on the IEEE 802.11a standard will be emerging in the near future. These products will support an even higher bandwidth and will not interfere with the cordless phones.

☑ Because the voice and data signals are integrated, products using the HomeRF standard should find voice recognition and automation applications easier to develop and support.

## Lessons Learned

☑ Building a simple home network is a relatively easy and inexpensive task that can be completed with technology available today. However, as with any network, you should complete a thorough process of investigation, analysis, and design before purchasing any wireless networking solutions.

☑ The advantages of wireless are that it offers you mobility and is available in locations where a wired outlet doesn't exist.

☑ The disadvantages of wireless include some minor interference problems and a quickly evolving and competitive group of standards.

# Index

2.5G technology, 150–151

30 Networks, 98

802 Standards Committee, additional
  initiatives of, 126–128

802.11 architecture, 135–138, 157
  developing WLANs and, 133–143,
    159–160

802.11 Frame Format, 125

802.11 network, 88, 123, 125, 140,
    159
  coverage zone in, 300
  and frequency diversity, 197
  infrastructure architecture, 134
  physical layer options for, 125
  possible interface sources in, 299
  and roaming between access points,
    141
  and vendor compatibility, 128–132

802.11a, 131–132, 281, 283,
    285–293, 297, 327, 334
  usable channels and, 132

802.11b, 103–133, 200–202, 254,
    264, 281, 312, 327, 333
  outdoor routers, 210, 229, 231

802.11d Working Group, 129

802.11f Working Group, 129

802.11g Working Group, 130

802.11h Working Group, 130

802.15 architecture, wireless personal
  area networks (WPANs),
  143–148, 158–161

802.3 standard, 85

## A

absolute horizon, 42

Accenture, Web site, 166

access point bridge placements, 218

access point devices, and routing
  functionality, 232

access points (AP), 57, 68, 113, 133,
    135, 157, 168, 211, 293, 308
  and equipment placement, 251–254
  installing, 258–259, 258

acknowledgment (ACK), 139
  and record keeping, 103

action plans, 179–180, 185

Active Member Address (AMA), 145

ad-hoc networks, 134, 163–164

address assignment, 105–106

address mapping, 86

Address Registry for Internet
  Numbers (ARIN), 114

Address Resolution Protocol (ARP),
    86

Advanced Mobile Phone Service
  (AMPS), 62, 160

agents, SNMP protocols, 105

Amplitude Modulation (AM), 29
  frequencies, 8

analog modulation schemes, 29–30

antennas, 49–55
  antenna gain, 71
  antenna point bridge placements,
    218
  quarter-wavelength momopole
    antennas, 51
  phased array antennas, 51
  planar array antennas, 53–54
  receiver antennas, 48
  transmitter antennas, 48

AP Manager software, 260

apparent horizon, 42

application layer
  and managing, 105–111, 113
  monitoring tools and, 105
  and network Address translation
    (NAT), 106–109
  protocols, 80–81, 112

application support, wireless networks, 194–196

Armstrong, Edwin Howard, 8

Asia/Pacific Network Information Centre (APNIC), 114

assessing the opportunity
campus case study, 271
industrial case study, 236–237

Asynchronous Transfer Mode (ATM), 10, 88, 110

attenuation, 36–39, 70

# B

Babbage, Charles, 9

bandwidth, 300

base stations, 56

baselining the existing network, 175

basic service set (BSS), 133–135, 157

beacon messages, 141

beams, directional antennas and, 51

Bill Of Materials (BOM), 170

binary, counting in, 91–92

bit streams, 31

Blaatand, Harold, 144

Bluetooth, 22, 131, 144–146, 161, 327, 333

bouncing, and radio signals, 39–41

bridges, and Dynamic Host Configuration Protocol (DHCP), 232

bridging, 82–85, 112
and Ethernet, 113

broadband access, 279

broadband configuration, 320–321

buffer zones, 60, 70

building-to-building connectivity, 220–221, 225–227

# C

cabling issues, 281

campus case study
assessing the opportunity, 271
constraints and assumptions, 277–282

defining scope of, 272

designing network for, 273–292, 297–298

detailed academic department requirements, 288–290

detailed administration requirements, 283

detailed athletic department requirements, 285–288

detailed design requirements, 283–292

detailed student requirements, 291–292

detailed student union requirements, 290–291

and functional design requirements, 273–277

and logical deployment, 294–295, 298

identifying assumptions and, 279–281

identifying constraints and, 281–282

implementing wireless campus networks, 292–298

and physical deployment, 293–294, 298

physical interface issues, 282

tracking the academic department needs, 276–277

tracking the administration needs, 274–275

tracking the athletic needs, 275–276

tracking student needs, 277

tracking student union needs, 277

campus network, See enterprise network

carrier sense multiple access collision avoidance (CSMA-CA), 138–139

carrier sense multiple access/collision detect (CSMA/CD), 77

carrier waves, 27–28

cell architecture, 149

cell phones, inventing, 11–12

cellular digital packet data (CDPD), 235

channel bandwidth, 59–60

channel offsets, 61

channel spacing, 60, 70

channelizing, 59–61
frequency spectrum, 57–64, 70

channels, 28
  extending the number of channels, 61-64, 70
checksum, 76, 90, 102, 104
coaxial cable, 47–48
Code Division Multiple Access (CDMA), 12, 41, 64, 148, 150, 161
collocation plan
  network architecture, 182
  network design, 178
Commercial off-the-shelf (COTS), 170
components, generic radio, 45–49
conducting the walk-through, 249
conduction, 6
configuring fragmentation, 140
connection-oriented protocols, 78–79, 89
connectivity
  building to building, 220–221, 225–227
  engineering connectivity, 290
  high-speed connectivity, 275
  inter-building connectivity, 294
constraints
  and campus case study, 277–282
  identifying constraints, 248–249
  identifying current technology options, 312
Continental Automated Buildings Association (CABA), 206
cosmic rays, 57
creating
  action plans, 185
  detailed design documents, 192, 240–242
  detailed operating model designs, 190–191
  detailed physical designs, 189–190
  detailed service collocation designs, 188–189
  detailed topologies, 187
  high-level designs, 239–240
  high-level operating models, 184
  high-level physical designs, 183
  site surveys of home, 309

training plans, 191–192
Custom Local Area Signaling Service (CLASS), 328
cycles, waveforms, 27
cyclical redundancy checksum (CRC), 76

## D

daisy-chained signals, 284
data and voice networks, 326–334
data flow diagram (DFD), 169
data-link layer, 75–77, 111
default address masks, 94
Delivery Services, and wireless technology, 14
Department of Defense (DoD) model, 74–81, 110–113
  managing the application layer, 105
  network access layer, 81–88, 112
design methodology, 172–192, 204–205, 225
design process, and wireless networks, 166–172, 203–204
design requirements, definition of, 299
designing
  data networks, 326–334
  voice networks, 326–334
  wireless home networks, 306–318, 333
  wireless networks, 239–250, 264–265
  wireless solution, 217–223, 230–231
Destination Access Service Point (DSAP), 85
detailed administration requirements, 283
detailed design documents, 192
detailed design of building links, 222–223
detailed design phase, 186–192, 205
  creating detailed design documents, 192
  creating a detailed operating model design, 190–191
  creating a detailed physical design, 189–190
  creating a detailed service collocation design, 188
  creating a detailed topology, 187

creating a training plan, 191–192

creating detailed services, 188–189

developing high-level implementation plans, 192

and maintenance plans, 192

and validating the network architecture, 186–187

detailed design requirements, 240–242, 283–292

detailed operating model designs, 190–191

detailed physical designs, 189–190

detailed service collocation designs, 188

detailed services, 188–189

detailed topology, 187

determining user density, 247–248

DHCP, See Dynamic Host Configuration Protocol

Digital Enhanced Cordless Telecommunications (DECT), 147, 328

digital modulation schemes, 30–34, 30

digital subscriber line (DSL), 10, 117

Dijkstra algorithm, 100

Direct Sequence Spread Spectrum (DSSS), 33, 125, 157, 160, 197

directional antennas, 49–55

    parabolic antennas and, 55

    planar array antennas, 53–54

    sectorized array antennas, 54–55

    Yagi array antennas, 52–53

director elements, 52

distance vector routing, 98–100

distribution services, 136–138

distribution system (DS), 133, 135, 157

Disturbed Coordination Function (DCF), 200

Domain Name System (DNS), 232

driven elements, 52

DS3 connection, 291

Dynamic Host Configuration Protocol (DHCP), 105–106, 111, 232, 241, 246, 291, 298, 317–318

    Client Tab, 325

    Server Tab, 325

    servers and, 258, 294, 312, 323

dynamic NAT, 107–109

dynamic routing, 96–98

## E

Eckert, John Presper, 9

electromagnetic (EM) waves

    definition of, 68

    transmitting radio signals over, 24–34, 69

    waveform anatomy and, 25–27

electromagnetism, 4–6, 20

    self-inductance theory and, 5

Electronic Numerical Integrator and Computer (ENIAC), 9

EM spectrum

    categories of, 57–58

    channelizing the frequency spectrum, 57–64, 70

engineering connectivity, 290

Enhanced Data Rates for GSM Evolution (EDGE), 151

Enhanced Specialized Mobile Radio (ESMR), 14

enterprise case study, 211–217, 230

    accessing the opportunity, 211–213

    assessing the satellite buildings' physical landscape, 214

    building to building connectivity, 225–227

    designing a wireless solution, 217–223, 230–231

    and detailed design of building links, 222–223

    evaluating the current network, 215

    evaluating the hospital conference room networking landscape, 216–217

    evaluating network requirements, 213–214, 230

    evaluating the outside physical landscape, 214–215

    and hospital's objectives, 227–228

network requirements and, 212–213
providing building-to-building connectivity, 220–221
providing satellite building access, 218–219
providing wireless technology to conference rooms, 219–220
testing the wireless solution, 224–231
enterprise network, 210–211
equipment placement, 265
  and access points, 251–254
  detailed design requirements, 283–292
  and implementing wireless networks, 255–256
  installing the wireless components, 258–262
  and IP addresses, 255
  planning, 250–262
  RF channel optimization, 254–255
  selecting hardware for, 256–258
Ethernet, 10, 110, 238, 284
  bridging and, 113
  carrier sense multiple access collision avoidance (CSMA-CA), 138–139
Ethernet connections, 250
Ethernet protocols, 85–86
Ethernet switch, 246–247, 289
evaluating network requirements, enterprise case study, 213–214, 230
evaluating the products, 184–185
extended service set (ESS), 133, 135–138, 157
extending the number of channels, 61–64, 70

**F**

Faraday, Michael, 5
FCC, 59, 65, 69, 122
  and cell phone frequencies, 11
  unlicensed transmitters and, 66–67
Fessenden, Reginald, 7

File Transfer Protocol (FTP), 81
Financial World, and wireless technology, 15
first octet rule, 93
fixed access unit (FAU), 121
fixed wireless technology, 117–133, 159
  Local Multipoint Distribution Service (LMDS), 119–120, 159
  Multichannel Multipoint Distribution Service (MMDS, 117·
  Point-to-Point (PTP) Microwave, 121–123, 157
  and wireless LAN standards, 123–124
  wireless local area networks (WLANs), 122–123, 159
  Wireless Local Loop (WLL), 120–121, 159
formalizing the detailed design phase, 186–192
fragmentation, configuring, 140
Frame Check Sequence (FCS), 86
frame formats
  Ethernet protocols, 85–86
Frame Relay, 110
free space optics (FSO), 156
fresnel zone, 118–119, 159, 164
frequency, and waveforms, 26–27
Frequency Division Multiple Accessing (FDMA), 59
frequency hopping, 328
Frequency Hopping Spread Spectrum (FHSS), 33, 125–125, 158–160, 202
Frequency Modulation (FM), 8, 29–30
frequency reuse, 61–64, 70, 148
  multiple accessing, 63–64, 70
  seven cell frequency reuse, 62–63
Frequency Shift Keying (FSK), 31–33
full-duplex communications, 61
full-duplex mode, 79
functional design requirements, 273–277
functional requirement, definition of, 299

# G

galvanometers, 5
gamma rays, 57
gap analysis, 176–177
Gauss, Karl Friedrich, 44
General Packet Radio Service (GPRS), 150–151, 155
generations, 148, 161, 163
generic radio components, 45–49
Global Positioning Systems (GPS), 15, 17, 19–20
Global System for Mobile Communication (GSM), 12, 63, 148, 150, 153–155, 161
ground wires, 27

# H

half-duplex communications, 61
half-duplex mode, 79
half-wavelength dipole antenna, 50
handshake process, 103
hardware
  installing, 321–322
  selecting hardware for networks, 256–258
Henry, Joseph, 5
Hertz, Heinrich, 7, 24
hidden nodes, 139
High Performance Radio LAN (HiperLAN), 147, 158
high speed connections, 279
high-level designs, 239–240
high-level implementation plans, 192
high-level operating models, 184
high-level physical designs, 183
high-level services network architecture, 182
high-level topology network architecture, 181
high-speed connectivity, 275
Home Firewall, 322–323
home location registers (HLR), 155

home networks, *See* wireless home networks
Home Phoneline Networking Alliance (HPNA), 328
HomeRF, 147, 161, 200, 202, 327–328, 333–334
hop counts, 98
horizontal applications, 16–17, 20
host-to-host layers, 101–104, 112
  transmission control protocols (TCP), 102–104
  User Datagram Protocols (UDP), 102
Hypertext Transfer Protocol (HTTP), 80–81

# I

identifying the design methodology, 172–192, 204–205
IEEE, 140, 144, 145, 229, 312, 327, 333
implementing wireless campus networks, 292–298
Incumbent Local Exchange Carrier (ILEC), 120
independent basic service set, 134
industrial case study, 235–239, 264
  and access points, 251–254
  assessing the opportunity, 236–237
  conducting the walk-through, 249
  defining scope of, 238
  determining user density, 247–248
  identifying constraints, 248–249
  and implementing wireless networks, 255–256
  and IP addresses, 255
  planning RF patterns for networks, 249–250
  planning the equipment placement, 250–262
  reviewing current situation, 238–239
  RF channel optimization, 254–255
  and RF interface sources, 249
  selecting hardware for, 256–258
  wireless components and, 258–262

industrial networks, 234–235
Industrial, Scientific, and Medical (ISM)
    frequency bands, 66
infrared light, 57
installing
    AP Manager software, 260
    hardware, 321–322
    Home Firewall, 322–323
    PC cards, 260
    software, 322–326
    Wireless Access Point, 324–326
    wireless components, 258–262
Institute of Electrical and Electronics
    Engineers' (IEEE's), 124, 157–159
integration plan, network design, 178
inter-building connectivity, 294
internal networks, 107
International Maritime Satellite
    Organization (INMARSAT), 14
International Mobile Equipment
    Identifier (IMEI), 154
International Mobile Subscriber Identity
    (IMSI), 154
International Radio Consultative
    Committee (CCIR), 64
International Telecommunication Union
    (ITU), 64
International Telephone Consultative
    Committee (CCIF), 64
Internet Control Message Protocol
    (ICMP), 101
Internet layer, 88–101, 110, 112
Internet Protocol (IP), 74, 89–101, 280
    classes of, 92
    conserving address space with Subnet
        Mask (VLSM), 93–95
    and Dynamic Host Configuration
        Protocol (DHCP), 105–106
    Internet Control Message Protocol
        (ICMP), 101
    IP addressing, 77, 91–93, 241, 246, 255,
        320–323
    obtaining range and, 113–114

and routing algorithms, 95–100
IP Headers, 89
    fields for, 90, 102
inventing computers and networks, 9–10
inventory control, 257
ISM radio band, 130
ITU Radiocommunication Sector
    (ITU-R), 64, 69

J

Joint Photographic Experts Group
    (JPEG), 80

L

line of sight, 42–43
link state routing, 98–100
link-state advertisements (LSA), 100
link-state protocols, 99
listening before talking (LBT), 138
Local Area Network (LAN), 10, 45, 87,
    238
    bridging and, 82–85, 112
    design types, 87
    and enterprise network, 210, 229
    LAN access, 224
    and multiple bridges, 84–85
    switches, 228
Local Multipoint Distribution Service
    (LMDS), 116–117, 119–120, 157,
    159
Logical Link Control (LLC), 76, 85, 136
logical ports, 109
low power transmitters, regulations and,
    66–67

M

maintenance plans, 192
management, needs of, 307
managing the application layer, 105–111,
    113
Marconi, Guglielmo, 7, 20, 24
Mauchley, John W., 9

media access control (MAC) addresses, 76,
    106, 125, 157, 219–220, 225, 232,
    258
  and Address Resolution Protocol, 86
  and security, 142
messaging, 17
metal, and EM wave penetration, 44–45
microwave spectrum, 57
mobile stations, 56
mobile switching center (MSC), 154
mobile wireless technology, 148–155, 158,
    161
  and digital transmissions, 163
modulation
  benefits of, 69
  radio signals and, 27–28, 69
monitoring applications, 16
Morse code, 7
Morse, Samuel, 5–6
Motion Picture Experts Group (MPEG),
    80
Motorola Talkabout Family Radio Service
    (FRS), 56
mounting radio-telephones in cars, 8
multicell roaming, 140–141
Multichannel Multipoint Distribution
    Service (MMDS), 116–117, 157
multichannel systems, 61
multipath reflection, 118–119, 159
multipath scattering, 42
  radio signals and, 41
multiple accessing
  code division multiple access (CDMA),
    63–64
  frequency reuse, 63–64, 70
  time division multiple accessing
    (TDMA), 63
multiple bridges, LANS and, 84–85

N

National Telecommunications and
    Information Administration (NTIA),
    59, 65, 69

NetBEUI protocols, 326
network access layer, 81–88, 112
  Address Resolution Protocol (ARP), 86
  bridging and, 82–85, 112
  and Ethernet protocols, 85–86
  and wireless protocols, 87–88
network address translation (NAT),
    106–109, 111, 323
network architecture, 180–186, 205
  creating a collocation plan, 182
  creating a detailed topology, 187
  creating a high-level operating model,
    184
  creating a high-level physical design, 183
  creating a high-level topology, 181
  creating an action plan, 185
  creating the deliverable, 186
  defining high-level services, 182
  defining the operations services, 183
  evaluating the products, 184–185
  understanding attributes from design
    perspectives, 193–205
  validating the planning phase, 181,
    186–187
network design
  and action plans, 179–180
  analyzing competitive practices and, 176
  baselining the existing network, 175
  campus case study, 273–292, 297–298
  collocation planning, 178
  creating a integration plan, 178
  creating a network plan, 173–174
  creating a technology plan, 177–178
  developing a detailed design, 317
  developing a preliminary design,
    315–316
  and functional design requirements,
    273–277
  and job costs, 206
  and operations planning, 176, 205
  performing a gap analysis, 176–177
  performing a risk analysis, 179
  planning deliverables and, 180

understanding attributes from design perspectives, 193–205
and wireless solutions, 217–223, 230–231
Network Engagement Methodology (NEM), 173, 203–204
Network Equipment Building Standards (NEBS), 188
Network File System (NFS), 79
network interface card (NIC), 77
network layer, 77, 88, 112, 77, *See* also Internet layer
Network Operations Center (NOC), 191
network plan
    creating, 173–174
    gathering requirements for, 173–174
network topology, 200–201
networks, *See* also wireless networks
    designing data networks, 326–334
    designing voice networks, 326–334
    inventing computers and networks, 9–10
    testing the network, 326
Nordic Mobile Telephone (NMT), 150

**O**

obtaining a physical map, 242–247
Oersted, Hans Christian, 4
omnidirectional antennas, 49–51
    half-wavelength dipole, 50
    quarter-wavelength momopole, 51
On/Off Keying, 31–33
Open Shortest Path First (OSPF), 100
Open Systems Interconnection (OSI) model, 74–81, 110–113
operations services, network architecture, 183
optical links, affect of rain and fog on, 163
optical wireless technology, 156, 158, 162
Orinoco RG1000, SNR levels, 196
Orthogonal Frequency Division Multiplexing (OFDM), 131
OSI model, 82
    and managing the application layer, 105

outdoor routers, 222
overloading, 107–109
overutilization, design constraints and, 175

**P**

packet numbering, 102–103
packets, 77
Palm Pilots, 19
parabolic antennas, 51, 55
Parked Member Address (PMA), 145
PAT, 114
PC wireless cards, 68
PCI/MCA cards, 265
    International Association (PCMCIA), 224, 256, 260, 321
PCS phones, 41
    signal strength of, 71
penetration, and radio signals, 43–45
Peripheral Component Interconnect (PCI) cards, 256–257
personal area network (PAN) devices, capabilities of, 2–3
personal communications services (PCS), 12
Personal Digital Assistant (PDA), 13, 143, 235, 305
Phase Shift Keying (PSK), 31, 33
phased array antennas, 51
physical interface issues, campus case study, 282
physical landscape, wireless networks, 197–199
physical layer, 75, 111
physical maps, 242–247
piconets, Bluetooth networks, 145
ping, and connectivity, 101
planar array antennas, 53–54
planning deliverables and network design, 180
planning phase, network architecture, 181
planning the equipment placement, 250–262
Point Coordination Function (PCF), 201

point-of-sale (POS) applications, 15–16
Point-to-Point (PTP) Microwave,
    121–123, 157
port address translation (PAT), 107–109
port numbers, 109
ports, 114
  radio port controller (RPC), 118
Post Office Protocol (POP), 81
POTS network, 154
power management options, 140
presentation layer, 79–80
price checks, 257
private address restrictions, 108
products, evaluation of, 184–185
providing wireless technology to
    conference rooms, 219–220
Public Safety, and wireless technology,
    14–15
Pulse Amplitude Modulation (PAM), 31,
    34

## Q

quality of service (QoS) functionality, 132
quantization errors, 30
quarter-wavelength momopole antennas,
    51

## R

radio, invention of, 6–7
radio components, 45–49
Radio Frequency (RF), 28, 75, 172, 241,
    261
  access points (APs), 293
  channel optimization, 254–255
  interface sources, 249, 263, 273
  leakage from microwave ovens, 309
  patterns, 252–254, 265
  planning for networks, 249–250
  ranges of, 24, 68
radio port controller (RPC), 118
Radio Signals
  analog modulation schemes, 29–30
  attenuation and, 36–39, 70
  bouncing, 39–41
  digital modulation schemes, 30–34
  and line of sight, 42–43
  modulation and, 27–28, 69
  and signal-to-noise ratio (S/N ratio),
    35–36, 69
  penetration and, 43–45
  refracting, 41–42
  signal propagation and, 34–45, 69–70
  transmitting over electromagnetic (EM)
    waves, 24–34, 69
radio spectrum, 57
radio-telephones, mounting in cars, 8
rain attenuation, 39
rain fade, 122
rake receivers, 41
Range Extender, 257
receiver amplifier, 49
receiver antenna, 48
receiver cable, 48–49
receiver channel filter, 48
receiver decoder, 49
receiver demodulator, 49
redundant links, 223
reflectors, 52
refracting, radio signals and, 41–42
registers, 155
regulatory agencies, 64–65
Remote Access Service (RAS), 143
Request for Comments (RFC), 101
request for information (RFI), 182
request for proposal (RFP), 182
Request To Send/Clear To Send
    (RTS/CTS) mechanism, 138–139
Reseaux IP Europeens (RIPE), 114
retail applications
  alternative handheld devices for, 266
  and wireless technology, 15–16, 267
  and wireless technology, 15–16
reviewing client's objectives, 261–262
RG1000 Wireless Access Points, 317, 319

right to send/clear to send (RTS/CTS), 87
risk analysis, network design, 179
routers, 88, 110–112, 238
    802.11b outdoor routers, 210, 229, 231
routing
    access point devices, 232
    distance vector routing, 98–100
    and Ethernet, 113
    link state routing, 98–100
    outdoor routers, 222
    static and dynamic routing, 96–98
routing algorithms, 95–100
routing information (RIF) cache, 83
routing information indicator (RII), 83
Routing Information Protocol (RIP), 99, 232
Routing Tabs, 325–326

## S

satellite building access, 218–219
satellites, signal reflection and, 40
scatternets, 145
scope changes, 292, 298
sectorized array antennas, 54–55
security, 232, 266, 280, 303–304
    and wireless networks, 201–202
    WLAN and, 141–143
self-inductance theory, and electro-magnetism, 5
serial links, 98
service provider networks, 173
Service Set Identifier (SSID), 142
session layer, 78–79, 112
Seven Cell Frequency Reuse, 62–63
Short Message Service (SMS), 17, 155
short-distance wireless networks, 144
signal-to-noise ratio (S/N ratio), 35–36, 69, 141
Simple Mail Transfer Protocol (SMTP), 81
single-mode communication, 79
sinusoidal waveform, 25

SNMP protocols, 105
SNR levels, Orinoco RG1000, 196
software
    Home Firewall, 322–323
    installation, 322–326
Source Service Access Point (SSAP), 85, 87
source-route bridging (SRB), 82–85, 112
source-route translational bridging (SR/TLB), 83–84, 112
source-route transparent bridging (SRT), 83, 112
Spanning Tree Protocol (STP), 84
spatial density, 199, 205
SPT1700, 257, 265
Standard Wireless Access Protocol (SWAP), 147
static, 36
static NAT, 107–109
static routing, 96–98
station services group, 136
Structured Query Language (SQL), 79
Subscriber Identity Module (SIM), 153–154, 161
subscriber relationships, 196–197
supported units, increasing number of, 267
Synchronous Optical Network (SONET) connections, 10, 88

## T

Tagged Image File Format (TIFF), 80
task tracking, 293, 298
testing the wireless network, 260–261
testing the wireless solution, 224–231
throughput, 300
Time Division Multiple Access (TDMA), 12, 63, 151
time to live (TLL), 90
Token Ring networks, 84, 110
Total Access Communication System (TACS), 150

traceroute, packet-tracking systems, 101

tracking the administration needs, 274–275

training plans, 191–192

Transmission Control Protocol/Internet Protocol (TCP/IP), 18, 102–104

  TCP/IP Properties window, 320

  TCP Header, 103–104

transmitter amplifier, 47

transmitter antenna, 48

transmitter cable, 47

transmitter encoder, 46

transmitter modulator, 46

transport bridging, 82–83, 82

transport layer, 78, 112, 78

transport layer protocols (TCP), 74, 89, 101, 110–112

TCP/UDP port assignments, 109

type of service (TOS), 90

## U

ultra violet light, 57

United Parcel Service (UPS), 14

Universal Plug and Play (UPnP), 329

unlicensed transmitters, regulations and, 66–67

Unshielded Twisted Pair (UTP) wiring, 213

  enterprise case study, 215

User Datagram Protocols (UDP), 78, 89, 101–102, 110–112

user density, determining, 247–248

## V

Variable Length Subnet Mask (VLSM)

  conserving address space with, 93–95

  and network address translation (NAT), 106–109

  and Routing Information Protocols (RIP), 99

vendor compatibility, 128–132

  choosing vendor solutions, 317

vertical markets, 13–14, 20

Virtual Private Network (VPN), 13, 143

visible light, 57

visitor location registers (VLR), 155

VLANS, 294

voice networks, 326–334

Voice over IP (VoIP) services, 132

## W

waveform anatomy, 25–27

wavelengths, 26–27

Web clipping, 194

Web surfing, 17–18

Wide Area Networks (WANs), 10, 16, 238

windowing, 103

Wired Equivalent Privacy (WEP), 142, 222, 232

Wireless Access Point, 324–326

Wireless Access Protocol (WAP), 150

Wireless Application Protocol (WAP), 17, 151–153, 161

wireless authentication, and association services, 137

wireless campus networks

  assessing the opportunity, 271

  constraints and assumptions, 277–282

  defining scope of, 272

  design of, 206

  designing network for, 273–292, 297–298

  detailed academic department requirements, 288–290

  detailed administration requirements, 283

  detailed athletic department requirements, 285–288

  detailed design requirements, 283–292

  detailed student requirements, 291–292

  detailed student union requirements, 290–291

  and functional design requirements, 273–277

and logical deployment, 294–295, 298
identifying assumptions and, 279–281
identifying constraints and, 281–282
implementing wireless campus networks, 292–298
and physical deployment, 293–294, 298
physical interface issues, 282
tracking the academic department needs, 276–277
tracking the administration needs, 274–275
tracking the athletic needs, 275–276
tracking student needs, 277
tracking student union needs, 277
wireless communications
    low power transmitters and, 66–67
    regulation of, 64–69, 71
wireless components, 258–262
    installing access points, 258–259
    installing the AP Manager software, 260
    installing the PC card, 260
    reviewing client's objectives, 261–262
    setting up IP information, 258
    testing the wireless network, 260–261
wireless devices, outdoor range of, 232
Wireless Equivalency Protection (WEP), 136
Wireless Ethernet Compatibility Alliance (WECA), 129
wireless home network
wireless home network case study, 305–336
    advantages of, 302–305
    analyzing existing environments and, 310–311
    assembling the network components, 319
    assessing functional requirements of, 310
    assessing the existing environment, 314–315
    assessing the opportunity, 305–306
    and broadband configuration, 320–321
    choosing vendor solutions, 317

creating site surveys, 309
    data and voice networks, 326–334
    defining scope of, 306
    designing, 306–318, 333
    determining functional requirements of, 307–309
    developing a detailed design, 317
    developing a preliminary design, 315–316
    and future solutions, 329–330
    and Home Firewall, 322–323
    identifying current technology options, 312
    implementing the network, 319–326, 333
    installing hardware, 321–322
    installing the Wireless Access Point, 324–326
    investigating costs of, 313
    investigating costs of, 313–314
    and needs of family, 308
    and software installation, 322–326
    and state of home wireless marketplace, 327–328
    testing the network, 326
wireless local area networks (WLANs), 68, 87, 122–123, 159, 294–295
    design types, 87
    developing with 802.11 architecture, 133–143, 159–160
    RF transmissions and, 88
    security and, 141–143
    standards for, 123–124
Wireless Local Loop (WLL), 116–117, 120–121, 157–159, 163
Wireless Markup Language (WML), 153
wireless networks
    and analysis of existing environment, 168, 204
    and application support, 194–196
    capturing the documentation, 171–172, 204
    cost of, 335

creating a detailed design, 240–242
creating a preliminary design, 169, 204
creating the high-level design, 239–240
design process and, 166–172, 203–204
designing and implementing, 239–250
executing the implementation, 170–171, 204
finalizing the detailed design, 169–170, 204
formalizing the detailed design phase, 186–192
identifying the design methodology, 172–192, 204–205
and network topology, 200–201
obtaining a physical map, 242–247
and physical landscape of, 197–199
preliminary investigation and, 167–168, 204
and security issues, 201–202
subscriber relationships, 196–197
testing the wireless network, 260–261
understanding attributes from design perspectives, 193–205
wireless personal area networks (WPANs), 143–148, 158–161
wireless propagation, 48
wireless protocols, 87–88
wireless services, verification of, 227
wireless solutions, LAN access, 224
wireless technology
  access points, 57
  antennas and, 49–55
  applying to vertical markets, 13–14, 20
  base stations, 56
  buffer zones, 60, 70
  channel spacing, 60, 70

channelizing the frequency spectrum, 57–64, 70
and cost savings, 266–267
and Delivery Services, 14
and electromagnetism, 4–6, 20
and exploring conduction, 6
and extending the number of channels, 61–64, 70
and Financial World, 15
generic radio components, 45–49
and horizontal applications, 16–17, 20
and industrial networks, 234–235
inventing cell phones, 11–12
inventing computers and networks, 9–10
inventing the radio and, 6–7
and messaging, 17
mobile stations, 56
and monitoring applications, 16
mounting radio-telephones in cars, 8
omnidirectional antennas, 49–51
and past discoveries, 4–12, 20
and point-of-sale applications, 15–16
present applications for, 12–18, 20
and Public Safety, 14–15
and Retail World, 15–16, 267
and Web surfing, 17–18
wireless voice, and differences to wireless networking, 21

# X

X Windows, 79
X-rays, 57

# Y

Yagi array antennas, 52–53

# Global Knowledge ™

## Train with Global Knowledge

The right content, the right method, delivered anywhere in the world, to any number of people from one to a thousand. Blended Learning Solutions™ from Global Knowledge.

## Train in these areas:

Network Fundamentals
Internetworking
A+ PC Technician
WAN Networking and Telephony
Management Skills
Web Development
XML and Java Programming
Network Security
UNIX, Linux, Solaris, Perl
Cisco
Enterasys
Entrust
Legato
Lotus
Microsoft
Nortel
Oracle

# Global Knowledge ™

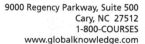

9000 Regency Parkway, Suite 500
Cary, NC 27512
1-800-COURSES
www.globalknowledge.com

At Global Knowledge, we strive to support the multiplicity of learning styles required by our students to achieve success as technical professionals. We do this because we know our students need different training approaches to achieve success as technical professionals. That's why Global Knowledge has worked with Syngress Publishing in reviewing and recommending this book as a valuable tool for successful mastery of this subject.

As the world's largest independent corporate IT training company, Global Knowledge is uniquely positioned to recommend these books. The first hand expertise we have gained over the past several years from providing instructor-led training to well over a million students worldwide has been captured in book form to enhance your learning experience. We hope the quality of these books demonstrates our commitment to your life-long learning success. Whether you choose to learn through the written word, e-Learning, or instructor-led training, Global Knowledge is committed to providing you the choice of when, where and how you want your IT knowledge and skills to be delivered. For those of you who know Global Knowledge, or those of you who have just found us for the first time, our goal is to be your lifelong partner and help you achieve your professional goals.

Thank you for the opportunity to serve you. We look forward to serving your needs again in the future.

Warmest regards,

Duncan M. Anderson
President and Chief Executive Officer, Global Knowledge

P.S.    Please visit us at our Web site www.globalknowledge.com.

# Enter the Global Knowledge
# Chrysler PT Cruiser Sweepstakes

**This sweepstakes is open only to legal residents of the United States who are Business to Business MIS/IT managers or staff and training decision makers, that are 18 years of age or older at time of entry. Void in Florida & Puerto Rico.**

## OFFICIAL RULES

**No Purchase or Transaction Necessary To Enter or Win, purchasing will not increase your chances of winning.**

**1. How to Enter:** Sweepstakes begins at 12:00:01 AM ET May 1, 2001 and ends 12:59:59 PM ET December 31, 2001 the ("Promotional Period"). There are four ways to enter to win the Global Knowledge PT Cruiser Sweepstakes: Online, at Trade shows, by mail or by purchasing a course or software. Entrants may enter via any of or all methods of entry.

[1] To be automatically entered online, visit our web at www.globalknowledge.com click on the link named Cruiser and complete the registration form in its entirety. All online entries must be received by 12:59:59 PM ET December 31, 2001. Only one online entry per person, per e-mail address. Entrants must be the registered subscriber of the e-mail account by which the entry is made.

[2] At the various trade shows, during the promotional period by scanning your admission badge at our Global Knowledge Booth. All entries must be made no later than the close of the trade shows. Only one admission badge entry per person.

[3] By mail or official entry blank available at participating book stores throughout the promotional period. Complete the official entry blank or hand print your complete name and address and day & evening telephone # on a 3"x5" card, and mail to: Global Knowledge PT Cruiser Sweepstakes, P.O. Box 4012 Grand Rapids, MN 55730-4012. Entries must be postmarked by 12/31/01 and received by 1/07/02. Mechanically reproduced entries will not be accepted. Only one mail in entry per person.

[4] By purchasing a training course or software during the promotional period: online at http://www.globalknowledge.com or by calling 1-800-COURSES, entrants will automatically receive an entry onto the sweepstakes. Only one purchase entry per person.

All entries become the property of the Sponsor and will not be returned. Sponsor is not responsible for stolen, lost, late, misdirected, damaged, incomplete, illegible entries or postage due mail.

**2. Drawings:** There will be five [5] bonus drawings and one [1] prize will be awarded in each bonus drawing. To be eligible for the bonus drawings, on-line entries, trade show entries and purchase entries must be received as of the dates listed on the entry chart below in order to be eligible for the corresponding bonus drawing. Mail in entries must be postmarked by the last day of the bonus period, except for the month ending 9/30/01 where mail in entries must be postmarked by 10/1/01 and received one day prior to the drawing date indicated on the entry chart below. Only one bonus prize per person or household for the entire promotion period. Entries eligible for one bonus drawing will not be included in subsequent bonus drawings.

| Bonus Drawings | Month starting/ending 12:00:01 AM ET/11:59:59 PM ET | Drawing Date on or about |
|---|---|---|
| 1 | 5/1/01-7/31/01 | 8/8/01 |
| 2 | 8/1/01-8/31/01 | 9/11/01 |
| 3 | 9/1/01-9/30/01 | 10/10/01 |
| 4 | 10/1/01-10/31/01 | 11/9/01 |
| 5 | 11/1/01-11/30/01 | 12/11/01 |

There will also be a grand prize drawing in this sweepstakes. The grand prize drawing will be conducted on January 8, 2002 from all entries received. Bonus winners are eligible to win the Grand prize.

All random sweepstakes drawings will be conducted by Marden-Kane, Inc. an independent judging organization whose decisions are final. All prizes will be awarded. The estimated odds of winning each bonus drawing are 1:60,000, for the first drawing and 1:20,000 for the second, third, fourth and fifth drawings, and the estimated odds of winning the grand prize drawing is 1:100,000. However the actual odds of winning will depend upon the total number of eligible entries received for each bonus drawing and grand prize drawings.

**3. Prizes:** Grand Prize: One (1) PT Cruiser 2002 model Approx. Retail Value (ARV) $18,000. Winner may elect to receive the cash equivalent in lieu of the car. Bonus Prizes: Five (5), awarded one (1) per bonus period. Up to $1,400.00 in self paced learning products ARV up to $1,400.00 each.

No substitutions, cash equivalents, except as noted, or transfers of the prize will be permitted except at the sole discretion of the Sponsor, who reserves the right to substitute a prize of equal or greater value in the event an offered prize is unavailable for any reason. Winner is responsible for payment of all taxes on the prize, license, registration, title fees, insurance, and for any other expense not specifically described herein. Winner must have and will be required to furnish proof of a valid driver's license. Manufacturers warranties and guarantees apply.

**4. Eligibility:** This sweepstakes is open only to legal residents of the United States, except Florida and Puerto Rico residents who are Business to Business MIS/IT managers or staff and training decision makers, that are 18 years of age or older at the time of entry. Employees of Global Knowledge Network, Inc and its subsidiaries, advertising and promotion agencies including Marden-Kane, Inc., and immediate families (spouse, parents, children, siblings and their respective spouses) living in the same household as employees of these organizations are ineligible. Sweepstakes is void in Florida and Puerto Rico and is subject to all applicable federal, state and local laws and regulations. By participating, entrants agree to be bound by the official rules and accept decisions of judges as final in all matters relating to this sweepstakes.

**5. Notification:** Winners will be notified by certified mail, return receipt requested, and may be required to complete and sign an Affidavit of Eligibility/Liability Release and, where legal, a Publicity Release, which must be returned, properly executed, within fourteen (14) days of issuance of prize notification. If these documents are not returned properly executed or are returned from the post office as undeliverable, the prize will be forfeited and awarded to an alternate winner. Entrants agree to the use of their name, voice and photograph/likeness for advertising and promotional purposes for this and similar promotions without additional compensation, except where prohibited by law.

**6. <u>Limitation of Liability:</u>** By participating in the Sweepstakes, entrants agree to indemnify and hold harmless the Sponsor, Marden-Kane, Inc. their affiliates, subsidiaries and their respective agents, representatives, officers, directors, shareholders and employees (collectively, "Releasees") from any injuries, losses, damages, claims and actions of any kind resulting from or arising from participation in the Sweepstakes or acceptance, possession, use, misuse or nonuse of any prize that may be awarded. Releasees are not responsible for printing or typographical errors in any instant win game related materials; for stolen, lost, late, misdirected, damaged, incomplete, illegible entries; or for transactions, or admissions badge scans that are lost, misdirected, fail to enter into the processing system, or are processed, reported, or transmitted late or incorrectly or are lost for any reason including computer, telephone, paper transfer, human, error; or for electronic, computer, scanning equipment or telephonic malfunction or error, including inability to access the Site. If in the Sponsor's opinion, there is any suspected or actual evidence of electronic or non-electronic tampering with any portion of the game, or if computer virus, bugs, unauthorized intervention, fraud, actions of entrants or technical difficulties or failures compromise or corrupt or affect the administration, integrity, security, fairness, or proper conduct of the sweepstakes the judges reserve the right at their sole discretion to disqualify any individual who tampers with the entry process and void any entries submitted fraudulently, to modify or suspend the Sweepstakes, or to terminate the Sweepstakes and conduct a random drawing to award the prizes using all non-suspect entries received as of the termination date. Should the game be terminated or modified prior to the stated expiration date, notice will be posted on http://www.globalknowledge.com. Any attempt by an entrant or any other individual to deliberately damage any web site or undermine the legitimate operation of the promotion is a violation of criminal and civil laws and should such an attempt be made, the sponsor reserves the right to seek damages and other remedies from any such person to the fullest extent permitted by law. Any attempts by an individual to access the web site via a bot script or other brute force attack or any other unauthorized means will result in the IP address becoming ineligible. Use of automated entry devices or programs is prohibited.

**7. <u>Winners List:</u>** For the name of the winner visit our web site www.globalknowledge.com on January 31, 2002.

**8. <u>Sponsor:</u>** Global Knowledge Network, Inc., 9000 Regency Parkway, Cary, NC 27512. Administrator: Marden-Kane, Inc. 36 Maple Place, Manhasset, NY 11030.

# SYNGRESS SOLUTIONS...

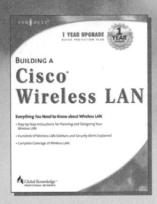

## Building a Cisco Wireless LAN

For individuals designing and supporting a Cisco LAN this book has detailed information on building a network design for the Cisco 340, 350, and UBR 7200 series and shows how to configure a Cisco WLAN.

ISBN: 1-928994-58-X

Price: $69.95 US, $108.95 CAN

## Hack Proofing Your E-Commerce Site

*From the authors of the bestselling Hack Proofing Your Network.* E-commerce giants, previously thought to be impenetrable are now being exposed as incredibly vulnerable. This book gives e-commerce architects and engineers insight into the tools and techniques used by hackers to compromise sites. The security of e-commerce sites is even more imperative than non-commerce sites, because of the added responsibility of maintaining customers' personal and financial information. This book will provide Web architects and engineers all the information they need to design and implement security measures.

ISBN: 1-928994-27-X

Price: $49.95 US, $77.95 CAN

## Configuring Cisco AVVID

AVVID (Architecture for Voice, Video, and Integrated Data) is a network architecture made up of hardware and software that transmits a company's data such as e-mail, Web traffic, file transfers, voice traffic, and video traffic over the same physical computer network. *Configuring Cisco AVVID* will introduce you to the new AVVID components from Cisco that can save hard dollars and increase a company's overall performance. This book will give IT professionals, ISPs, and engineers the first insight into how each piece of hardware and each software application function independently, as well as how they interoperate, forming a completely converged solution. It covers the many components of AVVID, including Cisco Routers, Cisco Catalyst Switches, Cisco IP Telephones, Cisco CallManager Servers, Analog and Digital Gateways, Voice Trunks, Voice Modules, CallManager 3.0, SoftPhone, WebAttendant, and Active Voice.

ISBN: 1-928994-14-8

Price: $59.95

solutions@syngress.com

SYNGRESS®